Imagining Robin Hood

Robin Hood: yeoman of the forest. This image, a late-fifteenth-century woodcut, was recycled both to illustrate Robin Hood in Chapman and Myllar's printing of the *Gest* in 1508 and to represent the knight's yeoman in Pynson's edition of *The Canterbury Tales* in 1491.

Imagining Robin Hood

THE LATE-MEDIEVAL STORIES IN HISTORICAL CONTEXT

A. J. Pollard

Routledge
Taylor & Francis Group

LONDON AND NEW YORK

First published 2004
by Routledge
2 Park Square, Milton Park,
Abingdon, Oxfordshire OX14 4RN

Simultaneously published in the USA and Canada
by Routledge
270 Madison Avenue, New York, NY 10016

Routledge is an imprint of the Taylor & Francis Group

© 2004 A. J. Pollard

Typeset in Weiss by M Rules
Printed and bound in Great Britain by
MPG Books Ltd, Bodmin

British Library Cataloguing in Publication Data
A catalogue record for this book is available from the British Library

Library of Congress Cataloging in Publication Data

Pollard, A. J.
Imagining Robin Hood: the late-medieval stories in historical context/
A. J. Pollard
272 p. cm.
Includes bibliographical references.
1. English literature – Middle English, 1100–1500 – History and criticism. 2. Robin
Hood (Legendary character) 3. English literature – Early modern,
1500–1700 – History and criticism. 4. Literature and society – England – History – To
1500. 5. Literature and history – England – History To 1500. 6. Ballads, English –
England – History and criticism. 7. Outlaws – England – History – To 1500.
8. Outlaws in literature. I.

ISBN 0-415-22308-3 (hbk)

In memory of Phyllis Porteous

CONTENTS

PLATES

(Between pages 48 and 49)

PREFACE AND ACKNOWLEDGEMENTS

I first encountered Robin Hood as impersonated by Errol Flynn. The 1938 movie *The Adventures of Robin Hood* was endlessly repeated by the BBC, it seems, along with *Bringing Up Baby* and *The Three Musketeers*, to fill Christmas schedules in the 1950s. Subsequently, I have assisted undergraduates with dissertations on various aspects of the legend. My scholarly interest was not really awakened until I was asked to contribute to a festschrift for Barrie Dobson. The editors set a theme, and all I could think of was something on Robin Hood. Out of that arose a contribution to *Pragmatic Utopias* edited by Rosemary Horrrox and Sarah Rees-Jones in 2001, an article written with Richard Almond in *Past and Present* in the same year, and now this book.

Scholarly interest in the subject of Robin Hood and his merry men as a cultural phenomenon at the intersection of history, literature and media studies has flourished in recent years. There is an International Association for Robin Hood Studies which holds biennial conferences alternating between Britain and North America; Rochester University maintains a Robin Hood website. Literary scholars have recently taken the lead in the analysis of the earliest texts as well as the continuing myth. But modern study of the early Robin Hood stories was launched in the early 1950s by historians particularly interested in them as the voice of the people in social protest. This work, tentatively, seeks to reclaim some of the ground for the historian. In so doing it tiptoes in the footsteps of giants: Barrie Dobson and John Taylor, Sir James Holt, and Maurice Keen in particular.

The book's premise is that the earliest knowledge we possess of what was said, sung and ultimately written of Robin Hood dates from the fifteenth century, probably well into that century. All we know is what was written down in the second half of the fifteenth century and the early sixteenth. They are late-medieval texts, very late medieval texts; it follows that they speak to us from that century or so and tell us about it. They do not tell us, directly, of an earlier period. If they do it is because they also carry a collective memory of earlier times. That itself would have been a late-medieval collective memory. There may or may not have been a 'real' Robin Hood some time two centuries earlier. If there were, we know nothing of him. We know there were stories in circulation in the late fourteenth century, but what those stories contained we do not know. They may have been like the stories recorded a century later; but we cannot be sure, especially since we know that after 1550 the stories did change. Thus the first Robin Hood we know was a literary creation that belonged to the fifteenth and early sixteenth centuries. This work is an exploration of what the hero meant to the generations who knew of him then.

I do not wish to imply that the fascinating search for an original Robin Hood is not worthwhile. At the end of 2003 it was as active as ever, with a long television programme presented by Tony Robinson reviewing effectively and entertainingly most of the enigmatic evidence, and an article in *Medieval History Magazine* by Vanessa Greatorex suggesting that he may never have existed, may have been an amalgam of several historical figures, or simply have been created as an archetype. That search will probably never end. However, this book is not about a possible real-life Robin; it is about his persona as a fictional creation as it existed when first we encounter it in the fifteenth century. It is about how Robin Hood was imagined then.

In endeavouring to relate the words of the late-medieval Robin Hood texts to the experienced world of people who first knew them, one encounters the 'postmodern bind'. The problem lies in truly knowing what that experienced world was. We have many historical sources on which to call, but they too are 'texts', interposing themselves between then and now, between the generations who created and used them and later generations who interpret them as historical evidence. And the interpretation of a historical source is never straightforward. Yet we cannot hope to understand the past but through the mediation of surviving texts and objects, of which the Robin Hood 'rymes' are themselves a handful. In essence, therefore, one is comparing text with text; the context in which we seek to set the texts, the creation of the historian, is in itself a construct from texts. The historian may be confident that the context he or she has created is well founded, and hopes that the reader will be convinced, but in the last resort it is only one person's perception, only one person's attempt to reinhabit that past. All that this historian can offer as qualification is a good part of a lifetime's study of the fifteenth century.

No historian is completely objective. The meaning of early Robin Hood stories, like almost all historical sources, is often obscure and ambiguous. As a result interpretations in several respects are controversial and contested. The texts can be read in many different ways. I do not expect that my interpretation will persuade all readers. I do not claim that it is the only reading. One judgement might be stressed at the start. Robin Hood, from the moment the first surviving written words were committed to paper, was perceived as a hero for all seasons, and could be all things to all men. Considerable debate has occurred as to whether he originally came from below or above; my view is that in the earliest surviving stories he already appealed to both gentry and the commons. There are elements of both chivalric romance and lewd ribaldries in them. The elements are bound together by a concern with putting wrongs right. What those wrongs were, and what the stories meant in putting them right towards the end of the middle ages, is the ultimate focus of this study.

The work starts with a discussion of the texts themselves and an attempt to delineate the economic, social and political context in which they should be set. It moves on to a detailed consideration of the meaning of the term 'yeoman', central to the understanding of all the texts. The following three chapters explore the significance of the locale of stories in the greenwood and in the north, examine the paradox underlying Robin Hood's life of violent crime, and consider the attitudes to religion, the Church and especially the monasteries revealed in the tales. The work then reflects on the meaning of 'good fellowship', a concept which runs through the stories and has a considerable bearing on their ideology. This leads to consideration of two related questions, whether the stories are subversive or affirmative of authority and what they reveal about historical memory and its uses in the fifteenth and early sixteenth centuries. Finally it is argued that, notwithstanding the many ambiguities of the texts, in their historical context, the early Robin Hood stories articulated a popular political outlook that challenged authority.

Finally, lest this emphasis on unearthing hidden meanings in the texts seems too intellectual, I hasten to acknowledge that they are first and foremost entertainments, not taken so seriously at the time, any more than the film *Robin Hood, Prince of Thieves*, when it first appeared, was seen to be pregnant with deep significance. The fifteenth-century stories are ripping yarns, woven around stock characters, with lots of action and adventures, in which the heroes triumph over the villains. Herein has lain the basis of their continuing appeal, from their first appearance, including to one who grew up in the Vale of Taunton Dean in the mid-twentieth century. It is because they also reveal, almost certainly unintentionally, much about the times in which they were first created and circulated, that they are worth close examination.

— *Preface and Acknowledgements* —

I owe many debts of gratitude and thanks incurred in the five years I have been engaged on this endeavour. To colleagues who sat through lectures, conferences and seminars at Aberdeen, Bristol, Champaign-Urbana, Durham, Liverpool, London, Norwich and York I am grateful for the opportunity to try out most of the chapters in progress and to benefit from their comments. In particular the following have given me specific assistance, encouragement or ideas: Caroline Barron, Linda Clark, Peter Coss, Sean Cunningham, Matthew Davies, Anne and Edwin DeWindt, David Ditchburn, Claire Etty, Peter Fleming, David Hepworth, Rosemary Horrox, Ronald Hutton, Hannes Kleineke, John Marshall, Mavis Mate, Malcolm Mercer, Tom Ohlgren, Mark Ormrod, Carole Rawcliffe, Colin Richmond, Felicity Riddy and Craig Taylor. Richard Almond, Ian Arthurson, Brian Barker and Amanda Richardson have been particularly generous in sharing their expertise with me and making available transcripts of documents. My thanks are also due to my editors at Routledge, Heather McCallum, who first signed me on; Vicky Peters, who has been both the most patient and the most enthusiastic of guides to completion; and Jane Blackwell, Christine Firth and Ruth Jeavons for overseeing the last stages through the press. My greatest debt is to Barrie Dobson and Maurice Keen, who read the manuscript, prevented many errors, subjected my argument to searching scrutiny, and made telling suggestions for improvement. While not agreeing with all that I have written, and those who know their work will have no difficulty in identifying what, they have been generous in their encouragement. What of merit there is to be found in these pages owes much to all these friends; its demerits are all my own.

Eryholme
20 *December* 2003

ABBREVIATIONS

Adam Bell — *Adam Bell, Clim of the Clough and William of Cloudesly*, in Dobson and Taylor, *Rymes*, pp. 260–73

BL — British Library

Chaucer, *Complete Works* — W. W. Skeat, ed., *The Complete Works of Geoffrey Chaucer*, 6 vols, 2nd edn (Oxford: Clarendon Press, 1900)

Death — *Robin Hood's Death*, in Dobson and Taylor, *Rymes*, pp. 134–7.

Dobson and Taylor, *Rymes*: — R. B. Dobson and J. Taylor, *Rymes of Robyn Hood: An Introduction to the English Outlaw*, 3rd edn (Stroud: Sutton, 1997)

EETS — Early English Text Society

EHR — *English Historical Review*

Gest — *A Gest of Robyn Hode*, in Dobson and Taylor, *Rymes*, pp. 79–112.

Guy — *Robin Hood and Guy of Gisborne*, in Dobson and Taylor, *Rymes*, pp. 141–5

HMSO — Her Majesty's Stationery Office

Malory, *Works* — Sir Thomas Malory, *Works*, ed., E. Vinaver, 2nd edn (Oxford: Clarendon Press, 1971)

Monk: — 'Robin Hood and the Monk', in Dobson and Taylor, *Rymes*, pp. 115–22

National Archives — The National Archives, Kew (formerly the Public Record Office)

Nottingham, Special Collections — University of Nottingham Library, Department of Manuscripts and Special Collections

PL — James Gairdner, ed., *The Paston Letters;* (6 volumes, London, 1904)

Potter — 'Robin Hood and the Potter', in Dobson and Taylor, *Rymes*, pp. 125–32

Rot Parl — *Rotuli Parliamentorum* (6 volumes, London, 1767)

Statutes of the Realm — *Statutes of the Realm* (11 volumes, London, 1810–28)

TRHS — *Transactions of the Royal Historical Society*

All quotations from and references to the early stories of Robin Hood are from the Dobson and Taylor edition, cited in italics (see *Death, Gest, Guy, Monk, Potter* above). However, the constituent elements of the *Gest*, which I have identified as 'Robin Hood and the Knight', 'Robin Hood and the Sheriff', 'Little John and the Sheriff', 'Robin Hood and the King' and 'The Death of Robin Hood' are cited in inverted commas. All other late-medieval texts are cited in italics.

Extracts from Julian Barnes, *England, England* are reproduced by kind permission of the author.

1

Texts and Context

————•◆•————

Everyone knows about Robin Hood is a myopic formula which makes an historian's hackles rise. Everyone knows, alas, what everyone knows. But the pearl richer than all his tribe is *You can't start messing around* with Robin Hood. What, my dear Jeff, do you think History is? Some lucid, polyocular transcript of reality? Tut, tut, *tut*. The historical record of the mid- to late-thirteenth century is no clear stream into which we might trillingly plunge.[1]

So pontificates Dr Max, a parody of a media don, in Julian Barnes' novel, *England, England*. The novel is a dystopia in which a media magnate, Jack Pitman, unmistakably based on Robert Maxwell, has turned the Isle of Wight into a themed heritage park encapsulating the quintessence of England. 'Robin Hood and his Merrie Men' came seventh in a worldwide survey (results adjusted by Sir Jack) of what people associated with Englishness, and so it becomes one of the main attractions, a team of actors performing 'Robin Hood and the Sheriff' daily at 4.00 p.m. to huge crowds.[2]

This book follows Dr Max's path and messes about with Robin Hood. On the other hand, it disagrees with his judgement that

1

the stories of Robin Hood provide a historical record of the mid-to late thirteenth century. It begins with the premise that the earliest surviving written version of the stories of Robin Hood dates from the fifteenth century, and probably the second half of that century. And it follows with the deduction that therefore they talk to us from and tell us about that century. Certainly history is no lucid, polyocular transcript of reality, and the book would not have been undertaken if I believed that everyone knew what I wanted to write. But history is nothing if not messing about with the past.

Everyone knows the story of Robin Hood. The Anglo-Saxon earl of Huntingdon, Sir Robin of Locksley, has been evicted from his estates by the Normans and outlawed. He lives by highway robbery and poaching. England is under the corrupt and oppressive rule of the wicked Prince John, regent while his brother the king, Richard I, is on crusade. Prince John is in league with the Sheriff of Nottingham and with Guy of Gisborne. They are terrorising the people. Locksley has taken to Sherwood Forest, and, as Robin Hood with his merry men leads the resistance of free-born Englishmen to the alien rule of the Normans, Robin runs rings round the sheriff. After many adventures, including an archery contest in Nottingham and fighting free of arrest, he triumphs. King Richard returns to England in disguise, observes what is amiss and discovers that Robin is his true subject. Prince John and his allies are removed. Locksley is restored to his lands, gets the girl (Maid Marian), good government is reinstated and freedom restored. This, with many variations on it, is the story that twentieth-century cinema and television audiences knew.

It is not, however, the story that was familiar to fifteenth- and early-sixteenth-century audiences. In fact, to begin with, they knew several stories, for Robin Hood the forest outlaw was a stock character on which different adventures were hung. One can identify as many as eight surviving stories, or 'rymes' as they were called, of Robin Hood set down in writing by *c.*1500, or containing elements which can be reasonably identified as of that time. We can look at them like episodes in a twentieth-century adventure series in 'comics', on radio, in film and on television, woven around stock characters – the hero, Little John, the sheriff, the monk, the king – in which the hero has various adventures, triumphing against the same set of villains in an infinitely changing set of circumstances. Plot lines, actions and incidents are endlessly repeated and varied. Outlaws go into Nottingham in disguise and fool the sheriff, there are archery contests, daring rescues and pitched battles between Robin's and the sheriff's men. In the eight 'stories' on which this study focuses the sheriff dies twice, a monk is robbed twice, the king intervenes twice. There were probably many more in circulation than have survived in writing. We have the testimony of the Scottish chronicler Walter Bower writing in *c.* 1440 to this effect. He wrote of Robin Hood and Little John and their companions: 'These men the stolid commons remember, at times in the gay mood of comedy, at others in the more solemn tragic vein and love besides to sing of their deeds in all kinds of romances, mimes and snatches'. He then proceeded to summarise a story, which has not itself survived.[3] Robin Hood was originally a popular (in the senses of both 'of the people' and 'enjoyed by many') late-medieval hero, about whom many tales were told. The survival of a number of different stories about him is the principal feature that separates Robin Hood from the other outlaw heroes of late-medieval England, such as Gamelyn or William of Cloudesly, about each of whom there survives but one self-contained narrative.[4]

The earliest stories of Robin Hood nevertheless contained features which everyone does know and which have survived the messing about of the centuries. Robin Hood is an outlaw. He is accompanied by his merry men, among whom are Little John (his principal lieutenant), Will Scarlet (or Scarlock) and Much the Miller's son. There is no Friar Tuck among his merry men, but there is a friar Tuck in a surviving play fragment. There is no Maid Marian, but Robin is devoted to the Virgin Mary. They reside in Sherwood Forest (but also float freely northwards to Barnsdale in south Yorkshire). They poach the king's deer, they hold up travellers through the forest whom they always invite to dine before they rob them. They are skilled archers, most of all Robin Hood, who can split the wand, the peg on which the target is hung in an archery contest. Robin in more than one story goes into Nottingham in disguise to take part in an archery contest, and in one he is recognised, betrayed and fights his way out. His arch-enemy is the Sheriff of Nottingham, who is frequently humiliated as well as killed twice. He is particularly unenamoured of monks, especially the Benedictine monks of St Mary's Abbey, York, who feature in two stories. He robs from the undeserving and helps the deserving, but he does not rob from the rich to give to the poor. He professes loyalty to his king, who in one story pardons him and in another condones his behaviour, but this is a King Edward, not Richard I. He is not an Anglo-Saxon, let alone a dispossessed earl. He is a plain yeoman.

A most significant moment in the development of the Robin Hood story was the drawing of five of these separate tales together in the fifteenth century into a compilation called the *Gest of Robyn Hode*, in which a single connecting narrative was supplied. One of the stories woven together is about 'Robin Hood and the Knight', sometimes known as the 'sorry knight' because of his plight. This provides the central thread. A second is about 'Robin Hood and the Sheriff' in which the hero goes into Nottingham to participate in an archery contest, is betrayed and fights his way out. A third is 'Little John and the Sheriff', in which Little John disguises himself as Reynolde Grenelefe and enters the sheriff's service and leads him into a trap in the forest. A fourth is 'Robin Hood and the King', which tells how the king pursues Robin, only catching up with him when he is disguised as a monk and is waylaid, and then pardons him and takes him into his service. And the last is 'The Death of Robin Hood' which tells how Robin, having abandoned the court and fled to the forest again, is finally killed through the treachery of the prioress of Kirklees, in Yorkshire.

After a few introductory stanzas, the narrative begins with Robin Hood's men waylaying the knight, who tells his sorry story. Robin lends him money to help redeem his mortgaged lands from the abbot of St Mary's, York. He goes with Little John to York, revealing that he has the money only after being humiliated by the abbot and the 'high justice', who had conspired to defraud him. Having recovered his lands he goes home, and a year later returns to the forest to repay the loan. But by this time Robin has waylaid the cellarer of the abbey, who was journeying south and relieved him of more than twice the amount. So Robin waives his loan. But when later Robin escapes from the sheriff in Nottingham and is pursued by him, he is given refuge by the knight in his castle, and the two withstand the siege. Now both the knight and Robin are outlawed. The sheriff seizes the knight, but he cannot capture Robin. So the king comes down to restore order, but not even he can catch him until he disguises himself as a monk who is waylaid by Robin. The king reveals himself, recognises Robin's loyalty, pardons him and takes him into his service. But after a year or so in royal service Robin flees back to the forest, where he remains at large for a further twenty years before his final betrayal and death.

The dominant narrative is thus woven together, in such a way as to form a coherent story in which Robin assists the knight, they are both pursued by the sheriff and in the end pardoned by the king. Yet close examination reveals the stitching as it were: the unnamed knight in the early part becomes Sir Richard at the Lee in the later sections. It is divided into eight 'fyttes' roughly representing the stories. Although the repetition of the call to the audience to pay attention is characteristic of these long recitations, sometimes they fail to disguise the joins. On the one hand the reminder to pay attention at the beginning of the sixth fytte,

> *Lythe and listen, gentlemen,*
> *And herkyn to your* [sic] *songe,*[5]

is followed immediately by the narrative where it left off at the end of the previous fytte, with the sheriff pursuing Robin to the knight's castle. On the other hand the third fytte, beginning with a similar refrain, is the beginning of a new story. This is the tale of 'Little John and the Sheriff', which seems to be included for comic relief. The tone is completely different. Whereas the thread provided by the dominant narrative is lofty and serious minded, 'Little John and the Sheriff', concerning the mockery of the sheriff, is knockabout farce. Even the story of 'Robin Hood and the Sheriff', while it is linked to the main narrative, is different in spirit, for this is an all-action, swashbuckling yarn in which Robin proves his fighting prowess. Their positioning in the compilation as the third and fifth fyttes, however awkwardly handled, suggests a deliberate change of key by the compiler to introduce light relief. 'The Death of Robin Hood' is but a short condensation of a longer story appended as an epilogue. An independent, longer fragment of the same story survives.

Nevertheless, as the first attempt to create a unified narrative, the *Gest* is clearly recognisable as the basis of all later versions of the story of Robin Hood. Textual and linguistic analysis has suggested a possible date of composition of the elements as early as *c.* 1400, and dates for the compositions to be committed to writing after 1450. The first surviving complete printed edition possible appeared in 1492. There are no earlier surviving manuscript copies.

6

Dating the *Gest* is complicated by the difficulty of distinguishing between what might have possibly been earlier, orally transmitted stories and the subsequent commitment of them to writing, of disentangling interpolations and adaptations at that stage, and of discerning manipulations of the text by compositors in setting the printed editions. Who was responsible for bringing this complex compilation together, when and why is not known. However, one can be reasonably certain that, while its constituent parts were in circulation earlier, it took the form we now have by the end of the fifteenth century.[6]

Of the other three, free-standing 'rymes', *Robin Hood and the Monk*, which survives in a manuscript version of the second half of the fifteenth century, and is probably the oldest surviving tale in writing, tells of how Robin is captured by the sheriff in Nottingham after he has been identified by a monk and how Little John rescues him. This has a sub-plot in which Little John rebels against Robin's authority, but is reconciled with his leader after he has rescued him. It ends with a speech by the king who had heard that Robin Hood had escaped the sheriff again, but concedes that Little John had in the end done his master good service.[7] *Robin Hood and the Potter*, also surviving in manuscript form, which has recently been dated to the last third of the fifteenth century, is more in the spirit of 'Little John and the Sheriff' and tells how Robin, switching places with a potter, goes into Nottingham, sells the pots deliberately at a loss, becomes engaged in an archery contest with the sheriff and tricks him into returning to the forest with him where the sheriff is relieved of his horse and goods.[8] *Robin Hood and Guy of Gisborne*, although the earliest surviving copy is much later, can be dated by its language and content to the late fifteenth century. It is a straightforward tale of how the sheriff hires a bounty hunter to hunt down and kill Robin and of how Robin reverses the tables and kills both of them.[9]

This then is the corpus of early Robin Hood stories. Inevitably the *Gest* has pride of place. As the first and influential attempt to construct one coherent story of Robin Hood, it quickly established the dominant narrative thread. It is also pre-eminent because it offered closure; it took the story to an end, Robin's return to the outlaw life, his betrayal and death, which give it an authority beyond the other tales of episodes in Robin's life. Later ballads, starting with the *Jolly Pinder of Wakefield*, *Robin Hood and the Butcher* and *Robin Hood and the Curtal Friar*, dating from the second half of the sixteenth century, may also be reworkings of pre-Reformation rymes. *Robin Hood and the Butcher* is so close to the story of the potter that it must be a variation on the same theme. *Robin Hood and the Friar* has many elements, which suggest an earlier, pre-Reformation origin. It is the tale that first introduces the story of Robin Hood and Friar Tuck, who appears as a character in the play text.[10] While these three have been excluded from the texts upon which this study is founded, they give further substance to the notion that there were many more tales in circulation before the mid-sixteenth century than have survived and been compressed into what became *the* story of Robin Hood in later centuries.

The surviving texts of the early stories, in rhyme, seem to have been originally composed to have been chanted or recited. They are addressed to, and might have been designed to appeal to, different audiences. The *Gest* calls upon freeborn gentlemen to take note and listen, an address which is repeated in the middle of the text.[11] It is a moot point whether this is to be taken literally. The storyteller might well be flattering his audience. The constituent stories, however, seem to have been originally addressed to different listeners. Both 'Robin Hood and the King' and 'Robin Hood and the Knight' have strong associations with a gentle audience and feature issues that would appear to have been of concern to the privileged. 'Robin Hood and the Sheriff' and 'Little John and the Sheriff', on the other hand, although amalgamated into the *Gest*, seem to be more appropriate for an audience of commoners. The mixed and wider audience seems then to be recognised in the envoi:

> *Cryst have mercy on his soule,*
> *That dyed on the rode!*
> *For he was a good outlawe,*
> *And dyde pore men much god.*[12]

This sits oddly with what has gone before, suggesting that it originally belonged to the separate story of the death of Robin Hood. It is also the only reference to Robin helping the poor.

Robin Hood and the Potter, on the other hand, in which the sheriff is again humiliated, is unequivocally addressed to good yeomen, ending with a blessing for all good yeomanry.[13] The comic action, in which Robin changes places with the potter to sell his wares in Nottingham and to be entertained, incognito, by the sheriff and his wife perhaps had an appeal to an urban audience. In this, as well as in 'Robin Hood and the King', mockery is made of commerce. Robin sells the pots for next to nothing; he gets his profit by liberating the sheriff of his horse and other equipment. In the *Gest*, too, the king is fitted out in a new livery in which the cloth is cut with lavish abandon by Little John. The target here, which perhaps both gentle and yeoman audiences would relish, seems to be the extortionate merchant.[14] Both *Robin Hood and the Monk* and *Guy of Gisborne*, in contrast, have no salutation or envoi at all. They stand as stories that do not seem to presuppose any particular audience.

Behind the written text lies the spoken word. One can be reasonably certain that Robin Hood stories were recited in halls, in taverns, in marketplaces and almost anywhere people gathered on special occasions. Late-medieval moralists disapproved of the ribaudiers, minstrels, jesters and histriones who entertained gentle and lewd people alike with their profane stories, dissolute innuendo, disrespectful jokes and their insistent cries of 'for largess, for largess'. They were little better than vagabonds and beggars, leading good Christians, and law-abiding subjects, astray. That goody two shoes Piers Plowman would have nothing to do with 'Robin the Rybauder for his rusty word'.[15] The Robin Hood stories were picked out early for special condemnation and there is a long string of complaint, from Langland in 1377 to the Reformation and beyond. Sloth, in *Piers Plowman*, is a personification of the indolent priest who did not know his pater noster well, but did 'rymes of Robyn hood'. In the first decade of the fifteenth century, the author of *Dives and Pauper* similarly disapproved of those who would sooner hear a tale or song of Robin Hood, or some other 'ribaudry' than go to mass or matins. It was the same a century later. Barclay complained in his early-sixteenth-century translation of *The Ship of Fools*:

> *For goodlie scripture is not worth an hawe,*
> *But tales are loved of ribaudry,*
> *And many are so blinded with their foly,*
> *That no scriptur think they so true nor gode,*
> *As is a foolish jest of Robin Hode.*[16]

The refrain was enthusiastically taken up by Protestants. William Tyndale in 1528 excoriated stories of Robin Hood, along with fables of love and wantonness, as ribaldries 'as filthy as heart can think'. Hugh Latimer was incensed, so he preached before Edward VI in 1549, to have found recently that he was locked out of church because it was Robin Hood's day and the parish had gone abroad to gather for him. He had actually to give way to Robin Hood's men. It was no laughing matter: 'under pretence for gatherynge for Robin hoode, a traytoure, and a thefe, to put out a preacher, to have his office lesse esteemed, to prefer Robyn hod before the ministracion of God's word'.[17]

Robin Hood became, literally, proverbial; the proverb 'many men speak of Robin Hood who never shot his bow' is first recorded at the beginning of the fifteenth century; the phrase 'Robin Hood in Barnsdale stood' had entered the language by 1429.[18] The relationship between written text as it emerged and spoken word was complex. We should not assume that an oral tradition preceded the written text. As recent study of the early-modern period shows, the two intermingled.[19] But it would be reasonable to suppose that the stories were far more frequently heard than they were read. Only after the development of print was it possible for those compiled as the *Gest* to be circulated in any number, and even then it would have been read aloud to a group more than privately alone. Whereas the author of *Dives and Pauper* castigated those who *heard* a tale or song of Robin Hood, Tyndale blasted those who allowed the laity to *read* (my italics) histories and fables, but forbade them to study scripture in the vernacular. The sentiment was the same, whether old catholic or new protestant, but for the protestant it was reading not hearing which was now central.[20]

The stories were not only recited and read, but also performed. Latimer was incensed that he had had to give way for a 'gathering' of Robin Hood. From as early as 1426–7, when there is a reference to a performance at Exeter, there is evidence, quickening after 1475, of dramatic presentation. We now appreciate, especially as a result of the Records of Early English Drama project, that plays, revels, gatherings and archery contests involving the impersonation of Robin Hood were being performed in parochial May Games almost as early as we know rhymes were being recited. It may be, as is generally assumed, that the rhymes came first; but by 1500 play and rhyme were interchangeable. A play text of *c.*1475 called *Robin Hood and the Sheriff* is remarkably like the

near-contemporary *Robin Hood and Guy of Gisborne*, which survives
only in a later version.[21] The language of the *Gest*, much of it in
dialogue, is the language of performance as well as the language
of storytelling; and the section which deals with the knight and
the abbot of St Mary's, York, structured in three acts, is dramatic.
We should not assume that Robin Hood performance was
restricted to parochial fund-raising. The case has been
convincingly made that the surviving play text was originally
among the Paston Papers and that it is the script for the play to
which Sir John Paston referred in a letter to his brother in 1473.[22]
And if a Norfolk gentry family enjoyed the play, why not other
venues, such as the revels of the Inns of Court, where we know
that plays were performed from the later fifteenth century. By the
end of the century the stories had become popular in the modern
sense of the word: all social groups, a few clerical kill-joys
excepted, shared the fun.

By the second half of the fifteenth century the Robin Hood
stories formed a body of popular literature that was declaimed,
performed and ultimately read at most levels of society and in
many different contexts. It is reasonable to suppose that
performances drew upon the same body of stories as have survived
as the rymes of Robin Hood and represented a wide
dissemination of their themes. How many there were, we shall
never know. But unlike the twentieth-century equivalent, such as
Batman, the hero is something of a chameleon. Even in the
surviving stories it is apparent that there were different Robin
Hoods: sometimes the fount of restorative justice ('Knight'),
sometimes a cold-blooded killer (*Guy*). Sometimes he is more
courteous ('Knight'), sometimes more common; sometimes he is
high-minded, sometimes he is a trickster (*Potter*). We are not
dealing with one Robin Hood character: we are dealing with
several. Little John, on the other hand, is more consistent. He is
the loyal servant, albeit his loyalty is tested in *Robin Hood and the*

Monk. He is also more consistently the trickster. Whereas in this tale Robin goes to Nottingham boldly, 'withouten layn',[23] and is quickly recognised, Little John in rescuing him pretends to be what he is not to the monk, to the king and to the sheriff. As the king acknowledges at the end:

> 'Little John hase begyled the schereff,
> In faith so hase he me.[24]

And the plot of 'Little John and the Sheriff' depends on Little John's pretence as Reynolde Grenelefe to hoodwink the sheriff. He is the master of disguise.

The Robin Hood stories were themselves examples of a wider collection of outlaw tales in circulation, some of which such as *Adam Bell, Clim of the Clough and William of Cloudesly* and *Gamelyn* dealt with similar themes. The story told in *Adam Bell* is exceptionally close to the Robin Hood stories. It survives in an early-sixteenth-century text. It concerns three outlawed yeomen, outlawed for poaching venison, who flee to Inglewood forest in Cumberland. The action centres upon William going to Carlisle to visit his wife, where he is betrayed, and after a good fight is captured by the sheriff and 'the justice'. He is rescued from the gallows by his brother outlaws, Adam and Clim, after another mighty conflict. They flee to the forest, but then travel up to London to seek the king's pardon, which they receive, only after William has performed the feat of shooting an apple placed on his son's head. The story ends with William becoming his bowbearer and chief riding forester of all the north, and his wife the chief nurse of the king's children.[25]

Gamelyn is more complex. This survives in a fourteenth-century text and is the story of how the youngest son of three is disinherited by his eldest brother after their father's death and forced to serve him. Eventually he rebels, assaults his brother and flees to the forest, pursued by the sheriff. There he and his faithful servant join an outlaw band of yeomen. Not long afterwards the outlaw chief is pardoned, and so Gamelyn is elected outlaw 'king' to succeed him. Soon his evil eldest brother is made sheriff; Gamelyn agrees to surrender because he is promised a fair trial by his honest middle brother, who stands bail. But he is double-crossed by the sheriff, who arrests the middle brother and puts him on trial in Gamelyn's stead before a packed jury and a bought judge. But Gamelyn comes to the rescue with his outlaw band, seizes his evil brother, the sheriff and the justice, has them tried and hanged. The king pardons both surviving brothers, making Gamelyn chief justice of his forests.[26]

Gamelyn links the Robin Hood tales and *Adam Bell* with an older tradition of exiled aristocratic outlaws exemplified in *Eustache the Monk* or *Fouke FitzWaryn*. As is apparent from these brief synopses, there are significant overlaps and borrowings between the stories. At the heart of all three is a story of a man outlawed, who flees to the forest where he lives by poaching before exacting revenge and receiving pardon from the king. Together they constitute the 'Matter of the Greenwood', a body of popular literature equivalent to the more refined Arthurian 'Matter of Britain'.[27] There are many details in common, but also some significant differences to which attention will be drawn later. But it is the stories of Robin Hood which are at the heart of it.

After the Reformation the Robin Hood stories changed. Protestantism significantly altered the context in which they circulated as popular literature. In brief the May Games were suppressed, but the tales resurfaced as ballads and broadsheets; print culture took over. The content also changed. Maid Marian entered the stories in the mid-sixteenth century: she was a migrant from other May Games, found associated with pre-Reformation Robin Hood games from the first decade of the century, but only after the Reformation did she replace the Virgin Mary in Robin's heart. Robin himself was promoted to the peerage as the dispossessed earl of Huntingdon in the last decade of the sixteenth century by Anthony Munday in his two plays, *The Downfall* and *The Death of Robert, Earl of Huntingdon*. Munday was responsible also for turning Marian into Matilda, daughter of Lord FitzWater, and transposing the plot to the reign of Richard I while he is absent on crusade, leaving his realm in the care of his wicked brother, Prince John.[28] Later, in the early nineteenth century, Robin became an Anglo-Saxon freedom fighter, throwing off the Norman Yoke. The publication in 1888 of Francis Child's edition of the *Gest* re-established it as the central early text and as a result, with the accretions and glosses of the intervening years, since the late nineteenth century it lies at the heart of the fixed story of Robin Hood familiar to the early twenty-first century.[29]

Robin Hood is essentially a fictional creation. A number of ingenious attempts have been made to discover the 'real' or 'historic' Robin Hood, even to identify some of the supporting cast as derived from people who once lived. The trail has led back to the third decade of the thirteenth century, to a record of 1230 in which the Sheriff of Yorkshire accounted for the goods he had seized from a fugitive called Robert Hood, and five years earlier to Robert of Wetherby, possibly the same man, an outlaw and evil-doer, whom the sheriff hunted down and hanged in 1225.[30] But another Robert Hood lived in County Durham in the early thirteenth century. He, Robert 'Hod' of Burntoft, gave surety to his neighbour, William Claxton, in 1244. Could he have later fallen foul of the law? His property, subsequently acquired by the Claxtons, was leased by them as 'Hodesplace' in the mid-fifteenth century. The matter is made more complex by the fact that from 1262, at the latest, the aliases 'Robehod' and Little John begin to appear in legal records, indicating the development of a convention whereby certain criminals adopted what had become known names. The existence of these aliases in the late thirteenth century suggest that stories about fictitious figures were already in circulation. But whose was a given name and whose an alias?[31] It is unlikely that it will ever be known for certain whether a 'real' Robin Hood ever existed on the same basis as we know, for instance, that Jesse James or Ned Kelly were 'real' outlaws in the nineteenth century.

The convention in the stories is indeed that 'he once walked on ground', but the earliest claims that Robin Hood was a real historical figure occur in fifteenth-century Scottish histories of English affairs. Andrew of Wyntoun wrote early in the century that Little John and Robin Hood were active in Inglewood and Barnsdale between 1283 and 1285; in the 1440s, Walter Bower placed them under the year 1266, linked to the defeated followers of Simon de Montfort. No fifteenth-century English chronicler made an attempt to place the outlaws in 'real time'. For these fifteenth-century commentators, Robin and Little John were nothing more than the central characters of vulgar tales, or lewd ribaldries.[32] It is the lewd ribaldries with which we are concerned. There is no doubt that some were in circulation well before 1400. What the content of these stories would then have been we do not know, but it is reasonable to assume that they were changing, and continued to change, just as they changed again in the century following 1550. Our texts are those captured at a particular moment, even though we do not know exactly when that moment was. But they are of the pre-Reformation century and they talk to us of that century. In so far as they seem to be set in an earlier age, they contain memories of that earlier era, which are refracted through and speak to the later fifteenth and early sixteenth centuries. The challenge, addressed directly in the final chapter of this book, is to identify that which was historic for the pre-Reformation century, and to establish the significance of it for contemporaries – what their past meant for their present.

What of that fifteenth-century present? Any attempt to

configure it in the twenty-first century is subject to the same catch as configuring the late thirteenth century in the early sixteenth. The past is seen from the present. This is perhaps nowhere more dramatically revealed in English historiography than in the history of the fifteenth century itself. As a result of successive layers of dynastic propaganda overlain by Shakespeare's dramatic influence, the century before Henry Tudor's victory on Bosworth Field was for long characterised as anarchic. The characterisation began in 1461 when Edward IV blamed Henry IV's usurpation of the throne for the subsequent 'unrest, inward war and trouble, unrighteousness, shedding and effusion of innocent blood, abuse of the laws, partiality, riot, extortion, murder, rape and vicious living', never experienced elsewhere in the world before. Successive usurpers, Richard III and Henry VII, recycled the same horrific vision to justify their acts. Fortuitously Henry VII was the last of three. His dynasty successfully established itself and so he, rather than either of his predecessors, became the great saviour from the chaos that had preceded him. What began as propaganda became accepted as historical truth by the end of the sixteenth century. Shakespeare used the history to hold up a mirror to his own age in his cycle of eight plays covering the end of Richard II's reign to the beginning of Henry VII's. Over the centuries, reinforced by Renaissance enlightenment, Protestant ideology and Whig political thinking, the fifteenth century as a whole came to be seen as uncivilised, blind and debased as well as anarchic. It was, and remains, a powerful characterisation of the last medieval century. During the twentieth century it was almost completely demolished by historians unbound by Victorian certainties and open to the evidence of contemporary sources. Nevertheless to this day one still finds, even in the works of influential British historians, repetition of the earliest caricature of the Wars of the Roses. Simon Schama commented in 1995 that it can hardly be an accident that the first printed editions of the *Gest* appeared 'at a disastrous moment in English history: the Wars of the Roses', while in 1999 Norman Davies wrote in a popular history of Britain, that 'From 1455 to 1485, the Wars of the Roses, between the rival proponents of Lancaster and York reduced England to chaos'.[33]

On the contrary the whole weight of twentieth-century historical scholarship was to stress that the later fifteenth century was neither chaotic nor a disastrous period. This is not to deny that there were in these decades periodic outbreaks of civil war. But the length, scale and impact of the conflict have been much exaggerated. There were rebellions and fighting in 1455, in 1459–64, in 1469–71, in 1483, in 1485, in 1486 and 1487. Some rebellions were short lived and easily put down, others succeeded with little opposition. Intense fighting between rival armies and sustained campaigning in the field in central, mainland England was restricted to 1459–61 and the spring of 1471. But none of the campaigns lasted more than a few weeks, battles were decisive, casualties, with the exception perhaps of Towton, were relatively light, the disruption and damage slight, and the impact largely restricted to the highest ranks of society and the rival royal families in particular. Civil war was intermittent. The disruption to normal civilian life, apart from the sustained upheavals of 1459–61 and 1469–71, was minimal; even then most people in most places were able to go about their daily lives without hindrance. For twelve years, between 1471 and 1483, peace and stability were fully restored. The crown changed hands several times as a result of battle, but most English men and women most of the time were unaffected by these events.[34] Far greater social and economic disruption was caused by the Great Civil War in the middle of the seventeenth century, and it is arguable that the conflicts of the reigns of Edward II and Richard II, as well as the struggle by Henry IV to establish himself on his throne after 1399, were as disruptive as the Wars of the Roses.

Beyond the realm of high politics and dynastic dispute, not finally put to rest until the peaceful succession of Henry VIII in 1509, England during the late fifteenth and early sixteenth centuries was growing in prosperity. The kingdom had passed through a period of trauma and crisis following the devastation of plague, which first arrived in the late summer of 1348. Successive outbreaks, not just the Black Death itself, had reduced the population by up to 40 per cent over four decades. In the wake of this almost unimaginable disaster, for which there seemed no remedy, as well as defeat and failure in war in France after 1369, which before 1360 had been so gloriously triumphant, the last decades of the fourteenth century were crisis ridden, politically, in religion and socially. Political crises in the reign of Richard II, who came to the throne in 1377, culminated in his deposition in 1399. Religious crisis came to a head in the heresy associated with John Wycliff, known as Lollardy, which was troubling the authorities by the 1380s. Heavy taxation to pay for a failing war, attempts by landlords to impose minimum wages and feudal obligations on tenants led to resentment which exploded in the Peasants' Revolt of 1381 and rumbled on in lesser protests thereafter. English society from top to bottom was jolted, confidence was shaken, and the very fabric of the social order seemed threatened. To shore up the established order a whole series of statutes were passed through parliament to control wages and employment, to fix the social hierarchy by prescribing the clothing people should wear according to their station (sumptuary legislation), to control leisure activity and social behaviour (football was banned, hunting in open land, tennis and bowls restricted to the better sort), to curtail educational opportunity, and carefully to delimit political enfranchisement to exclude the non-gentle. As the old 'feudal order' (for want of a better phrase) in their eyes faced collapse, parliament and the crown stepped in to construct a national code of social control, more explicitly class based, to buttress it.[35]

But during the fifteenth century matters stabilised. Continuing high death rates and low birth rates ensured that the population did not recover to its previous level. Indeed it was probably not until the mid-sixteenth century that it rose again to its early-fourteenth-century level. The Lancastrian dynasty, for a while, especially under Henry V, restored political confidence and brought even greater victories in the long-running war in France. The Lollard challenge was faced down, and the remnant of its followers driven underground. But most important of all the economic structure was transformed and stabilised on a new basis. The loss of population led in the long term to a contraction of output, especially agricultural output, a significant reduction of land under cultivation, the shrinkage and desertion of villages, the abandonment of direct farming of their own demesnes (or home farms) by landlords exploiting labour service, the withering and virtual disappearance of serfdom (the legal basis on which the obligation to render labour service stood) and a general rise in wages and fall in rents. In this new equilibrium, in which tenants and labour were in short supply, the advantage switched marginally away from the landed elite towards tenants and labourers. Market forces did not operate entirely smoothly, and in many places social conflict and tension continued, but all in all the landed elite accepted the new relationship.

Alongside the changes in the countryside, towns suffered mixed fortunes. There was a general contraction, especially of those dependent on local agriculture. Many small towns, with only limited markets, virtually reverted to villages. Fierce competition locally led to survival of some at the expense of their neighbours. A shift in international trade patterns also affected the great seaports. The rise of the Hanseatic League led to the effective exclusion of English shippers from the North Sea/Baltic trade routes. The once great port of King's Lynn was a major victim here. At the same time a major shift took place in the nature of English exports from raw wool to half-finished cloth. By the end of the century certain districts, especially East Anglia, the Cotswolds, Somerset and Devon, were flourishing on the basis of this new industry. On the back of it London grew at the expense of its provincial rivals, especially York. While Southampton and Exeter briefly flourished, a growing proportion of international trade focused on London and the sea route across the Straits of Dover to the ports of Flanders and Brabant. During the fifteenth century London entrenched itself as the unchallenged metropolis of the kingdom.

In all this the social order survived. The late-fourteenth-century social legislation may well have helped, but in essence it became apparent that social revolution was a long way off. The gulf between the resources of the very rich, the peers of the realm, the wealthiest gentry and the great religious houses and institutions and the income of those who worked for their living remained huge. While much of the legislation designed to check social mobility and fix social relationships in an old mould proved futile, fearful contemporaries discovered that the social order could absorb change. There was a general rise in the living standards of those who were skilled labourers in regular employment, tenant farmers, artisans and craft workers. Paradoxically the per capita wealth of English people increased while national income declined. As the century progressed, right through the ultimate defeat in France in mid-century and the 'chaos' of the Wars of the Roses that followed, the disposable income of ordinary men and women grew. This is shown in improved housing, a growth in horse ownership, an increase in the consumption of meat, dairy products and ale, the acquisition of decencies such as brass and pewter vessels, and more time spent simply in leisure. There was widespread amelioration as the benefits of a redistribution of income spread down the social order. New definitions were adopted for that social order, and given legal form by the Statute of Additions of 1413. Men below the level of gentleman were to identify themselves in any legal transaction as yeoman, or husbandman, or labourer or by their craft. The stratification was not in itself new, but it is clear from the end of the fourteenth century that a recognisably modern occupational structure existed in the countryside. The greatest beneficiaries were what came to be called the middling sort – yeomen, substantial husbandmen, self-employed craftsmen, small-scale traders, brokers and factors (many were employed in the cloth industry, which flourished in the countryside where costs were lower).

The question thus arises as to whether this was in any meaningful sense a peasant society. A peasant is usually identified as a self-sufficient smallholder, with a strong attachment to the land over several generations, who lives on the resources of his own family and whose way of life is rooted to the soil. This is a husbandman in the social terminology of the fifteenth century, who worked his own smallholding (some thirty acres or so) with his family and generated from it an income upon which in normal years they could live. To call him a peasant (or 'rusticus' as it was rendered in some accusations presented before the local courts), however, was a much resented slander.[36] A forthright case has been made, drawing a contrast with the model of more recent eastern European peasantries, that England from the moment from which written records survive, never had a peasantry.[37] This is a view that would seem to have been shared by Sir John Fortescue. England, he told the young Lancastrian prince of Wales in exile in France in the late 1460s, was a place that unlike France was virtually productive without the need of labour. Hence, the English

> are not very much burdened with the sweat of labour, so that they live more spiritually . . . For this reason the men of that land are made more apt and disposed to

investigate causes, which require searching examination than men who, immersed in agricultural work, have contracted a rusticity of mind from familiarity with the soil.[38]

Sir John viewed his native country nostalgically, especially in his imagined rural Arcadia, but it is revealing nevertheless that he saw a connection between independence of mind and liberation from toil. The English countryman did not have a peasant outlook, because, in Fortescue's eyes, he was not a peasant.

Nevertheless historians of the medieval economy continue to use the word to describe a particular category of smallholder. Jane Whittle has maintained that there were through to the sixteenth century 'small-scale agricultural producers . . . in possession of land which is farmed primarily with family labour and with the main aim of providing the family directly with a means of subsistence', who can be called peasants. And Phillipp Schofield, in an incisive discussion of the topic, while acknowledging the difficulty of accommodating traditional and narrow definitions of peasantry and emphasising the multiplicity of the experience of country people across time and between regions, judges that the term 'peasant' still seems entirely appropriate.[39] But was late-medieval England a peasant *society*?

The test applied here is the degree of market penetration. All agree that the rural economy was commercialised. Countrymen, Christopher Dyer argues for example, had moved away from simple self-sufficiency by 1200 and by the end of the thirteenth century were producing for sale on a considerable scale. They responded to market demand by changing farming practices. The market promoted a greater degree of specialisation. A vibrant land market flourished. However, although influenced by the market, countrymen had not fully developed a commercial mentality and were only partly integrated into it. Or, as Whittle puts it, they are not market dependent. This seems to be the test: rural society ceased to be a peasant society only when market production dominated over subsistence production.[40]

It all depends on the degree of commercialisation. By 1300 England had undoubtedly reached a high degree of commercial development. It was already a highly urbanised society, if by town one accepts the broad definition of a settlement whose inhabitants lived by other means than agriculture. While it has been estimated that 20 per cent of the population was urban, a far larger proportion lived within a day's walking distance to and from the nearest market town. Much manufacturing production was already rural, including stages of the cloth-manufacturing process, clothes making, metal working, pottery, brewing and of course milling. The English economy was to a significant degree commercially driven and market oriented. And so it remained through the great economic crises of the fourteenth century.[41]

Might it not, therefore, be more appropriate to describe England as already a capitalist economy? Characterised by the operation of market forces, the dominance of consumer demand, new investment, specialisation and concentration of industry (in the country as well as in the town), the English economy in the fifteenth century showed many of the features of incipient capitalism. It may not have been a fully fledged capitalist economy, but the transition was well under way. Some individuals emerged in the late-fifteenth-century countryside, such as the grazier Roger Heritage of Burton Dassett in Warwickshire, who produced on a large scale for the market, employed a considerable labour force, invested in buildings and equipment, and made a significant profit. Northern Norfolk, the most advanced economic region of England, was already by the early sixteenth century in effect a capitalist economy. In lowland southern and eastern England generally, town and country, market and hinterland, were so integrated and interdependent, structured in an interlocking network of regional urban hierarchies, all dominated by the great city of London, that the distinction between urban and rural society was already blurred. As Dyer has concluded, it was not yet a capitalist economy, but capitalists and potential capitalists thrived in fifteenth-century England.[42]

These issues are important because we need to have as clear an idea as possible of the social characteristics and outlooks of the popular audiences to which the Robin Hood stories appealed. They were neither 'peasants' in the generalised use of the word, nor 'capitalists' in any modern sense of that word. No doubt husbandmen enjoyed them, and so perhaps did graziers, but so too did gentlemen, yeomen, artisans and labourers, as did men and women of all ranks. From whatever precise social category readers, listeners and performers were drawn, they shared one thing in common; the benefits of an improved standard of living. One must be careful not to paint a picture of a pre-Reformation golden age. Disease and death rates remained high, harvests failed (spectacularly in the late 1430s and early 1480s); trade stoppages were common. The middle decades of the fifteenth century were a time of deep recession, brought on first by agrarian crisis, and then by a gathering slump in international trade, from which recovery did not really begin until after 1470.[43] But thereafter, in an international climate in which English rulers generally sought to avoid war, and to maintain peaceful relationships with England's principal markets in the Netherlands, despite periodic interruptions, prosperity continued to increase. Although sporadic in their movement, some indicators of economic growth have been found which have suggested an overall annual increase of just under 1 per cent per annum between 1471 and 1529. By twenty-first-century standards this is a modest growth rate. But by comparison with what had gone before, and what could be expected of a pre-industrialised economy, sustained growth of any level might be considered impressive. The signs of increasing national wealth, if only patchily distributed, are to be seen today most vividly in building works, especially in the improvements to parish churches, whether by new furnishings of pews and rood screens, the addition of new porches (Tiverton, Cirencester), the building of new chapels, the erection of bell towers (most notably in Somerset and East Anglia) or even complete rebuilding (Lavenham). Prosperity had its limits. Political circumstances (at home and abroad) and economic conditions were still volatile and uncertain.[44] The world was often unsettled. But there is some foundation to the notion, which arose after the upheavals of the mid-sixteenth century, the break with Rome, the imposition of Protestantism, the beginning of inflation and an apparent increase in poverty, that this had been a happy and prosperous time: that this had been Merry England.

Robin Hood was reckoned to be the best archer that was in Merry England.[45] This book cannot seek to encompass all that can be said of him. The expressly literary dimensions, the exploration of the stories as a manifestation of a particular genre of writing and the provenance of the texts are expertly handled elsewhere.[46] Certain elements of the stories are played down. Little is said of archery contests, or wrestling, or pluck buffet and other competitive games in which the outlaws revelled. There perhaps should be another chapter here on popular sports in the era before the Reformation. Nor does the book address adequately the absence of women. Apart from the Virgin Mary and the repeated convention that Robin honoured all those of her sex, and the wives and widows who crowd around to buy the potter's cut-price pots in Nottingham market, only three individual women appear in the stories. One is the sheriff's wife, with whom he flirts, and who is a bit of a sport. When the sheriff returns to Nottingham at the end of *Robin Hood and the Potter*, having been relieved of his horse and all his gear, he brings with him a gift of an ambling palfrey for her. When her husband bemoans the way he has been tricked and humiliated, she bursts into laughter and remarks that they have now paid for all the pots Robin gave to her. She seems to be drawn from the same tradition as Noah's wife and the wife of Bath.[47] The knight's wife, fair and free, appears twice as a dutiful and supportive lady, welcoming her lord home at the gate when he returns having recovered his property, and coming to the greenwood to beg Robin to free her lord, who had been captured by the sheriff.[48] Lastly there is the prioress of Kirklees, a mysterious kinswoman who is also described as a widow, but who betrays Robin. She is the very antithesis of the Virgin Mary.[49] Women in the stories are highly conventional. These are boys' stories for boys of all ages.

The scene for almost all that follows is set in the opening stanzas of the *Gest*.[50] It begins with a call to the audience to pay attention, in which the narrator informs his listeners that Robin, when he lived, was a yeoman and an outlaw; in fact, a good yeoman and a proud outlaw. Robin is found leaning against a tree, probably his trystel tree, in Barnsdale (it later becomes apparent that Barnsdale in southern Yorkshire merges into Sherwood Forest). With him are his principal confederates: Little John, Will Scarlock and Much the Miller's son, also good yeomen all three. Robin declares that he will not dine until they have waylaid a traveller through the forest and invited him to share his table, for which, of course, he is expected to pay handsomely. Nor will he eat, as is his custom, until he has heard three masses. Who, Little John asks (as if he did not know), should they rob and assault ('beat and bind')? Why, Robin replies, earls, barons, knights and esquires, bishops, archbishops and abbots, and especially the hye sherif of Notyingham'. However, they are not to molest women, husbandmen, good yeomen and any knight or esquire 'that wol be a gode felawe'. And so they walk to Sayles on Watling Street to find a guest for dinner. We do not hear of Robin's professed loyalty to his king or of his poaching the king's deer. And we are not told yet that it is the merry month of May when the leaves be green and the birds do sing. These appear later. We have, however, entered Robin Hood's world. And so in we 'trillingly plunge'.

2

Yeomanry

————•◆•————

Herkens, god yemen,
Comley, cortessey, and god,
On of the best that yever bare bou',

His name was Roben Hode
Roben Hood was the yeman's name,
That was both corteys and ffre

So runs the second and repetitive beginning of the third stanzas of *Robin Hood and the Potter*, a story which most clearly and unambiguously identifies Robin as a yeoman and his audience as composed of those who were, or would like to be thought of as, yeomen, and whose self-esteem and aspirations are flattered by the minstrel in his greeting to them as comely and courteous. The emphasis is repeated at the very end:

God haffe mersey on Roben Hodys sole,
And safe all god yemanrey[1]

'From the moment he first steps on the historical stage', wrote Dobson and Taylor in 1976, 'Robin Hood is presented as a yeoman hero for a yeoman audience'.[2] But what precisely constituted a yeoman and yeomanry in the fifteenth and early sixteenth centuries, and especially what precisely is meant in the description of Robin Hood himself as the personification of good yeomanry has been and remains hard to pin down. Essentially there are two distinct usages of the term. The first and oldest is that of a household rank; the second and more recent was the extension of the term to describe a social status. In the fifteenth and early sixteenth centuries both were in common use

It is perhaps not surprising therefore that the meaning of the terms yeoman and yeomanry in the rymes of Robin Hood has been the subject of sustained discussion since the late 1950s. Debate began with the publication in *Past and Present* of Rodney Hilton's ground-breaking article on 'The Origins of Robin Hood' in 1958. Hilton, who received initial support from Maurice Keen, conceived of the ballad hero in terms of medieval class conflict. Robin the yeoman was identified as a free peasant representing peasant ideology for a peasant audience.[3] Hilton's intitial hypothesis was roundly challenged by Sir James Holt, first in his rejoinder to Hilton, and subsequently in his *Robin Hood*. Holt argued that the term was used in the sense of a household officer and that the stories were nurtured in the halls of castle and manor, and were not for peasant ears.[4] Since then the argument has moved on. The specific identification of the term yeoman within a peasant context has been significantly modified in the light of the understanding that fifteenth- and early-sixteenth-century rural society was considerably more complex than a simple peasant economy and that there was a growing and influential body of *mediocres*, or middling sorts, for whom the word peasant is not applicable, and with which the yeomanry as a social group can be equated.

More recent writings on the ballads have accordingly stressed this social context. Peter Coss has expressed himself broadly in agreement that the term employed in the *Gest* describes a social gradation between the armigerous and the tillers of the soil. He has concluded that the *Gest* was composed for an audience that was not knightly and detected in the work elements of parody of knightly rituals.[5] Colin Richmond has associated Robin Hood with an intermediary and transitional status of 'yeomanliness'. Not 'gentle', he embodies the dreams and aspirations not only of the emergent rural elite of prosperous farmers of medium-sized holdings, but also of the downwardly mobile younger sons of gentry who joined their ranks.[6] In their most recent thoughts on the subject, Dobson and Taylor have reiterated the centrality of Robin Hood's status as a yeoman. By the mid-fifteenth century he had emerged:

> not only as a new sort of hero but as a hero for a new and large social group, the yeomanry of England. Above all it seems to have been the outlaw's association with that large if ill-defined section of late-medieval society which provided him with what were to prove his most distinctive and enduring characteristics.[7]

The early-twenty-first century consensus is that Robin Hood was the personification of non-gentry aspirations and of the hopes of 'people of handicraft',[8] artisan as well as husbandman, urban as well as rural, of fifteenth-century England.

Even so, Holt, while acknowledging that from the late fourteenth century the term had been extended to incorporate a social status between gentleman and husbandman, was dismissive of any attempt to identify yeomanry with a new social group emerging in the later middle ages. He has continued to insist that the ballads did not express the outlook of any new social group;

indeed he doubted that society in the fifteenth century was any more diversified than in the thirteenth, suggesting that the word yeoman was but a new label for a long-established social status. Only later, at the end of the fifteenth century, were the stories adulterated and contaminated for a more popular 'yeoman' audience.[9]

First, the point at issue has been whether the term yeoman was initially used in the stories and continued to be used primarily as a description of a household rank on to which the meaning of a social status was grafted, or whether the term was from the beginning primarily used to identify a social status. On this hangs a wider debate as to whether the Robin Hood stories are to be perceived as deriving from gentle circles or as having popular roots, and thus as to whether they subsequently became popularised, or in the course of time became gentrified. In the debate as it has been conducted so far, these have largely been seen as alternatives, and the two mutually exclusive. In the process there has also been a tendency to make no distinction between the yeomanry of Robin Hood, and of his merry men and some of his associates, and the yeomanry of the audience to which the stories were supposedly delivered, and in at least one surviving text explicitly addressed. But the two need not have been the same. Robin Hood could have been one sort of yeoman, the audience as a whole composed of others, and not just yeomen. Second, there has also tended to be an assumption that all the different stories drew upon one meaning of yeoman and yeomanry, whichever it was. But this too is not to be taken for granted. As we have already seen, there were different sorts of stories in circulation in the later middle ages, about Robin Hoods with different characteristics. It is thus possible that the stories in their first recorded versions incorporated and encompassed both the yeoman of the household rank and the yeoman of intermediate social status either in the personification of the hero or the membership of the audience. A discussion of the 'yeomanliness' of Robin Hood and the social world in which he is set needs to keep all these considerations in mind.

Part of the problem is linguistic. The English word 'yeoman' is derived from the Old English 'yonger man'. The phrase 'yonge men' in fact appears twice in place of 'yeomen' in the printed version of the *Gest* at the beginning of the story of 'Robin Hood and the Sheriff'; here his followers are his 'mery yonge men' and 'seven score of wyght yonge men'.[10] A similar usage is found in *Gamelyn*; the outlaws in the forest whom he joins are 'seven score yonge men', sometimes merry men, but always young men not yeomen. In *Gamelyn* an emphasis is placed on their age. They are indeed young, as is the hero.[11] They are also in the service of their master, the king of the outlaws, whose service Gamelyn also joins. There is implicitly a dynamic element in the use of the phrase in the sense of indicating a stage in a career, the stage through which a young man in service passes on the way to becoming a squire or master, as does Gamelyn, who soon becomes the king of the outlaws himself.[12] The usage of 'yonge man' in this way was extended to great London companies of the late fourteenth and fifteenth centuries such as the tailors. The word was adopted to identify those who had completed their apprenticeships, but were not yet masters, probably unmarried and working as wage-earners, or journeymen. In the late fourteenth century they formed their own fraternities, which, at first distrusted by the livery, were in time absorbed into the structure of the company. The membership also widened to incorporate small-scale masters who were on their way to becoming livery men, or, in many cases, were never going to make it. Thus in this urban context too the meaning of the word shifted from being a life stage to a social and economic status.[13]

In the fourteenth century the word 'yeoman' also began to be used as a translation of the French *valet*, or Latin *valettus*, as a rank.

As such it lay between esquire and groom in a noble household. Valets or yeomen, as household ordinances and lists reveal, occupied a distinct position in the hierarchy. Ralph Neville, earl of Westmorland, provided in his will drawn up in 1424 for legacies of 10 marks for each of his squires, £2 for each of his valets and £1 for each of his grooms.[14] In this context, too, the word probably began as an indication of a life stage, but by the end of the fourteenth century, while it probably implied an unmarried man, it did not necessarily mean a stage in career development (although in the case of Geoffrey Chaucer it did). There were probably some aged valets in Earl Ralph's household, just as there were ageing yeomen in the ranks of the Merchant Tailors in London. Such an aged yeoman is to be found in the household of Richard Clervaux of Croft, a Yorkshire squire who in 1449 granted to William Cabery on his retirement free board, lodging and livery after a lifetime of service to Richard and his father.[15]

In the later fourteenth and early fifteenth centuries, an age of rapid social mobility and growing differentiation of wealth, in which the governing classes were anxious to preserve the status quo, the use of the term yeoman was extended to an intermediary social category between husbandman and gentleman in the country. Some sense of the transition of meaning is to be found in the provision in 1386 by William Claxton of Claxton, County Durham, of the same livery for his new tenants of his manor of Hulam as he was accustomed to provide for the yeomen of his household.[16] The defining moment was the Statute of Additions of 1413, which laid down that social status or occupation had to be specified in all legal transactions. Craftsmen were to be known by their trades; but countrymen appearing before the courts who were of greater wealth and higher standing than mere husbandmen gave to themselves, or had ascribed to them, the loose designation of yeoman.[17] As a social category 'yeoman' was primarily applied to men who in the modern sense of the word were substantial and prosperous farmers. It was a status akin to that enjoyed by certain rural artisans and tradesmen. Many occupations such as clothier, or fuller, or butcher, or smith, or even potter, in town and country generated as much income, or more, and endowed a similar social status. Moreover in late-medieval villages and small towns, where the same men were often occupied in both husbandry and a craft or trade, the distinction was blurred: they all were handicraftmen, men who practised a craft with their hands. Additionally, the manner in which the act was applied led to multiple ascriptions, or aliases, whereby the same person could be identified in separate legal actions by different designations, both by social status and by occupation. There was therefore considerable confusion of nomenclature.

In the late fourteenth century yeomanry also implied freeborn blood and free tenure. Robin, the storyteller reminded his audience, was both courteous and free. But it is evident that a century later substantial customary tenants, some even of questionable birth, styled themselves yeomen and were accepted by their neighbours as such. William Hawler, who leased and worked the small Durham manor of Pontop from Robert Claxton in 1435, was identifed as a yeoman in his lease. In 1470 a tenant of a holding of sixty acres in the Tees valley could describe himself uncontroversially as a yeoman. Bishop Latimer preaching before Edward VI reminisced about his father being one such yeoman with his own farm, one or two labourers and a comfortable standard of living.[18] A yeoman was in the later fifteenth and early sixteenth centuries a respectable local worthy, a man whose income, if it exceeded 40 shillings a year, might even, and if the returning officer did not inquire too closely into his tenure, entitle him to vote in parliamentary elections. He was one who might serve as churchwarden, as a juror on his local manorial court, or even find himself empanelled by the king's sheriff or escheator onto one of the many local juries of inquiry. When Sir John

Fortescue, in exile, praised the virtue of his kingdom, he only exaggerated when he claimed that there were in England many yeomen sufficient in patrimony to serve on a jury who could spend more than 600 'scutes' (£100) a year. Yeomen belonged to the social group which a century later came to be known as the 'middling sort'.[19]

Not a gentleman, still a working farmer, artisan or tradesman who worked with his hands, he was nevertheless a man of local substance and importance, employing one or two of his own servants. The privileged were anxious to draw a clear distinction between a gentleman and a yeoman, even though in practice, at the margins, it was sometimes difficult to discern. No gentleman, it was asserted, worked with his hands. The distinction was even extended to objects; there were yeomen sheets, which were rougher than gentlemen's sheets, there were horses suitable for yeomen to ride, but not gentlemen.[20] A yeoman might aspire to gentility, and indeed on occasion seek to pass himself off as better than he ought; if so he was usually found out. His son, however, might be put to school and so prosper in the law, or at court, or in noble service, or on the field of battle that he became a gentleman. Yet the distinction was clear. One knew a gentleman from a yeoman. Richard Calle, the son of a Framlingham grocer, loyal bailiff and servant to the Pastons, discovered in 1469 to his cost that a yeoman presumed too much above his station if he eloped with his employer's daughter.[21] Yet yeomen liked to think of themselves as being sufficiently courteous and free to be a cut above the common sort. Some may have had pretensions to gentility, but they were all proud to be respectable.

The numbers of yeomen, at least proportionally to a reduced population, grew during the fifteenth century in line with the rise of the standards of living of those in the intermediate ranks of society, and they were swollen by downward as well as upward mobility. In a world of primogeniture, the younger sons of gentlemen, and even more so their grandsons, came to rest in the same social group. They were to be found throughout England, in Weardale as well as in the Thames valley. It is arguable, too, that those who styled themselves yeomen were becoming more self-conscious and articulate. Some may even be described as proto-capitalists; they were certainly not averse to investing in trade and industrial production.[22]

Yet the word yeoman was still current at the end of the fifteenth century in its older and original meaning. It still continued to be employed in noble and royal households. In the great noble households there remained three grades of servant – now gentlemen, yeomen and grooms (sometimes knaves). A list has survived of those present in John, Lord Howard's household on a visit to London on 22 January 1467. There were sixteen 'gentlemen' (three of whom were knights), forty-eight yeomen and twenty-seven grooms. The number of yeomen seems excessive, for sixteen years later, when he had risen to be duke of Norfolk, he was accompanied on a journey to London on 2 September 1483 with fifty-four men, no more than nineteen being yeomen. Greater detail of the household staff and their functions is given of the similar riding, or travelling household, of Henry Percy, earl of Northumberland, in 1511. It was laid down in his household statutes that when he set out on a journey a group of five servants would go ahead to set up the lodgings, three would accompany the baggage (also in advance) and another much larger party would follow to prepare the hall and chamber for his arrival. The rest would travel with him. Three yeomen, a yeoman usher of the chamber, a yeoman usher of the hall and a yeoman cook would be in the first party. Accompanying the baggage would be a yeoman porter for keeping the gate. A yeoman cellarer travelled with the third party. In the retinue of the earl himself rode a yeoman of the robes, a yeoman of the horse, a yeoman of the chamber, a yeoman of the pantry, a yeoman of the buttery, an unspecified number of yeoman waiters and finally 'all other yeomen to ride behind the lord', presumably as the party's escort.[23]

The official ordinances of the household of Edward IV, issued in 1478, give full details of the duties, perks and rewards of such yeomen. The yeomen of the chamber, of whom there were four in the king's household, were to make beds, to hold torches, to set boards (tables), to apparel all chambers and to carry out all other such tasks as ordered by the chamberlain or ushers of the chamber, taking the accustomed wages and receiving the usual livery (clothing allowance). Other royal yeomen, some duplicated in noble households, were the yeoman of the stool (the chamber pot), the yeoman of the armoury, the yeoman of the bows and a yeoman of the king's hounds. The royal household was the model for all others. The ordinances in fact laid down the nominal sizes of noble households, specifying, for instance, that a duke should have eighty men. It is clear too from Edward IV's ordinances, explicitly drawing upon similar ordinances laid down by Edward III, more than a century earlier, that the yeomen had a specifically military function. The twenty-four yeomen of the crown, who carried out all these various functions, had also to be the 'most semely persones, clenly and strongest archers, honest of condicions and of behavoure, boldmen, *chosen and tried out of every lordes house in Yngland for theyre cunyng and vertew*' (my italics). They were chosen men of 'manhoode [and] shootyng'. In the noble Edward's statutes, the ordinances further noted, they were called the 'xxiiij archers a pe currauntz enchierment deuaunt le roy pur payis pur gard corps du roy', called also 'the kinges watchement'. Thus it was laid down that 'whan they make wache nyghgtly they should be gurde with theyr swerdes or with other wepyns redy and harneys about them'.[24] This was an elite corps, the yeoman of the guard as they were to be later styled, whose responsibilities combined waiting on the king in various functions with maintaining the security of the palace. One assumes that the yeomen of the noble households, from which they were recruited, carried out similar duties. Thus one might envisage that the yeomen who followed on the earl of Northumberland in 1511 were his armed guards, employed to protect him.

It is not hard to find examples of the term being used in the stories to denote service rank. In *Robin Hood and the Potter*, when Robin, in disguise, is in Nottingham, has sold the pots, and dined well with the sheriff and his wife, takes part in an archery contest. Since Robin had no bow with him,

> *The screfe commandyd a yemen that stod hem bey*
> *After bowhes to weynde;*
> *The best bow that the yeman browthe*
> *Roben set on a stryng.*[25]

Was this the sheriff's yeoman of the bows? In the story of 'Little John and the Sheriff', Little John disguises himself as Reynolde Grenelefe to join the household service of the sheriff. Though the role he assumes is not specified, a post such as yeoman of the hall or chamber is envisaged, otherwise the comic action in which he assaults the steward and butler would make no sense. The cook, with whom he fights and finally absconds, is an equal, and proves himself an equal in combat. He is subsequently praised by Robin Hood as a 'fayre' yeoman.[26] At another point in the story of 'Robin Hood and the Knight', also incorporated into the *Gest*, Little John plays the role of a household yeoman in service to the knight as he sets off to repay his mortgage. Having been elaborately equipped by the outlaws, the knight finally departs with Little John standing in for his entire entourage:

> *'It were greate shame', sayde Robyn,*
> *'A knight alone to ryde,*
> *Withoute squire, yoman, or page,*
> *To walk by his syde*

'I shall the lende Littell John, my man,
For he shal be thy knave;
In a yeman's stede he may the stande,
If thou greate nede have.'[27]

The knight should have an honourable escort, worthy of his dignity. It might be smaller than that with which the duke of Norfolk or earl of Northumberland moved about the country, but the yeoman fulfils the same function. A similar sense of propriety is at play in an incident later in the story when, having lost an archery contest to the king in the disguise of an abbot, Robin prepares to take the customary forest penalty of a blow to the head. But the king refuses:

'It falleth not for mine order', seyd our kynge,
'Robyn, by thy leve,
For to smite no good yeman,
For doute I sholde hym greve.'[28]

Neither a king nor an abbot should strike an honest servant. The distinction between the two types of yeomen is apparent in the texts. The same is found in *Adam Bell*, even more explicitly. At the end the three outlaws are received into the king's household. The king declares:

William, I make the a gentleman
Of clothing, and of fe:
And thi two brethren, yemen of my chamber,
For they are so seemly to me.[29]

Some yeomen in the stories of Robin Hood do, as Holt argued, hold household office.

Finally we can find the term being used simultaneously to

describe both a yeoman by office and a yeoman by status. In 1386 Isabella Claxton of Horden, the widow of Sir William Claxton, agreed a complex twelve-year lease of her manor of Hulam and its appurtenances in County Durham with three Betonson brothers who were to work the land. Among the clauses she undertook to provide clothing such as she gave her yeomen (*valetti*), and of the same livery, and if she failed to do so would make an allowance as a deduction of the rent to the value of clothing received by her own yeomen, or other yeomen in the neighbourhood. Thirty-four years later she entered into a similar agreement over the site of the manor of Claxton, in which again the tenant farmers were to receive annual robes of livery. In 1465 Henry, Lord FitzHugh retained Abraham Metcalf, yeoman, at Ravensworth in north Yorkshire, who was to have the lease of the demesne at Askrigg and other tenements in exchange for his sworn service at all times and to be 'good tenant and agreeable and of good reuill and demenynge to all the seid lord tenants'.[30] In an era of social flux, therefore, when contemporaries frequently complained that no one knew their place any more, the term yeoman encompassed several overlapping shades of meaning and incorporated diverse social groups. As Coss has stressed, the use of the term 'yeoman' in the stories is often hard to disentangle from the contemporary confusion of status and status terminology.[31]

There is, however, a specific further use of the term yeoman, 'yeoman of the forest', which brings official rank and social status even closer together and has particular relevance for the social world of the stories. Holt drew attention to a particular association between yeomen and the forest as early as his original article on the subject. As he pointed out, one of the earliest references to 'yonger men' is to be found in the twelfth-century *Pseudo-Cnut de Foresta*, in which they are under-foresters drawn from the middling ranks of freemen. But neither in his initial article nor in his later book did Holt develop the significance of the explicit description of Robin and his men as foresters, or examine the terminology of forest and hunting which recurs in the ballads. In his first article, he stressed the manner in which Robin poached the king's deer, thus to be seen in the thirteenth-century context of conflict over forest rights between king and lords. But while he noted the probability that Robin's earliest audiences thought of him as an outlawed forester, he did not there, or subsequently, develop the idea further.[32] He was more concerned to establish what he perceived as the broader aristocratic milieu of the ballads and Robin's rank as a household officer than to explore his particular identification as a specific kind of yeoman.

Coss noted too that Robin and his men are sometimes described as 'yeomen of the forest', but concluded, nevertheless, that the phrase applies to the outlaws' situation rather than their status. The term forester, he added, was used by way of contrast to a man specifically in royal service. By implication, were they foresters by occupation, the legendary outlaws would be described as such. Robin and his men are thus not yeomen *of* the forest, but outlawed yeomen of an intermediary social status who have sought refuge *in* the forest. We are thus to picture Robin and his fellows as prosperous countrymen in flight from justice who have banded together in the woods.[33] Yet the key to Robin Hood's own yeomanry, and his being equally at home in rural society and in household service, lies in his identification by the audience as a yeoman of the forest.

In the *Gest*, Little John holds up the cellarer of St Mary's Abbey, York:

> *'Who is your mayster?' sayd the monke*
> *Lytell Johan sayd, 'Robin Hode',*
> *'He is a stronge thefe', said the monke*
> *'Of hym herd I never good'.*

'Thou liest', than sayd Lytell Johan,
'And that shall rew the;
He is a yeman of the forest,
To dyne he hath bode the'. [34]

A yeoman of the forest is the antithesis of a strong thief. This angry exchange can make sense only if one appreciates that it was the yeoman of the forest's role to apprehend common criminals; in Little John's eyes his master did not break the law, he upheld it. He is, in short, a forester. The specific meaning of a forester is reinforced when, later in the *Gest*, Robin himself with his men behind him holds up the king, who is disguised as a monk. He declares

We be yemen of this forest,
Under the grenewode tre,
We lyve by oure kynges dere,
Other shyft have not we. [35]

He too identifies himself and his men as honest foresters, whose sole duty is to protect the king's deer. Furthermore, he and his men now claim to be explicitly yeomen of *this* forest; they are, the king/abbot is to believe, his serving foresters of Barnsdale/Sherwood. [36]

Late-medieval foresters, the yeomen of the forest, were part of the extended household of the king and great lords; the household out of doors as it were. They exercised a wide range of duties. The responsibility for preserving the vert (the vegetation) and venison (the game) in all forests, seigneurial as well as royal, lay with them. Each belonged to an elaborate establishment. At its head, the keepership, was usually an office occupied as a sinecure by a courtier or retainer. The principal man on the spot was the chief forester, who was himself assisted by a team of riding or mounted foresters, whose responsibility extended over the whole forest, and by dismounted or walking foresters, each of whom kept a division of the forest known also as a walk, ward or bailiwick. The first duty of the yeoman forester was the protection of the deer in his 'division'. He needed to know that division like the back of his hand. He had to be alert for poachers, to provide winter feed for the deer, and to take care of the hinds and newly dropped calves during the 'fence month' (the equivalent to the close season) around Midsummer Day. But he had also to preserve the vert, which included the prevention of unlicensed grazing, the detection of illegal logging and the management of woodland in all its aspects. He walked or, if he were mounted, rode round his section of the forest protecting the game and the vegetation.[37]

There were nine working foresters employed in the New Forest at the end of the fifteenth century, nine in the forest of Clarendon, six employed by the earls of Westmorland in their Durham forests and sixteen, including parkers and woodwards, in the seigneurial forest of Wensleydale. The New Forest establishment, for instance, was headed by the Keeper, a sinecure held by the earl of Arundel in the 1480s. He employed a lieutenant and a deputy lieutenant. Beneath them came a chief forester, the riding forester, two rangers and the bowbearer. Then there were the nine foresters each responsible for a separate bailiwick. The office of forester was of local importance, sometimes held by members of minor gentry families, but more characteristically in the fifteenth century by those of lesser families, yeomen by status as well as occupation, bearing names in Wensleydale such as Forster, Hunt and Hunter. The post carried with it rights of pasture and pannage, the concession of cutting a number of standing trees and the privilege of taking one or two deer a year. Some, reckoned always to be on duty, were paid a salary of two pence a day. Other forest officials, such as verderers, woodwards, rangers and agisters, were also of yeoman status, as were the parkers of the enclosed parks both within and separate from the forests themselves. Taking all the forests and chases throughout England, there were literally hundreds of them in the kingdom at large.[38]

Sir John Fortescue in his idealised descriptions of England had a special word to say for these men. Discussing the king's officers he comments,

> the least of them, although he be only a parker, taking but two pence a day, yet he has yearly £3 and 10 pence, besides his dwelling in his lodge, his cow for his milk, and such other things about him, and the fees of his office, so that the office is to him as would be 100 shillings of fee or rent, which is a fair living for a yeoman.

Thus, *mutis mutandis*, for a forester who received the same fee, and enjoyed similar benefits. And so also for those employed not by the king, but by great lords such as the third earl of Westmorland, whose parkers and foresters on his Durham estates enjoyed the same rate of pay. Fortescue valued them, he wrote, because in them, after the might of the great lords, lay the might of the land. 'Some forester of the king's', he asserted, 'who has no other livelihood, may bring more men to the field well arrayed, especially for shooting, than may some knight or squire of very great livelihood, dwelling by him but having no office'. This applied, too, as Fortescue knew, to his 'overmighty subjects', the great lords of the realm. As archers, and the leaders of archers, foresters provided a significant part of the kingdom's military reserve.[39]

These are the same yeomen, foresters, whom Little John and his fellows are not to molest. They can prey on churchmen and the Sheriff of Nottingham,

> *But loke ye do no husbonde harme,*
> *That tylleth with his ploughe.*

No more ye shall gode yeman
That walketh by grene wode shaw.[40]

These yeomen are *not* substantial farmers of an intermediary status between husbandmen and gentry, as has usually been supposed. An unambiguous distinction is drawn, in the conventional terminology of estates, between those who work the land and those who patrol the forest. Confirmation that walking 'by grene wode shaw' is a job description is to be found in the surviving records of Sherwood Forest itself. A late-fifteenth-century transcription of the oath made by foresters includes the undertaking to 'kepe and walke the office of forestership and trewe watche make bothe erly and late both for vert and venyson'.[41] An eighteenth-century copy of the charge of the court of swanimote likewise refers to the foresters and walkers within the forest.[42] The occupational description is made even more explicit in the opening two stanzas of *Adam Bell*:

Mery it was in grene forest
Among the leves grene,
When that men walke both east and west
Wyth bowes and arrowwes ken:

To ryse the dere out of theyr denne;
Such sightes as hath ofte bene sene;
As by yemen of the north countrey,
By them it is as I meane.[43]

And then Adam Bell, Clim of the Clough and William of Cloudesly are named. They come from the same background as Robin Hood and Little John.

Robin is not just a forester: he is himself the self-proclaimed 'chief governoure' of the forest, the master in outlawry of a fabulous 140 'wight' yeomen, as if all the foresters of the north had flocked to his side. When, at the end of the *Gest*, he deserts the court and returns to the life of a forest outlaw, he blows his horn, and all the old gang reassemble, duff their hoods, kneel and welcome their master back. He is the forest king. So knowledgeable of his kingdom is he that he is able to lead not only the sheriff but also the crowned king a merry dance from forest to forest. Only another 'proud' forester in the royal service knows how to track him down, and that is by the ruse of the king disguising himself as a monk, a guest Robin can never resist inviting to dinner.[44]

As befits the self-proclaimed chief governor of the forest, Robin needed a bowbearer, for in all forest administration a bowbearer was appointed to carry the keeper of the forest's bow when he came to hunt, or to accompany the king when hunting, and possibly also to act as his personal bodyguard. He was also his deputy, charged with overseeing the administration of the forest law in his absence.[45] This is a role, however, which Little John rejects at the beginning of the story of *Robin Hood and the Monk*. Robin, planning to go into Nottingham to participate in an archery contest, is advised to take an escort of twelve men. But no,

> *'Of all my merry men', seid Robyn,*
> *'Be my feith I will none have,*
> *But Litul John shall beyre my bow,*
> *Till that me list to drawe'.*

To which Little John, asserting bluntly that there is no room in the greenwood fellowship for such aristocratic hierarchy, replies,

> *'Thou shall beyre thin own, Maister,*
> *and I will beyre mine'.*[46]

William of Cloudesly, on the other hand, is happy after he is pardoned to accept the role of king's bowbearer, with a fee of 18 pence a day and the additional office of Riding Forester of the North.[47]

Finally, Robin and his men, as no one needs reminding, dressed in green. They don the uniform when they go into action. Thus in the fourth fytte of the *Gest*, part of the story of 'Robin Hood and the Knight', when the outlaws go up to Sayles to lie in wait for an unsuspecting guest, they go with bow in hand, and Little John, as Robin's lieutenant,

> *Gyred hym with a full god sworde,*
> *Under a mantel grene*[48]

At the climax of 'Robin Hood and the King', the king and his men cast away their robes in which they had come to the forest disguised as monks and clothe themselves in Lincoln green; dressed as foresters they descend with the outlaws on Nottingham.[49]

Robin was, as Chaucer put it in his description of the Knight's yeoman, 'a forster . . . soothly' (modernised by Coghill as a proper forester). 'Of wodecraft wel coude he al the usage'. That is to say he was a master of the handicraft of forestry. Chaucer described a riding forester, mounted on horseback. He is dressed accordingly 'in cote and hood of grene' and carries the forester's tackle of bow, arrows, shield, sword and dirk, complete with a horn; even 'the bawdric' (baldric), the belt on which his horn was carried, 'was of grene'.[50] This yeoman forester, now on foot, reappears in the 'Friar's Tale', all in green again, carrying a bow and standing under a 'leafy shaw'. The reader may mistake him for Robin Hood himself, for he passes himself off to the summoner, whom he hopes to entertain one day, as a man like himself, a grasping bailiff from far away in the north. But the joke is on the reader as well as his new companion, for the mysterious forester soon reveals himself to be a fiend come to take the summoner down to hell.[51]

1 **The yeoman as household officer**: in this detail from January in the calendar in *Les Très Riches Heures du Duc de Berry*, a household yeoman, or valet, an usher of the chamber in his English equivalent, can be seen bringing a visitor to the household (*top left wearing a red hat*) into the duke's presence (*far right*). (See p. 37.)

Musée Condée, Chantilly, France.

2 **The yeoman of the crown**: this brass effigy, recovered from the bed of the Thames in the nineteenth century and now in the possession of the Society of Antiquaries, has been identified as depicting a yeoman of the crown of Edward IV, whose duties were set down in the king's household ordinances known as 'The Black Book'. His armour emphasises the role of the yeoman as the royal bodyguard. (See p. 38.)
Society of Antiquaries.

3 **The yeoman as forester**: this misericord in the choir stalls of St Mary's, Beverley depicts a scene in the type of hunting known as 'bow and stable'. The huntsman, assisted by a forester acting as his bowbearer, awaits the deer driven towards them at their trystel tree, just as Robin Hood put on a hunt for his king. (See pp. 51–2.)
Photograph © Christopher Hairsine, with permission from Revd David Hoskin, Vicar of St Mary's, Beverley.

4 **The yeoman as forester**: in this detail from Lucas Cranach's *The Stag Hunt of the Elector Frederick the Wise* (1529), huntsman and bowbearer stand at their trystel tree. In Germany they bear cross bows rather than long bows. (See pp. 51–3.) Kunsthistorisches Museum, Vienna, Austria, <www.bridgeman.co.uk>

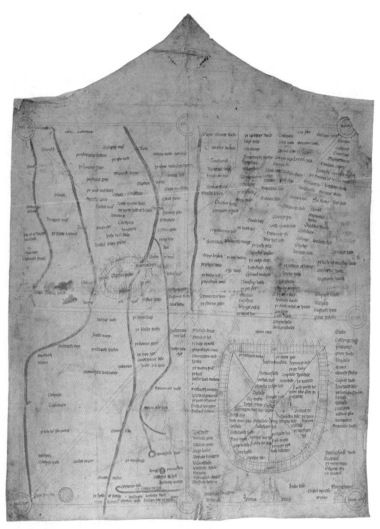

5 Sherwood Forest: this late-fourteenth or early-fifteenth
century map is difficult for modern eyes to read. Little John
and Robin Hood, who knew the paths 'each one', unlike the
fictional Sheriff of Nottingham, had no need of it. (See p. 59.)
Archives of the Duke of Rutland, Belvoir Castle, Map 125. Reproduced by
permission. Photograph held at the British Library MS Facs. Suppl. IV(t)
and Maps 4640 (2).

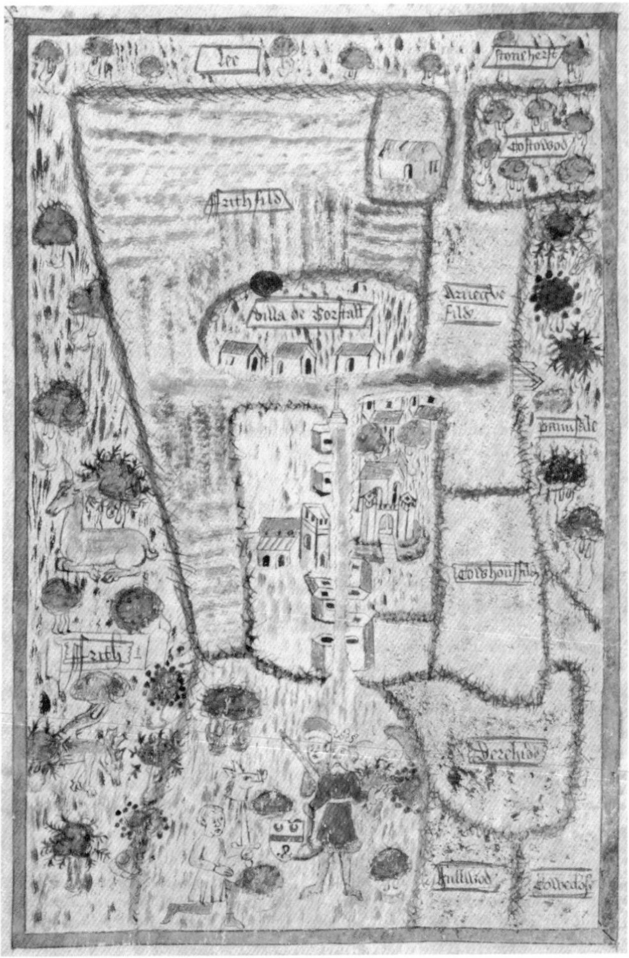

6 **Bernwood Forest**: this map of Boarstall within the forest of Bernwood from the Boarstall cartulary of 1444–6 shows how developed most English forests were in the fifteenth century. Deer lurk in the woods surrounding the village and its fields. In the foreground Edward the Confessor presents a shield bearing the coat of arms of the Fitz-Nigels to the ancestor of the forester-in-fee. A forester-in-fee is not to be confused with a working forester. (See p. 59.)

7 Floriala: Botticelli's *La Primavera*, evokes the festival of floriala, the season of rebirth and renewal, as does the perpetual spring of the greenwood, when 'Mery it was in the grene forest / Amonge the leves grene'. Flora is ushered into a grove, garlanded in flowers and greenery. Chaucer celebrated the same ritual in 'The Knight's Tale'. (See pp. 73–4.)
Uffizi Gallery, Florence, © The Art Archive.

8 Maying: in Maytime it was customary for everyone, noble and commoner, to go out collecting greenery and bring it back to bedeck the home. Here, in the calendar entry for May in a mid-fifteenth-century book of hours, a nobleman and woman return from an expedition. (See pp. 75–6.)

From a French *Horae* c. 1480 (vellum), Fitzwilliam Museum, University of Cambridge, <www.bridgeman.co.uk>

9 Maying: a more complex image is to be found in the Golf Book of Hours. The border illumination of men at archery shooting at a target above their heads suggests a link with May Games, and is a reminder of the prominence of archery contests in the Robin Hood stories. The painter of second version in the possession of the Victoria and Albert Museum, now removed from its calendar and without the border, has been identified as Simon Bening. (See p. 76.)
© The British Library.

10 A forest feast: the hunting day started with the hunt breakfast, here depicted in Gaston Phebus' *Livre de Chasse*. The huntsmen and foresters take their meal in the foreground. Robin Hood, however, when he entertained his guests to dinner, feasted like a lord at the main table. (See pp. 51–2, 146–7.)

Bibliothèque nationale, Paris, France.

11 A chivalric feast: the ceremonial feast was an important ritual for chivalric orders such as the knights of the Order of the Knot of Naples. Robin Hood's forest fraternity shared many of the same values, albeit at a far lower social level. (See p. 153.)

Order of the Knot of Naples (detail) Bibliothèque nationale, Paris.

13 Good fellows: Maximus Valerius points out to a ruler the contrasting behaviour of the temperate and the intemperate, in an illustration from a late-fifteenth century edition of the *Faits et dits memorables des romains*. The temperate, respectable, literally upright, better sort dine in a sober and orderly fashion, as did the men and women of fraternities at their fraternity feasts and the knight in his castle when he returned Robin Hood's hospitality. The intemperate, riotous, common sort eat and drink in a drunken and disorderly manner, as they would in the ale houses they habitually haunted. The Robin Hood of the surviving stories appealed to the former. Did another kind of unrecorded Robin Hood appeal to the latter? (See pp. 148–9, 166, 176.)

'The Temperate and the Intemperate' (detail), Master of Dresden Prayer Book, Flemish, 1475–80, Bruges, Belgium © Paul Getty Trust.

(Opposite) **12 Cakes and ale:** the Church House at Crowcombe near Taunton in Somerset built soon after 1515. A similar, less well preserved building, substantially remodelled in the nineteenth century as a school house, still stands in the church yard at Croscombe near Wells. Baking and brewing took place on site. Such buildings, village halls as they would be today, were the focus of parochial fund-raising events, which at Croscombe included well-documented playing at Robin Hood. (See pp . 169–71.)

Photograph courtesy of Bob Dunning.

14 'Oure comly kynge': Edward III, the flower of kings past and the glory of kings to come, here portrayed as the venerable founder of the Order of the Garter. He was the most likely of the first four Edwards to have been the model for the king in the early stories. Yet memory of the ultimate failure of even this paragon, embedded in the narrative of the *Gest*, reminded audiences to put their trust in Robin Hood rather than princes. (See pp. 200–1.)
© The British Library.

Fifteenth-century men and women of all ranks, not just the poet, who was himself briefly absentee Forester of North Petherton in Somerset (Quantock Forest) in the 1390s,[52] are likely to have been familiar with the forest world to which Robin Hood belonged. Forests, seigneurial as well as royal, existed in almost every county of England. Some were extensive. Foresters were still significant local officials. They were, as servants of their lord or of the king, members of their extended households, receiving fees from them. At the same time they were also of their local communities, frequently landholders themselves. In some districts, service when the king hunted was one of the conditions of tenure.[53] There were thus few parts of rural England where husbandmen and labourers did not know and deal with foresters and hunters, seigneurial or royal. Sometimes relationships were amicable and peaceful; sometimes they were not. But the yeoman forester was a familiar figure, a member of both the society of countrymen and the world of aristocratic service. While he occupied a higher social status than his occupational descendant the gamekeeper, like him his role gave him a foot in both camps.

The extent to which a forester belonged to the world of the gentle as well as the commoner is demonstrated by the need for him to be familiar with the code of aristocratic hunting. Paralleling the local forest administrations of the crown and great lords were local hunt establishments. In 1408, Edward, duke of York, the author of the early-fifteenth-century translation of the *Livre de Chasse* as the *Master of Game*, entered into a contract with Henry IV as his master of hart hounds in Somerset and Dorset. He agreed to retain two yeomen berners at horse (*valets de chiens* or *kennelmen*) at four pence daily, four yeomen berners at foot at two pence daily, two yeomen fewterers (who held the greyhounds ready to let slip the leash at the appropriate moment in the hunt) also paid two pence a day, and four groom fewterers. In Chapter XXXVI of the *Master of Game*, entitled 'Of the ordinance and the manner of hunting when the king will hunt in forests or parks for the hart with bows and stable', the duke states that the master of the game, the organiser of the royal hunts, is required to arrange with the master forester where the king will hunt. The master forester is to advise the master of the game where the deer are to be found, and to direct his foresters to set up the hunting positions, and to meet the huntsmen and escort them to their posts so as to avoid disturbing the game.[55] The foresters who worked alongside the huntsmen needed themselves to know how to conduct a hunt and how to deal with the quarry when it was killed. They were required, as part of their craft, to know the specialised terminology of hunting and to be able to participate in the formalised rituals involved in virtually every aspect of this aristocratic pastime.

As expected of foresters, Robin Hood and his men are fully conversant with the art of venery. They understand the hunting terminology and practices employed, such as the correct description of a 'great hart' or a 'dun deer', the way to 'undo' the carcass, and are familiar with the dining customs, especially the eating of the numbles or offal.[55] And they practise the different types of hunting. On one occasion Robin stalks his prey like a poacher, common or gentle. This is on his return to the forest after his flight from court at the end of the *Gest*, when he goes out alone to shoot 'a full grete hart'. In this respect he is like Bell, Clim and Cloudesly, who, after they have fought their way out of Carlisle, celebrate their return to the forest by each slaying a 'hart of graece' the best there were.[56] Once, too, hunting 'par force', the chasing of a hart by mounted huntsmen with hounds, occurs. But this is a lampoon in which the sheriff is gulled by Little John, alias his servant Reynolde Grenelefe, who offers to lead him as a forester should to a 'ryghte fayre hart', his colour all of green, with a herd of seven score deer, each with sixty sharp tyndes (tines, the points of the antlers). Of course the hart is Robin with his merry men armed with bows and arrows. In this mockery of aristocratic hunting, the stupid sheriff is led into an ambush by 'the mayster herte' at his tryst.[57]

The use here of the word 'tryst' is a reference to the other, and increasingly favoured, form of aristocratic hunting, 'bow and stable', in which herds of deer, red and fallow, hinds and does as well as younger males were driven towards standing huntsmen. The principal huntsman took up his stand, accompanied by his yeoman of the bows (or bowbearer) and the fewterers with their hounds ready to be let slip. In a large (especially royal) hunt, courtiers and gentle companions were directed to their own stands nearby, each with their own bowbearers and fewterers. Other hunters, including the professional hunt staff and foresters were stationed around the boundaries of the section to drive any 'great deer' (harts) back towards the hunting party and to take lesser game for themselves. The place, or station, where the gentle huntsman stood with his bowbearer and fewterer to receive the deer was also called the tryst. It was frequently placed beside or in front of a prominent tree. Thus occasionally the word 'tree' is used for 'standing' or 'tryst'. In a great hunt, especially when the queen or ladies were accompanying the king or noble hunter, a lodge, or hide, of green boughs was constructed by the fewterers at the tryst for shelter and camouflage.[58]

Knowledge and practice of bow and stable hunting by the outlaws is clearly implied. In the *Gest*, after he has intercepted and invited the king, disguised as an abbot, to dine, and having discovered that he carries the king's seal, Robin lays on a hunt.

> *'Syr Abbot, for thy tydynges,*
> *To day thou shalt dyne with me,*
> *For the love of my kynge,*
> *Under my trystell tree.'*

Forth he lad our comly kinge,
Full fayre by the honde,
Many a dere there was slayne,
And full fast dyghtande.[59]

The abbot/king does more than dine at the trystel tree. Robin leads him there courteously by the hand, just as the yeoman of the bow is instructed in the *Master of Game*. And *there* many deer are slain before being 'undone' (dyghtande) for eating. In other words Robin organises a hunt by bow and stable and then breaks up the carcasses in the proper manner, before providing the feast. The outlaws are also accustomed to organising a bow and stable hunt for their own entertainment, or larder. In a passage in *Robin Hood and the Monk*, Little John and Much set out to ambush the monk. But before they leave, it seems, John instructs the other outlaws to have some sport:

'*Loke that ye kepe wel our tristil tre,*
Under the leves smale,
And spare non of this venyson,
That gose in this vale'.[60]

Poaching is done in style.

This trystel tree has more uses than as a hunting spot where deer are killed. Little John proposes that Robin waits under a trystel tree while he goes forward to challenge Guy of Gisborne. Robin himself, disguised as the potter, boasts to the sheriff that he has had a hundred bouts with the great outlaw under his trysting tree. The lodge fulfils a similar role. Robin welcomes the knight and the cellarer of St Mary's at the lodge door. Before the knight leaves he undertakes to repay Robin for his loan a year later, 'under this greenwood tree'. On his return, he is welcomed again by Robin 'under my trystell tre'. It would seem that in this tale the greenwood tree, the trystel tree and the lodge are one and the same place. The trystel tree and associated lodge are the symbolic places where Robin exercises his authority as the 'king' of the forest. Thus it would appear that the game played by the young Henry VIII on Shooters Hill on 1 May 1515, when he, dressed all in green, and the queen were welcomed by Robin Hood at his 'arbour of boughs' was a more meaningful playing out of a scene from the tale of 'Robin Hood and the King' than has usually been supposed.[61]

The symbolism of the trystel tree depends on Robin being clearly identified by the audience, gentle and common, as an outlawed forester. The stories are nevertheless ambivalent in their attitude to hunting. They present Robin Hood as a dutiful and diligent forester, organising a hunt for the abbot/king; they casually refer to his fellow outlaws hunting themselves by bow and stable. They portray Robin stalking, the manner of poaching practised by nobleman and commoner alike. On the other hand they mock the aristocratic method of hunting par force in the gulling of the sheriff. The outlaws sometime dine as gentlemen, sometimes as foresters. They adopt the same hierarchy as legitimate foresters. Little John might at first refuse to be Robin's bowbearer, but in the end he accepts his position as a subordinate. These ambiguities, all apparent in the stories which make up the *Gest*, nevertheless all derive from the status of Robin Hood and his men as outlawed yeomen of the forest.

The ambivalence in the texts is matched by the contradiction between knowledge of hunting assumed by them and the social exclusiveness claimed for hunting in romance and treatise. Books VIII–X of Malory's *Morte D'Arthur* concern Sir Tristram de Lyonesse's exile in the forest. Corinne Saunders suggests that Malory depicts him as the epitome of a huntsman, 'the chief chacer of the worlde and noblyst blower of a horne'. As such he is the pattern of gentility.[62] Indeed, the author adds a much quoted digression to his tale when he reminds his readers that Sir Tristram devised the terminology of hunting and for that reason the book of venery was called the book of Sir Tristram. Thus

> all jantylmen that beryth old armys ought of right to honour sir Trystrams for the goodly tearmys that jantylmen have and use and shall do unto the day of Dome, that thereby in a maner all men of worship may discever a jantylman from a yoman and a yoman from a vylane.[63]

Leaving aside the question of what kind of yeoman Malory had in mind, Robin Hood, as a yeoman of the forest, evidently broke this rule. He also knows all the terms of hunting. The *Master of Game*, a stickler for correct terminology, also makes it clear that one can tell a gentleman from others because he refers to a 'great hart', not to a 'big' or 'large' hart, and can distinguish correctly the three different coat colours of brown, yellow and dun.[64] It is reasonable to suppose that, notwithstanding Malory's snobbish assertion that only a gentleman should know the finer points of distinction of venery, those from lower social groups, to whom the tales were often addressed, were also familiar with them. The Oxfordshire gentleman, Peter Idley, moaned that nowadays, 'a man shall not know a knave from a knight, for all be alike in clothing and array'; he could probably have added that they could tell a brown hart from a dun too.[65]

Around the figure of yeoman forester could be created different, even contradictory situations, for different audiences. In 'Robin Hood and the King', for instance, hunting is treated with respect; the forester plays his proper role in laying on a hunt for his master. In 'Little John and the Sheriff', another story incorporated into the *Gest*, aristocratic hunting is parodied. In both 'Robin Hood and the Knight' and 'Robin Hood and the King', the social order is treated with solemnity: rank is recognised and loyal service is rewarded. But in 'Little John and the Sheriff', the conventions of courtesy, good service and household order are lampooned. In the first the figure is constructed to conform with social norms and hierarchy, and thus perhaps to appeal, not only to those of gentle blood themselves, but also to those worthy and respectable yeomen who may have had aspirations to gentility. In others he is made to be more subversive, and thus perhaps appeal to those who had no time for such pretensions, or even for the gentry themselves. The wider appeal to all yeomen is most clearly reflected in *Robin Hood and the Potter*. The potter himself, an artisan, is recognised as a good yeoman and becomes, as it were, an honorary outlaw. *Guy of Gisborne* is the most directly focused on the forest world itself, having as its theme the conflict between good and bad foresters. Guy, another 'wight yeoman', is a bounty hunter, hired by the sheriff to kill Robin, who had been 'many a mans bane', and has 'done many a curst turn'.[66] He meets his richly deserved and grisly end, his head treated as a hunting trophy. The sheriff is shot in flight as if he were the hunted beast. Is this a ballad which yeomen of the forest themselves would have appreciated most?

The yeomanry of Robin Hood is thus a complex, if not to say confusing, matter. The identification of the outlaws as yeomen lies at the cusp of a significant change in the usage and meaning of the term from a descriptor of household rank to a descriptor of social status. In fifteenth- and early-sixteenth-century society it meant both things and was on occasion used at the same time in both senses. And so too in the stories, where the uses of the word to describe Robin Hood himself and as an invocation to the audience are not necessarily calling upon the same meaning. But the particular and unambiguous identification of Robin Hood as a very specific kind of yeoman, a yeoman of the forest, or forester, provides a fixed point of reference in this fluidity. His status as a forester, a figure familiar to both gentle and common audiences, who practises a skill, shooting, which is admired by both and sustains himself by an activity, hunting, which is exercised by both, brings the heterogeneous elements of audience and narrative together. He is both of intermediary rank and of intermediary status. The liminal character of this situation means that Robin Hood is a hero cut for all. As a fifteenth-century literary figure, therefore, Robin need neither be seen exclusively as belonging to the milieu of the aristocratic household, nor solely as a representative of a new middling sort. He reaches out beyond precise social categories. When we first come across him in the fifteenth-century versions of the stories, he is already all things to all men, and the idealised greenwood in which he operates is an appropriate milieu in which all men can imagine him.

3

A Greenwood Far Away

———•◆•———

Robin Hood's forest, as everyone knows, was Sherwood Forest. But it was not just Sherwood. It was also the ill-defined district of Barnsdale further to the north in southern Yorkshire. Robin and his men moved freely between these two locations in a manner that presupposes that no listener or reader had local knowledge or, if they had, were not concerned about mere geographical accuracy. The forest itself, as conjured up, was similarly unreal. Take the opening stanzas of *Robin Hood and the Monk*:

> *In somer, when the shawes be sheyne,*
> *And leves be large and long,*
> *Hit is full mery in feyre foreste*
> *To here the foulys song*
>
> *To se the dere draw to the dale,*
> *And leve the hilles hee,*
> *And shadow hem in the leves grene,*
> *Under the grene wode tre.*[1]

The same setting is established in every text and the season never changes, Even in the *Gest*, in which the action takes place over many years, it is always perpetual early summer. The forest is 'full merry', a safe, benign and fruitful haven in which to live without need of toil or shelter.

Yet the forests of England, northern or southern, so constructed as the 'Greenwood', were not and never had been Arcadia. Everyone knew that rough winds sometimes shook the darling buds. There are other paradoxes. In literary imagination the greenwood is a wilderness, unpopulated except by outlaws. While a road runs through it, only the outlaws themselves are familiar with the paths and secret tracks beyond. None of his pursuers can find Robin in this unmapped terrain. Yet no forest in England was an impenetrable wilderness. By being north of the Trent the greenwood is also distant from metropolitan and southern England. Its northern location neatly fits the literary stereotype of the remoteness, wildness and lawlessness of the late-medieval north. Yet there is abundant contemporary evidence that northern England was none of these things. It is likely that audiences were aware that Robin Hood and his merry men inhabited only an imagined forest in an imagined northern world. What did the imagined greenwood far away mean to them?

As Simon Schama has pointed out, the great forests of eastern Europe were impenetrable, inhospitable and uninhabited wildernesses. Medieval English forests, on the other hand, were tame affairs, not really forests at all. Tamed as well as tame, for they were in his words, 'vigorous working societies', different but not separate from the open-field manorial societies with which they rubbed shoulders.[2] Forest was essentially a legal concept, land set aside and separated from the rest in which game, especially deer, was protected for the sport of kings and aristocrats. Settlement was not excluded. Pockets of arable husbandry existed within forests. But for those inhabiting and making a living in the forest, there were three essential differences to living outside the forest: there was more woodland, there was more pasture and all were subject to a specific code of law designed to protect the vert and venison – the vegetation and the deer which depended on it. The forest was man-made, created by Norman kings and the holders of great feudal liberties for hunting. The term 'chase' was employed to define seigneurial forests, but otherwise they were identical to royal forests, subject to the same code of law, but administered by the feudal lord rather than the king. It was so that the game could be preserved that all forest was outside the common law.

The extent of royal forest expanded in the twelfth century, reaching its peak under Henry II, and leading to conflict with the baronage. At its widest extent all forest took up approximately a quarter of English land. Thereafter, in the face of opposition, noble and popular, and growing population, which put pressure on resources, it shrank. Henry II's extensions were the first to succumb. Some sections of forest were legally disforested; in others assarts for conversion to arable and enclosures for pasture gradually ate at the woodland from inside. Some, such as Arden, became so settled and developed that they virtually ceased to exist as forest. In the forest of Bernwood a town, Brill, was established and flourished in the high middle ages.[3] In the north, too, great stretches were being enclosed and leased for pastoral husbandry. Inglewood, which occupied practically the whole of central Cumberland between Carlisle and Penrith, was partially settled and enclosed by the end of the middle ages, although it was not until the second half of the sixteenth century that it was systematically developed.[4] Knaresborough Forest too was being transformed by the end of the fourteenth century, and Galtres, to the north of York, had almost disappeared by 1500. Even Sherwood itself was much transformed by settlement. There were ten townships belonging to the ancient demesne of crown owing rents and a great number of assarts and prepestures listed in the late-fifteenth-century Forest Book. Only on the high northern moorlands, which were less easily converted to agriculture and less hospitable to settlement, did the forest remain substantially unchanged through the later middle ages.[5]

Domestic animals of all kinds rubbed shoulders with the game, especially pigs in the southern lowland forests and cattle in the northern moorland tracts. The forest was a pastoral economy before it was imagined as a pastoral ideal. The standing trees were felled for timber or to make charcoal for iron, copper and lead smelting, woods were coppiced, stone was quarried for building and clay pits dug for pottery, as at Brill in the heart of Bernwood Forest. Commercial exploitation and revenue generation became more important in the long recession of the later middle ages. In the northern moorland forests, where vaccaries, or cattle stations, were well established, pastoral farming was the only buoyant sector of the agrarian economy in the early fifteenth century. There were twelve in the forest of Wensleydale, fourteen in the neighbouring New Forest of Richmond and a further twelve in the forest of Lune on the south side of Teesdale. A vaccary supported some 80–100 head of cattle. Unlike sheep they could coexist with deer, but even so restricting their grazing was a perennial headache for forest administrators seeking to balance conflicting demands.[6] It is difficult to discern whether the forests were more prized by their lords for the hunting they provided or the revenue they yielded from rents, quarries, timber, dairy products and beef.

Concurrently the process of deforestation and commercial exploitation seems to have led to a continuous and irreversible decline in the numbers of wild red deer. Far fewer red deer are to be found in the forest record. Almost all the deer poached from the New Forest between 1484 and 1488 were fallow.[7] It might have been that the northern forests were better stocked than those of the south. To some extent this was so. Camden in the late sixteenth century reported that the high Pennines of Richmondshire, at the head of Swaledale, were still safe living for 'deer and stags which for their bulk and branchy heads are very remarkable and extraordinary'. Earlier in the sixteenth century, Leland, who did not penetrate far up the dales, remarked, cautiously, that the king had a forest of red deer at Middleton (in Teesdale) and more specifically that there were 'many red deer in the mountains of Weardale'. Henry VII was very concerned about the Forest of Pickering, the eastern part of the North York Moors. By 1499 red deer stocks had declined to no more than 100, largely because the local nobility and gentry had been allowed to hunt the king's deer at will. A strict regime introduced on the king's behalf by a new chief forester, Sir Richard Cholmley, managed to increase stocks to 300 in four years. Other lords gave up the struggle. By the end of the fifteenth century administration in the bishop of Durham's forest of Weardale had become so lax that the master forester had ceased to present his rolls of the forest for inspection. The red deer, the preservation of which in the wild was the raison d'être of the forest, were no longer as numerous as they had been.[8]

The park emerged as an alternative hunting ground. The park had originally been developed, as within the New Forest, Knaresborough or Pickering, as a special deer reserve. By the fifteenth century no self-respecting gentleman would be without his own park and many early enclosures which saw the destruction of settlements were undertaken to create a park around the manor house. In 1476, for instance Sir William Gascoigne of Gawkthorpe in the West Riding received a licence from the crown to empark 2,600 acres which resulted in the destruction of the old village. The enclosure commissioners of 1517 reported many such acts. The park was predominantly the home of the fallow deer. They were more easily hunted and the park was a more convenient larder for venison. Most of the gifts given by aristocratic patrons to religious corporations and cities were of bucks and does culled from their parks, not harts and hinds hunted in the wild. Yet while some lords such as the earls of

Northumberland were careful to maintain the stocks in their parks, many, in the face of declining revenues, began to lease them out for pasture. The FitzHugh and Beauchamp parks in Teesdale, at Thringarth, Mickleton and Barnard Castle were tenanted by the early fifteenth century. Some were subject to piecemeal settlement. Linda Drury has shown in detail how Stanhope Park, created within the forest of Weardale, and belonging to the bishops of Durham, was transformed in the later middle ages from a hunting reserve to a leased-out pastoral estate.[9]

The English forest had never been what forest was imagined to be, and in the fifteenth century, when the stories of Robin Hood were recorded, it was in the process of further contraction and change. Yet the forest, as a legal entity, was still a reality for the many people throughout England who lived within its bounds and in its environs. Deer, which damaged crops in the purlieus (the surroundings of the forest into which they might roam), continued to be protected. Timber could not be taken without permission; licences for grazing had to be sought. It was both a managed resource and an administrative system, interwoven into the structure of late medieval society. As a physical feature, also, the forest was still visible. There was more woodland to be found in Sherwood, or in the New Forest, woodland in which it was easy to lose one's way, than in champion country. It was reported by the Westminster Chronicler in the late fourteenth century that William Beckwith had been able to escape the law by hiding in the depths of Knaresborough Forest.[10] It was not difficult to imagine forests as refuges for those fleeing the law. The very distribution of forest and chase reveals that there was hardly a person in England who did not live close to one. Thus, although the very peculiar English forest was not quite as it was imagined in the stories, it was never very far removed. Londoners had Epping Forest on their doorstep, and Windsor where Edward IV was wont to entertain the leading citizens in a day's sport was a short trip up river. York was close to Galtres, Southampton to the New Forest, and Nottingham, of course, stood on the edge of Sherwood.

The changing character of forest and park is reflected in the incidental detail of the stories. The hunted beast whose flesh was consumed was traditionally a red deer, the most prestigious quarry being a great hart (a male of at least six years with a rack of antlers of ten points or more), such as Robin killed when he returned to the forest from the court, or a hart of grease (at its prime), three of which were slain by William of Cloudesly and his associates after they had escaped from Carlisle back to the forest.[11] But the outlaws frequently fed on fallow venison too. Little John and the cook ate the numbles of a doe, not a hind; the king is particularly incensed that Robin has virtually cleared Plumpton Park of the fallow deer with which it had been stocked; the justice reports to the king that Adam Bell, Clim and Cloudesly had 'broken his parks, and slain his dere'.[12] In this respect the ballads reflect the changing deer population and hunting customs of the fifteenth century. The later ballads put even more stress on the fallow deer. Thus in the seventeenth-century ballad of 'Robin Hood and the Curtal Friar', Robin challenges his men to shoot deer five hundred feet away. Will Scarlock killed a buck, Midge a doe and only Little John a hart of grease.[13] The great hart, perhaps already a rarity in the English forests in the fifteenth century, long remained a symbolic creature in both romance and ballad.

The forests and parks in which Robin Hood poached the king's deer were specifically northern forests. It is said in the *Gest* that the king pursued him round all the forests of the north. The great forests stretching along the Pennine chain were less developed than southern forests. And while in decline there as well, the red deer were still more plentiful on the high ground of the north than in the lowlands of the south. However, the image of the north itself, rather than specifically its forests, was perhaps more important in the setting of the stories. Almost all the surviving English references to the stories of Robin Hood were by southern authors, who took the northern context for granted. Although the stories reveal specific and accurate knowledge of the area of Yorkshire around Wentbridge, suggesting a northern genesis of some elements woven into them, there is frustratingly little evidence of their circulation in northern England itself. It is true that the first reference to Robin Hood's Stone, on the main road north near Barnsdale, is to be found in 1422, but this highway marker may equally have been named by travellers from the south, who were aware of the connection between the area and the fictional outlaw, as by locals proud of the legendary association. One cannot conclude from the absence of further evidence that Yorkshire people were not familiar with tales of Robin Hood associated with Barnsdale; it would be surprising if they were not. On the other hand it may well be that the stories when they were first committed to writing were by then stories with a northern setting compiled for and circulated predominantly among southern English audiences.[14] As such they could draw upon a long-standing stereotype of the 'north'.

The north generally was perceived as wild, uncivilised and lawless. It was a deep-rooted image owing something to literary convention and biblical exegis. William of Newburgh, writing in the mid-twelfth century, described the site of Fountains Abbey at its foundation as 'a dreadful spot in the deserted wild'. It does not appear so today. Such a perception may have derived in part from early Cistercian ideology which stressed the Christian virtue of withdrawing to deserted places; it also perhaps reflected the condition of Yorkshire after the harrowing of the north by William the Conqueror. It is even possible that the desert was created, as Walter Map claimed, to match the ideal; some six nearby settlements were cleared to make room for Cistercian granges.[15] But it was a persistent image. The uncouthness of northerners was reflected also in their language. From William of Malmesbury in the early twelfth century sophisticated southerners commented on their virtual inability to understand what on earth northerners were talking about. The difficulties of communication grew in the telling. In the fourteenth century it was repeated by Ranulph Higden of Chester, translated and expanded a few decades later by the Cornishman, John de Trevisa:

> Al the longage of the North-humbres, and specialich at York, is so scharp, slytting and frotting [piercing, rasping and unshapely] that we southeron men may that longage unnethe understand. Y trowe that that is because that a beth nigh to strange men and aliens, that speketh straunglich [the Scots?], and also because that the kinges of England woneth alwey fer from that contray.[16]

Before this the author has remarked how in his own time, even in the year of writing in 1385, English was being transformed by the introduction of grammar teaching in the vernacular. It would seem that the civilising influence of the court, bringing the teaching of proper English in its wake, was yet to penetrate the benighted north.

The mythology was reinforced by biblical text of almost proverbial status. Writing in April 1486, the commentator known as the second continuator of the Crowland Chronicler remarked in horror of news that had just reached him:

> And although by these means [the marriage of Henry VII and Elizabeth of York], peace was graciously restored, still the rage of some of these malignants was not averted, but immediately after Easter a sedition was set on foot by these ingrates in the north, whence every evil takes its rise.[17]

'Whence every evil take its rise' is taken directly from *Jeremiah*, 1:14, 'Then the Lord said unto me, Out of the north an evil shall break forth upon all the inhabitants of the land'. The same text was in the mind of John Hardyng earlier in the century when he wrote of Scotland, 'though scripture saith of north all evil is showed', and is surely reflected in Polydore Vergil's comment in the early sixteenth century concerning the 'folk of the north, savage and more eager than others for upheaval'.[18]

There was a powerful literary tradition which shaped late-medieval perceptions of the north. Its influence can be seen dramatically at work in late-fifteenth-century political propaganda. A rattled Clement Paston, writing from East Anglia where he had heard rumours of a huge Lancastrian army marching south, told his brother John on 23 January 1461 that his neighbours were willing to take up arms under the Yorkist lords because 'the peppill in the northe robbe and styll, and ben apoyntyd to pill all the sowthe cwntre'. The earl of Warwick in London was not slow to play the same tune, prefacing appeals for support with the warning that the 'misruled and outrageous people in the north parts of this realm' were threatening the destruction of the land. After it was all over and Edward IV was installed on the throne, royal propaganda stressed how he had saved the south country not only from pillage but also from rape. And so it echoed down the years, with Henry VII responding in 1489 to a localised tax revolt in the North Riding of Yorkshire (which had also led to the death of the earl of Northumberland) with the claim that the rebels were intending to 'rob, despoil and destroy all the south parts of his realm'. Men and women, one is supposed to believe, were lying awake at night in fear of these wild savages from the north.[19]

There can be no doubting that a distinction was made conventionally between the north and south countries. By the fifteenth century the dividing line had broadly settled on the river

Trent, especially as far as administrative boundaries were concerned. Ecclesiastically it divided the provinces of York and Canterbury. It divided the organisation of the royal forests and the duchy of Lancaster into northern and southern parts. Lesser landowners imitated the crown and the great magnates: the Fitzhughs employed receivers and auditors for their estates *partes boreales* and *partes australes*. Heraldically it divided the responsibilities of Norroy and Clarenceaux Kings of Arms. Nottingham, where so much of the action in the Robin Hood stories took place, was the gateway to this north. Nevertheless the sense of where the north (or the south) began varied. The University of Oxford divided its students into northern and southern 'nations' for disciplinary reasons; all those who came from north of the river Nene in Northamptonshire were northerners. On the other hand, to arbitrators in a violent dispute in northern Northumberland, the south, to which one participant was banished, began at York.[20]

By the same token the north was not one homogeneous region. Although the counties north of the Trent, from Derbyshire and Nottinghamshire northwards, shared a common responsibility to raise levies to defend the kingdom against incursions by the Scots in time of war, little else united them. There were very significant differences, socially, economically and legally between the marches towards Scotland in Cumberland and Northumberland and the rest of the north. When Aeneas Sylvius Piccolomini, the future Pope Pius II, undertook the hazardous journey from Scotland through England in 1436, so he recalled later, the immediate border country was indeed wild and lawless, described by him as 'rude, uncultivated and unvisited by the winter sun'. But he also recollected his relief when he arrived in Newcastle upon Tyne, there 'to see again a familiar world and a habitable country'.[21] The high Pennines, Lakeland fells and North York Moors were likewise rude and uncultivated, characterised by scattered settlements, large parishes and pastoral farming. The East Riding, the vale of York and other lowland areas were in contrast more densely populated with nucleated villages, were more highly manorialised and, like midland England, were the focus of arable husbandry. Equally significant was the division between town and country. York was the second city of the kingdom. A description of late-medieval England north of the Trent as a whole as backward, wild and lawless is wide of the mark.[22]

Yet during the later middle ages the economy of the north country passed through an economic crisis more severe than the rest of the kingdom. In addition to the shared tribulations of epidemic disease and commercial recession, which reduced population and output dramatically, the north was further assailed by the ravages of the Scots in the first half of the fourteenth century and major harvest failure in the fourth decade of the fifteenth, the combined effects of which were to hasten the shift towards a more pastoral economy in the lowland areas. Additionally the combined impact of the rivalry of the Hanseatic League which closed the Baltic and North German ports to northern merchants and the remorseless growth of London as the focal point of English commercial life, whose merchants stretched their tentacles into northern markets and cornered northern supplies, especially of woollen cloth, undermined the independence of the northern economy. What had been in the fourteenth century part of a thriving North Sea economic zone was by the sixteenth subordinated to London; a development symbolised by the trade of coals from Newcastle to London. York, which in the fourteenth century had been a great regional metropolis, was by the early sixteenth century sadly reduced in wealth and international significance.[23]

The gradual emergence of a more integrated national economy in the later middle ages further broke down barriers between north and south. Not that there had ever been a fundamental division. Northerners migrated south for clerical career opportunities as students at the universities. Durham Priory had its own hall at Oxford where it sent its brightest men; Chaucer's lusty Cambridge students in 'The Reeve's Tale' were, he informed his audience, from far in the north and swore by St Cuthbert. Sons of the gentry flocked to the Inns of Court in significant number. The sons of the less privileged were admitted to apprenticeships in the great London companies: 46 per cent of apprentices admitted by the Skinners and Merchant Tailors in the last two decades of the fifteenth century were from north of the Trent. If it was the case, as has been forcefully argued by some scholars, that the genesis of the Robin Hood stories is to be found in the London companies, then many of the audiences would have been familiar with the setting in which the outlaw hero was placed.[24]

Communications may have been slow, and normally leisurely, between London, York and points north, but it had always been frequent. Men and women of all walks of life, merchants and lawyers, churchmen and estate administrators, soldiers and vagabonds, cattle drovers and pilgrims, were for ever on the move. As indeed were highwaymen, who operated up and down the main routes.[25] The Robin Hood stories drew heavily on this, for travellers through Barnsdale and Sherwood were the outlaw's reluctant guests. Southern men and women went north as well as northerners south. In July 1409 the earl of Warwick's receiver-general travelled to Barnard Castle where he supervised repairs to the castle. The bursar of Merton College, Oxford, embarked in 1464 on a two-month round trip which took him as far north as Embledon in Northumberland, where among other business he supervised the collection of tithes and surveyed the estate for recent war damage. Marjorie Kemp visited York and other Yorkshire places on pilgrimage, creating, according to her ghost-written autobiography, the usual stir. In 1462–3 John Paston III served in the company of the duke of Norfolk against the Lancastrians and Scots in Northumberland. Although his brother John II, who enjoyed the Robin Hood stories, is not known to have been in the north himself, he is unlikely to have been as misinformed about the region as his uncle Clement appears to have been in the panic of early 1461.[26]

Twenty-five years later, many of the southern nobility and prominent gentry of the kingdom accompanied Henry VII on what an attendant herald described as the first progress of his reign. This took them to Nottingham and then after Easter onwards towards York. On 10 April,

> And by the way in barnesdale, a littil beyonde Robin Hoddez stone, therle of Northumreland with right a great and noble company, mete and yave his attendaunce upon the kiing – that is to say with xxxiii knightes of his feed men, beside esquires and yeomen.[27]

The herald knew that this was a tense political moment, for there had been risings in Yorkshire, whence, as the nervous author of the second continuation of the Croyland Chronicle was shortly to remark, all evil arose. The earl of Northumberland, who had only three months earlier been released from prison, was still on probation. He and his feed men had stood, although they had not been engaged, on Richard III's side at Bosworth Field the previous August. Was there something pre-planned and stage-managed about the earl and his meyny coming to 'submit' and welcome his king at Robin Hood's Stone, just as Robin Hood in the story had been pardoned and welcomed into the king's service in Barnsdale? Or was the detail added by the herald himself, who was struck by the manner in which life on this royal progress seemed to have imitated art?

Southerners, heralds, East Anglian gentry, or college bursars, were neither ignorant of what the north was really like, nor unaware that the Robin Hood stories were set in an imaginary north. The portrayal of the north as wild and unruly, and its inhabitants as savages, was, by the fifteenth century, a well-established literary convention. It was a convention, moreover, which could be called upon quite shamelessly for political propaganda when it suited governments so to do. This is nowhere more transparent than in the manner by which in early 1461 Richard Neville, earl of Warwick, the scion of a great northern family, whose roots lay in northern Yorkshire, so as to rally support in the home counties cynically called up the image of wild and hairy northerners about to descend on the peaceful and prosperous south intent on rape and pillage. But the idea of the north as a distant wilderness where outlaws could resist corrupt authority and dispense true justice was attractive. Is it a coincidence that the great ballad sequences of the later middle ages celebrate the northern forest as an imagined setting for escape from and defiance of evil government? It is not the north as it was known and experienced by well-travelled and well-informed southerners that infuses the stories; it is the stereotypical north of literary convention. This is important. It is because the north was and could be imagined as different and distant, when it was known to be neither, that its reputed wildness and lawlessness could be called to mind as the setting for the violent but cleansing lives of bandits, outlaws, poachers and highwaymen.[28]

Thus we return to Arcadia. The north, like the greenwood, was strictly a literary locale. Just as most late-medieval English people were in a position to know that the north was not the savage wilderness of literary imagination, so also everyone was aware that neither Sherwood Forest nor Barnsdale enjoyed perpetual spring. The audience willingly suspended belief when they were called upon by the storyteller to imagine the greenwood in the merry month of May. All the texts either start with or contain a reminder of this basic convention. *Robin Hood and the Potter* begins:

> *In schomer, when the leves spryng,*
> *The bloschems on every bowe,*
> *So merey doyt the berdys syng*
> *Yn wodys merey now.*[29]

The opening stanza of *Guy of Gisborne* reads:

> *When shales been sheene, and shradds full fayre,*
> *And leeves both large and longe,*
> *It is merry, walking in the fayre fforrest,*
> *To heare the small birds singe.*[30]

And after Robin abandons court in the *Gest*:

> *When he came to grene wode,*
> *In a mery morning,*
> *There he herde the notes small*
> *Of byrdes mery syngynge.*[31]

The setting in the greenwood on a merry morning when the birds are in full song is a common literary trope. It recurs in the opening stanza of *Adam Bell*, set in the Cumberland forest of Inglewood:

> *Mery it was in grene forest*
> *Amonge the leves grene,*
> *Where that men walke both east and west*
> *With bowes and arrows kene.*[32]

The convention is by no means restricted to outlaw tales. The narrator/dreamer in the *Parlement of the Thre Ages* also goes to the greenwood one morning in the month of May and stalks and kills a great hart. Like Robin he is capable of performing the extraordinary feat of dispatching his quarry with one bow shot which kills the beast stone dead. Having concealed his prey, he rests on the grassy bank and falls asleep, dreaming of youth, maturity and old age.[33] The narrator in John Russell's *Book of Nurture* likewise rises early in the morning in the merry month of May to take sport in the forest. Here he falls in with a youthful poacher; their conversation develops into his advice to him, and all men like him, on how to advance in the world through knowledge of courtesy and the ability to render good service.[34] In these prose works calling up the greenwood is an invocation to enter an imagined or dreamed world: an explicit sign that what is to follow is fictional not fact. Yet the dreaming has a further implication, for these uses of the merry month of May link explicitly to youth. Spring, the season of rebirth and renewal, is a time of hope and expectation, and thus prompts the listener/reader to turn optimistically to thoughts of the future.

While the association of spring with rebirth, youth and hope are universal, the ultimate source for this literary device is specifically Floralia. Floralia was the ancient Roman festival of the Ludi Florae on 27 April, which celebrated Flora, the goddess of flowers and vegetation. Her cult was first marked with a temple in the middle of the third century BC, and under the empire was honoured by circus games which lasted six days and thus into May. Being a fertility cult they were associated with sexual licence and lewdness, some Roman commentators such as the younger Cato expressing their disapproval of striptease shows and the adoption of the festival by prostitutes.[35] In later Christian Europe the festival was retained as a specific celebration of May Day, 1 May, in which young people, both noble and commoners, would forage in the neighbouring woods for green boughs and branches, which they would bring home to decorate their palaces and homes. It was also a day of courtship, dalliance and, no doubt, more. Botticelli's allegorical painting *Primavera*, drawing on classical sources, depicts Flora as a woman garlanded in flowers and greenery being ushered into a grove where Venus presides over perpetual spring, while Cupid prepares to shoot his arrow at one of a group of three maidens who look admiringly at a handsome youth.

The courtly rituals of the celebration of Floralia in late-medieval northern Europe were evoked by Chaucer in one passage of 'The Knight's Tale'. Having described the dawn, the poet recounts:

> *And Arcite, that is in the court royal*
> *With Theseus, his squyer principal,*
> *Is risen, and loketh on the myrie (merry) day.*
> *And, for to doon his observaunce to May,*
> *Remembring on the point of hys desyr,*
> *He on a courser, sterting as the fyr,*
> *Is riden in-to feeldes, him to pleye,*
> *Out of the court, were it a myle or tweye;*
> *And to the grove, of which tht I yow tolde,*
> *By aventure, his way he gan to holde,*
> *To maken him a gerland of the greves,*
> *Were it of wodebinde or hawethorn-leves;*
> *And loude he song ageyn the sonne shene:*
> *'May, with alle thy floures and thy grene,*
> *Wel-come be thou, faire fresshe May,*
> *I hope that I som grene get may.'*[36]

The theme of maytime and renewal is also to be found woven into Malory's *Morte D'Arthur*. Book IV of 'Launcelot and Guinevere' begins with a hymn to May:

> The moneth of May was com, when every lusty harte
> begynneth to blossom and to burgyne. For lyke as trees
> and erbys burgenyth and florysshyth in May, in lykewyse
> every lusty harte that ys ony maner lover spryngeth,
> burgenyth, buddyht and florysshyth in lusty deeds.

It was a time, Malory explains, especially for the renewal of love:

> For than all erbys and treys reneewyth a man and a
> woman, and in lyke wise lovers callyth to their mynde
> olde jantylnes and olde servyse.

'So it befelle in the moneth of May', the narrative begins,
Guinevere calls upon ten of the knights of the Round Table, 'on-
maying in the woodys and fyldis besydes Westemynster',
commanding them to be dressed all in green. And she would bring
ten ladies with her. But when they were 'bedaysshed with erbis,
mossis and floures in the freysshyste maner' they were ambushed
by Sir Mellygaunte and eight score men, and the queen carried
off.[37] Henry VIII's much publicised May Day expedition in 1515,
when the court, all dressed in green, rode into the woods to play
a game of Robin Hood, fits into the same tradition. On the way
back, one reporter commented, the royal entourage was
accompanied by a pageant car with singing girls dressed as Lady
May and Dame Flora, along with their attendants Humidity, Vert,
Vegetative, Pleasaunce and Sweet Odour.[38]

The scenes described here were frequently alluded to in
calendar illustrations for May. It is never a month of labour. Some
calendars show aristocratic ladies and gentlemen dallying in a
garden; some show the expedition to the countryside to gather
the greenery. A mid-fifteenth-century book of hours held by the
Fitzwilliam Museum at Cambridge, for instance, depicts a
nobleman and lady riding together on a white horse, both bearing

a bough of greenery.[39] A more complex image in the Golf Book of Hours, a Flemish work of the early sixteenth century, shows young ladies and gentlemen returning to the city laden with green boughs by both boat and horseback. The boaters are about to pass under the bridge which the riders are crossing as they are about to enter through the city gate. In the boat there is music making; one man plays a recorder, and a lady accompanies him on a tamboreen. The Golf Book of Hours takes its name from one monochrome illustration of commoners at play in the bottom margin. For the month of May men are shown in an archery contest shooting at a target above their heads, all but one with long bows. Here it seems the association between Maying and May Games is being made explicit.[40]

The May Song, which also carried the more sombre warning of a *memento mori* and advice to seize the day, opens:

> *We have been rambling all of the night,*
> *The best part of this day.*
> *We are returning here back again,*
> *And we've brought you a garland gay.*
>
> *A bunch of may we bear about.*
> *Before the door it stands.*
> *It is but a sprout, but its well budded out,*
> *And it is the work of God's own hands.*
>
> *Oh wake up, you, wake up, pretty maid,*
> *And take the Maybush in.*
> *For it will be gone ere tomorrow morn*
> *And you will have none within.*

The next verse, which begins with the line, 'The Heavenly gates are open wide', barely leaves anything to the imagination by way of sexual innuendo.[41] No wonder that at the end of the sixteenth century William Stubbes thundered, salaciously, against this filth:

> All the yung men and maides, older men and wives, run gadding overnight to the woods, groves, hills & mountains, where they spend all the night in pleasant pastimes; and in the morning they return, bringing with them birch and branches of trees, to deck their assemblies withal . . . I have heard it creditably reported (and that *viva voce*) by men of great gravite and reputation, that of fortie, threescore, or a hundred maides going to the wood over night, there have scarcely the third part of them returned again undefiled.[42]

Went out the maid, that in a maid never more did come.

The well-documented customs, literary allusion, pictorial presentation and later criticism of Floralia, traceable back to early Roman practice, needs to be distinguished from the much more speculative associations in folklore with the Green Man, the world of faery and supposed suppressed woodland deities such as Robin Goodfellow (alias Puck), Jack-in-the-Green and Hob. The fantastic image of the foliate head, or the Green Man, as a decorative sculptural motif in medieval cathedrals and churches has itself been traced back to Roman art in the first century AD, and is to be found in several places in northern Europe, including Britain. Adopted by Christians, the images in time came to represent demons, sometimes with their 'unruly member', the tongue, sticking out. An analysis of the late-medieval versions in Devon churches has led to the suggestion that few can be interpreted as a symbol of regeneration in springtime. More telling might be the image in Exeter Cathedral of the Virgin treading a Green Man underfoot. In the words of Kathleen

Basford, 'He represents the darkness of unredeemed nature as opposed to the shimmering light of Christian revelation'.[43]

There may well be something in the notion that other figures such as Robin Goodfellow also reflect a memory of suppressed pagan deities: the literary evidence for Robin Goodfellow also stretches back to the later middle ages. Moreover Robin Goodfellow was a prankster, and, as we have seen, Robin Hood himself takes on the shape of a prankster in at least one story. One cannot therefore dismiss out of hand the links between Robin Hood, the green outlaw and the Maytime setting with hidden and deep-rooted folk memories. But this is a long way from arguing, as many folklorists have, that Robin Hood is essentially the personification of a pagan deity, the mythic Green Man who encapsulated the power of nature and man's oneness with the earth. Robin Hood might represent a prehistoric rite of the summer king struggling against the winter king to capture the spring maiden, but the historical evidence, as in much of folklore, is regrettably very skimpy.[44] It is easier to trace how the ideas have been invented in succeeding centuries than to show their existence in pre-Reformation England.[45] For fifteenth-century audiences these matters are as likely to have been as obscure to them as they are to us today. Yet there is sufficient evidence for us to conclude that the setting of the Robin Hood stories in perpetual spring, in the merry greenwood in the merry month of May, had well-understood symbolic meaning. Floralia represented renewal and 'the hope of happy day'. The season is captured perpetually in the stories of Robin Hood, just as Botticelli in *Primavera* freezes Flora at the moment in time when she is led into Venus's grove.

But always the hope of renewal and of happy days is at the same time tinged with the knowledge that it cannot last. The May Song continues with the sentiment that

For the life of man is but a span;
He's cut down like a flower.
He makes no delay; he is here today,
And he's vanished all in an hour.[46]

Malory, too, was well aware that the merry month of May is but a passing season: 'For, lyke as winter rasure dothe allway arace and deface grene summer, so faryth hit by unstable love in man and woman'.[47] The final tale, of the death of King Arthur, begins with a similar ominous reminder:

> In May, whan every harte floreshyth and burgenyth (for as the season ys lusty to beholde and comfortable, so man and woman rejoysyth and gladyth of somer cuommynge with his freyshe floures, for wynter with hys rowghe wyndyis and blastis casuyth lusty men and women to cowre and sit by fyres), so thys season hyt befelle in the moneth of may a great angur and unhapp<e> that stynted nat tyllle the floure of chivalry of [alle] the worlde was destroyed and slayne.[48]

In the renewal of hope there lies also the intimation of disappointment. Just as in nature summer eventually gives way to winter, so also the expectations of social and political renewal are invariably undermined by the cold reality of human behaviour.

There was, moreover, an alternative cultural tradition in which the forest was uncomfortable and friendless, used in works critical of outlaws who took to the woods and preyed on the local inhabitants. The Nut Brown Maiden warns against the life:

Yet take good hede, for ever I drede,
That ye coulde not sustain
The thoorney ways, the depe valeies,

The snow, the frost, the reyne,
The cold, the hete, the drye or wete
We must lodge on the plan;
And, us above non other roue,
But a break, bussh, or twayne. [49]

A variation of this theme underpins *As You like It*, Shakespeare's play nearest to the Robin Hood tradition. Owing more to *Gamelyn* in fact, it is itself a winter play in which good Duke Senior and his loyal entourage are banished to a cold and unwelcoming Arden to live like 'Robin Hood of old'. Here the resolution comes in spring, when the invented goddess Hymen, standing in for Flora or Venus, unites the lovers, and ushers in a restoration of the true order and the promise of renewal. Shakespeare gives us both the hardship of exile in the forest *and* rebirth in the spring. Jacques nevertheless sceptically reminds the duke, and the audience, at the end, that it will end in tears again. He remains in the forest:

I am for other than for dancing measures . . .
To see no pastime, I: what you would have
I'll stay to know at your abandoned cave. [50]

It is just such a request, to return to a chapel he has founded in the forest for a period of retreat, that Robin Hood uses to escape the court and take up his old ways towards the end of the *Gest*. He returns to the greenwood on another merry morning, but this time he knows there is no going back, no second pardon.

For all drede of Edwarde our kynge
Agayne wolde he not goo. [51]

Robin Hood has a touch more of Jacques than Duke Senior.
   The forest as perpetual spring represents the hope of better

times to come; the forest as raw nature represents the hard and imperfect world, which men and women know in their hearts it is. In the merry May morning when the leaves are shining green and the birds do sing, this knowledge is briefly suspended. Yet, come autumn, as everyone knows, leaves will fall and birds will cease to call. In the hope for better times ahead lies the knowledge that they cannot last. The greenwood is thus an ambiguous setting. On one level it is a conventional Arcadia, a place to which one escapes from the venality and the corruption of politics and the world. But it is more than this, as it is more than an elegy for a lost world of liberty and justice; and it is not simply the setting for a forlorn dream of an alternative, yeomanly society.[52] The representation of the forest in perpetual spring cannot be separated in the listener's or reader's mind from the knowledge that spring is transient. Thus it is also a reminder that there is no escape from the world as it is and that there is little hope that the world will ever change. This subliminal dimension to what the imagined greenwood signified, gives a sharper edge to the Robin Hood corpus as a discourse on justice and the late-medieval social order.

4

Crime, Violence and the Law

———◆———

Everyone knows that the hero of the greenwood was an outlaw. The cellarer of St Mary's Abbey had no doubt that he was a common criminal. As he roundly informs Little John, 'He is a strong thefe, Of hym herd I never good'.[1] Robin Hood was indeed the leader of a gang of violent criminals who terrorised travellers through the forest in open defiance of the king and his authority. The stories, however, transform a gang of hardened highwaymen and poachers, who do not hesitate to kill even innocent children when they get in their way, into jocular, heroic, swashbuckling adventurers. What resonance did the idealised criminal life and the disdainful attitudes to the law portrayed in the stories have for listeners and readers? Were the crimes, however glossed, typical of the everyday experience of the fifteenth and early sixteenth centuries? How closely do the stories represent the audience's attitudes to the law, and more specifically law-enforcers? To what extent do they reflect contemporary concepts of justice? The questions are not easy to answer because the evidence from surviving legal records is incomplete. Much of the evidence is of indictments, not of verdicts, and is by its very nature partisan. Many crimes were alleged, but not so many, one suspects, committed. However, indictments do reveal what people believe to have been credible criminal offences. Similar problems exist with comment on the effectiveness and impartiality of the law. Criticism is stereotyped and common, not only in the literature of complaint but also in private letters. But what we do know is that contemporaries were deeply concerned that the law was administered properly, and felt, sometimes justifiably, that often it was not. The depiction of crime and the administration of the law in the Robin Hood stories is part of this discourse.[2]

When Robin declares to the king in disguise that

> *We be yemen of this forest*
> *Under the grenewode tre,*
> *We live by the kynge's dere*
> *Other shyft have not we*[3]

King and audience no doubt appreciate the irony that living by the king's deer actually means poaching them, not protecting them. In their own eyes, perhaps, they are still legitimately foresters, but in their straitened circumstances they have no other shift but to poach. In fact even here Robin is economical with the truth, for, as king and audience also both know, given the irony of the situation in which Robin has just held up a man he believes to be the abbot of a monastery, they have another far more profitable shift – highway robbery. Poaching and highway robbery are the bases of the outlaws' livelihood. First, let us consider poaching.

When the king was based at Nottingham vainly seeking to track Robin down,

> *But always went good Robyn*
> *By balke [hiding place] and by hyll,*
> *And always slew the kinges dere,*
> *And welt [took] them at his wyll.*[4]

The outlaws are portrayed as living year by year off the fruits of the forest: not just the deer, but also every kind of bird (taken by snares and nooses rather than by hawks), and feasting on swans as well as venison. They have denuded the king's northern forests. In the *Gest* the king discovers that the merry men have destroyed all the herds of deer in his Lancashire park of Plompton. For six months he pursues the poachers round his northern forests, but they elude him, all the time killing his deer.[5] Poaching is a different order of crime and more likely than any other to strike a sympathetic chord with rural audiences.

How much poaching took place in royal and seigneurial forests in the fifteenth century is impossible to tell because of the paucity of the evidence. Before 1320 poaching from royal forests was rife and fully documented in the forest eyres (circuit courts). The conflict over rights to game in the thirteenth and early fourteenth centuries between local inhabitants and lords of the forest, fuelled by growing scarcity of resources and enforced vigorously by foresters and keepers, was intense.[6] But the reign of Edward III witnessed the decline of the forest eyres. The last commission was issued in 1368, although their ineffectiveness was becoming apparent long before the legal process fell into disuse.[7] The decline of the eyre and other aspects of royal administration was but a reflection of the decreasing pressure on resources in mid-century and of a growing rapprochement between crown and landed subject over the matter of the forest. Throughout the century the crown had been extending the prerogative of hunting to favoured persons, especially tenants in chief, by allowing the creation of seigneurial forests (chases), licensing emparkment and granting the rights of free warren (the entitlement to hunt for lesser game on the demesne land of the grantee). Two linked and fundamental changes thus took place in the fourteenth century. Hunting ceased to be primarily a forest-based privilege, and conflict between crown and nobles over the right to hunt in the forest virtually came to an end. But for the local inhabitants there had never been much difference between a royal forest and a seigneurial forest, or a royal or seigneurial park. They were excluded from them all. Crown and landed society closed ranks to enforce their hunting privileges against the commons everywhere, in forests, in parks and in free warrens.[8]

There is no doubt that hunting remained a popular pastime for all classes of men. No one would claim that it was less popular in the fifteenth century than the thirteenth. Kings continued to hunt, though circumstantial evidence suggests that the Lancastrians hunted rather less than either the Plantagenets before them or the Yorkists and early Tudors after them. Lords and gentry chased deer in forest and park as much as they could. The growing dissemination of the key manuals, eventually printed in English, attests not only to hunting's special role in gentle culture but also to its wider social appeal. Nonetheless, fifteenth-century lords, royal and seigneurial, seem to have shown curiously little anxiety to preserve the game through prosecutions in their forest courts. Surviving swanimote and forest court records reveal a singular lack of prosecution of cases against the venison. The principal concern of forest courts in the fifteenth century was the vert, and even here it seems that the main interest appears to have been to make sure that no one grazed in the forest without payment, either in advance by agistment, or in arrears by amercement.[9] In this context it is perhaps significant that the late-fifteenth-century compiler of the Sherwood Forest Book, who had access to royal records, did not include an example of a forest eyre after the mid-fourteenth century, but chose to transcribe from nearer his own time a summary in English of Geoffrey Kneeton's account as clerk of the forest for 1446–7, which records the collection of rents from its townships and parks.[10]

It is inconceivable that poaching ceased; poaching was the gentleman's sport and the common man's fair game. From time to

time poachers were presented in forest courts, as were Thomas
Beckwith and his associates for taking deer from Haverah Park in
the forest of Knaresborough in March 1460. Others received
royal pardons, as did Philip Pagham, gentleman, for his trespasses
of venison in the royal forest of Bernwood, Buckinghamshire, in
1438–9.[11] The real scale of the taking of illegal game, to which
perhaps a blind eye was frequently turned during the fifteenth
century, is revealed only after the accession of Henry VII. Henry
instituted a revival of vigorous royal forest administration with the
objective of bringing poaching under control and restoring the
numbers of deer. The forest eyre was revived. Thanks to the zeal in
executing his wishes and the care in keeping records shown by his
chancellor of the duchy of Lancaster, Sir Reginald Bray, and steward
of his household, John Radcliffe, Lord Fitzwalter, co-justices of the
forests south of the Trent, evidence of his impact has survived.[12] At
New Forest swanimotes in 1487 and 1488, and at a meeting of the
forest eyre held at Salisbury before the two justices of the forest in
August 1488, well over a hundred presentments, almost all for
offences against the venison, were made. Poachers ranged from the
knightly through yeomen, butchers, bakers and bucket makers to
vagabonds. Most offences were committed by men on their own,
or with no more than four confederates, who took no more than
one animal. There were some serial poachers, notably William
Holcombe, gentleman, late of Lymington, who in fourteen separate
incidents between 2 June 1484 and 30 January 1488 killed eighteen
deer, as well as cutting down a large oak for himself in January 1487.
With other gentle offenders, he received a pardon at the forest eyre
under a bond of £10 for his future good behaviour. At the same
Salisbury forest eyre in August 1488 presentments were also heard
from the forest of Clarendon, although the offences revealed were
less grave than those in the New Forest. The most serious was a
gang of six (a yeoman, a husbandman and labourers) who broke
into the park to take game.[13]

Most damage to the venison in the New Forest seems to have been done under Richard III. It was claimed by the forester of the In Bailiwick in 1488 that, at various times during the reign, the suspiciously rounded number of 500 deer had been taken by the northern men and their servants from his bailiwick. Some of these men were identified by the foresters of Battramsley and Burley bailiwicks in February 1487, who presented John Hoton esquire, late of Bisterne, and six yeomen servants for killing without warrant, at various times in the first two years of Richard III's reign, no fewer than 190 animals. Hoton hailed from Hunwick, County Durham. He had been granted Bisterne and the keepership of the New Park by Richard III; he and his servants benefited greatly from royal largesse, being the king's officers in the forest. Two of those indicted alongside Hoton were identified as forest officials: Henry Smith, one of the riding foresters, and Robert Vascy, the bailly of Burley. Vascy may well have been the same Robert Vascy, gentleman of Newland, County Durham, who had been indicted in 1472 with his kinsmen for assaulting the sheriff of the county. One may doubt whether Hoton and his foresters truly took deer without authorisation, and one would be even more surprised if they had been viewed sympathetically by the local inhabitants as heroic greenwood outlaws transplanted from their native north. They did not denude the forest, for in preparation for an early hunting expedition by the king himself, 400 deer were driven from the In Bailiwick into the park.[14]

Poaching did not only take place from forest and chase, where the game was protected by forest law. Game in parks and free warrens were protected by the common law. Here the principle was developed that while the game itself did not belong to the owner, the means of killing it, or the infringement of another law in the act of killing, or the act of entering an enclosure, could be used as an action. Thus the breaking of the palisades of a park could be presented as a riot, or the taking of game from free warren as a trespass. Until 1390, however, the commons, who did not possess a privilege to hunt on reserved ground, could freely take game from all land that was not protected by forest, not within free warren and unenclosed: a significant right. A statute of 1390, which established the modern game laws, swept this away.[15]

The act was part of that raft of legislation passed in the late fourteenth century, including labour laws, sumptuary legislation and legislation restricting leisure activities, whereby matters which had been regulated informally through feudal relationships were taken up in what has been described as a national code of social control.[16] Collectively the legislation represented a hardening of class boundaries, pushed through by the landed classes themselves, who sought to protect their material interests and privileged positions in the face of the unprecedented economic, social and religious changes following in the wake of demographic crisis. The preamble to the act, and the petition on which it was based, reflect these anxieties. Picking up the fear of heresy, the act alleged that poaching took place especially on holy days, when good Christians should be in church, and claimed that sometimes under the colour of poaching the commons made assemblies, confederacies and conspiracies to rise and destroy their allegiance. The petition asserted that artificers, labourers and others went hunting with greyhounds in the parks, coniegries (rabbit warrens) and free warrens of lords where they did great damage and requested that the crown enact that no artificer or labourer, or any other layman with lands worth under 40 shillings a year, or clergyman with a living worth less than £10, should keep greyhounds and hunt with the same. In the process of becoming law, however, the prohibition was extended from the more limited protection of parks, coniegries and warrens, to the blanket taking of deer, hares, rabbits and 'other gentlemen's game' without limitation to land. This was a radical extension of the existing law, for under it hunting was restricted by income on all unenclosed land, not just by special privilege on some of the demesne land of lords. The vaguely expressed gentlemen's game enabled the justices of the peace, gentlemen themselves, to determine for themselves what was or was not permitted.[17]

The 1390 act greatly extended the crime of poaching and had the potential to inflame wider class conflict. Yet it appears that throughout the first century of its existence it was only sporadically enforced. There are only six cases in the proceedings of the justices of the peace published by Bertha Putnam of indictments under the act, all from Worcestershire in the period 1392–6. None of the 199 indictments made before the Shropshire justices of the peace between 1400 and 1414 was made under the statute of 1390. Not one indictment appears in four surviving gaol delivery proceedings for Hampshire between 1409 and 1427. In the surviving rolls for Durham in 1471–3, to take another example, just two out of a hundred and six presentments were made under the act. These eight indictments in total concern hunting of hares by labourers, husbandmen and yeomen, one vicar and two chaplains. Six were in fields and woods, one in a warren and one in a 'manor'. This is not a large sample from even the surviving records of the justices of the peace, but it does not suggest a rush to prosecute.[18]

Poaching in the fifteenth century was potentially a widespread offence. The reason why under both forest and common law it was so little enforced at the time probably lies in the prevailing economic and social conditions. Put simply, from 1390 there was plenty of game to go around. In the circumstances of population decline, village desertion and the reversion to waste of much land, more game could be supported than there were hunters, of all classes, to kill it. A blind eye could be turned to the casual taking of a deer, or a hare, or other game for the pot, because it did not seriously reduce stocks or hinder gentlemen's pleasure. Only when organised gangs started to poach on a large scale did the authorities endeavour to prosecute in a determined manner, and then possibly more because of the general threat to public order than the threat to stocks of wild life. This, the recurrence of larger scale poaching in the Weald, was one of the justifications of the re-enactment of the 1390 Game Law in 1485.[19]

Henry VII reissued the 1390 act with a new clause to prohibit hunting at night. At the same time he revived the forest eyre and instructed his justices of the forest to restore effective forest administration and to institute the zealous prosecution of poachers.[20] It is not that social and economic conditions changed over night. One cannot be sure whether the decision to clamp down on poaching was Henry's initiative or whether he was reacting to pressure from his landed subjects – pressure which his predecessors had ignored. Henry VI, although he appears to have enjoyed hunting personally, was not of a character to assert royal authority in his forests. Edward IV, perhaps an even more enthusiastic hunter, was for other reasons uninterested. Richard III, as far as one report by John Rous suggests, was more inclined to relax forest laws than to tighten them. While staying at Woodstock in August 1483, the king responded to a local petition to disafforested land which Edward IV had annexed to Wychwood.[21] It may be that the king's landed subjects wished to see a renewed drive against poaching, but judging from the number of them who subsequently found themselves presented in the swanimotes and forest courts, one doubts it. A special inquiry held at Pickering in 1495 found that over the preceding five years the earl of Surrey, Lord Latimer, Sir Ralph Bigod, Sir William Eure, John Hotham, Sir Ralph Salvin and several other local gentry had been hunting in the king's duchy of Lancaster forest at will. The deer stocks themselves were in danger. Moratoria, which seem to have had only limited success, were imposed in 1489 and 1494. Successive chief foresters seem to have lacked the determination or desire to impose the king's will. Eventually Sir Richard

Cholmley, chief forester from 1499, was able to establish royal authority, but only after he had come to an agreement with the lords and gentry neighbouring the forest that they could take a quota of deer so that they would be 'loving and favourable' to the rest. Subsequently stocks recovered.[22]

It seems to have been Tudor royal policy to enforce the laws against poaching more rigorously, especially in the royal forests. At first it seems to have been an uphill struggle. As the sixteenth century progressed, however, the pressure on resources grew, and the stocks of red deer dwindled in the forests and chases, conflict over game resurfaced. Violent gangs of poachers once more became more common, often led by disaffected and marginalised lesser gentry and yeomanry.[23] Thus by the second half of the century the exploits of Robin Hood and his merry men, who were, if nothing else, an organised gang poaching on a large scale, once more struck a familiar chord. However, in the intermediate period when the stories were first put into writing and widely circulated, the hunting of game, whether in forest, park or open field, was not, it seems, a source of intense social tension. The laws against poaching then were honoured more in their breach than in their observance. In these years Robin Hood's life of organised crime as a poacher did not have an immediate frisson; only gradually after 1485 did the poaching gang once more become a familiar feature in life as well as in literature.

Robin Hood and his merry men had other shift than to live by the king's deer, as many a monk knew. There are six robberies or planned robberies featured in the early ballads, of which five are highway robbery. There is no doubt that highway robbery was a frequent occurrence in the fifteenth century and the sums involved were as large as those stolen by Robin Hood. Rosemary Hayes has revealed a rash of incidents in northern England in the years 1462–72. Five approvers, described as yeomen, grooms, labourers and a hosteler, confessed to a dozen robberies in

Durham, Lancashire and Yorkshire, stealing cash and goods from merchants, churchmen and other unidentified travellers to the value of 300 marks, £300, £700 and in one case £1,000. Robberies took place anywhere on the open road, including the Stockton Road leading out of York towards Sheriff Hutton, but two actually took place in, or on the edge of, Barnsdale, on the great north road near the very spot in southern Yorkshire where the legendary outlaws themselves were wont to intercept their victims. William Robinson, alias Robert Robertson, labourer, and two others held up a canon and stole a casket containing £400 between Pontefract and Wentbridge in May 1472. On 9 September 1466 Alan Greneside and two accomplices lay in ambush at Wentbridge, where they held up a passing jeweller, William Jackson, and relieved him of £20 in cash as well as his stock of silver pieces and jewels to the value of £60.[24]

There were other notorious haunts of highwaymen in late-medieval England. One was the Pass of Alton in Hampshire. The heyday of its notoriety was in the thirteenth century. The pass, a mile or so south-west of Alton, close to Chawton Park, was on high ground as the main road from Winchester to London crossed the watershed between the rivers Itchen and Wey. Matthew Paris described in detail an incident in 1248 when two Brabantine merchants were held up and a whole criminal world preying on travellers was revealed, leading the king, Henry III, to intervene personally. The king's own household was ambushed there in 1261. The justices in eyre agreed eight years later in view of 'the number and heinousness of the crimes daily committed in the pass called the pass of Aulton [sic]' to lobby the crown to clear and widen the road. It seems as though one of the provisions of the Statute of Winchester in 1285, to widen highways leading from market town to market town, was a response to this and other local pressure to improve security on the road. But the pass remained a danger spot. The wardens of the annual fair of St Giles at Winchester continued to maintain a guard of five mounted sergeants during the fourteenth century and Langland in *Piers Plowman* remarked ironically that Poverty might even pass through the Pass of Alton without peril of robbing. It was probably at the pass that King John of France was 'ambushed' as he journeyed from Winchester to London in late May 1357. The author of the *Anonimalle Chronicle* told how, as the royal cavalcade passed 'near a forest', 500 men dressed in green in the guise of robbers intercepted it. The king, who was somewhat alarmed, asked the prince of Wales who they were. They were, the prince replied, English foresters living in the wild and it was their custom to do this every day. And so, no doubt, the king realised that this was one of the pageants put on to entertain him. Whether the pass remained such an infamous spot in the fifteenth century is hard to determine. A preliminary search of legal records has drawn a blank.[25]

Northern highwaymen in Edward IV's reign operated in groups of two or three. But then so did Robin Hood's men when delivering invitations to guests to dine with them. It was Little John, Much and Scarlock, 'these yeomen all three', who waylaid the knight. It was the same three who held up the cellarer of St Mary's Abbey and fifty-two men later in the tale; and it was Little John and Much who intercepted the monk in *Robin Hood and the Monk*. Robin on his own faced the potter, but watched by Little John and others, who intervened when they thought the potter was getting the better of him. It was only when Robin faced the king, disguised as a monk, that he stood in the way with 'many a bolde archere'.[26] While, as the audience is reminded from time to time, there were 'seven score of wight yonge men' in the outlaw band, it was their leaders who customarily laid in wait. In this respect Robin's fictional activities were very much in accord with fifteenth-century experience.

There were, however, few if any bands of outlaws numbering

140 men lurking in forests for years on end in the fifteenth century. Even in the late thirteenth and early fourteenth centuries, when gangs such as those led by the Folvilles gained notoriety, they were difficult to hold together for any length of time and tended to melt away again quickly. The depredations of William Beckwith and his gang in the honour of Knaresborough in the late fourteenth century were, it seems, exceptional. Beckwith's criminal career is worth comment since it took place in a northern forest and its context was hostility between the inhabitants of the forest and their lord, John of Gaunt. Gaunt had entered the lordship in 1372 and had instituted a drive to improve administrative efficiency and increase revenues, which had led to resistance. Violence erupted in the late 1380s when discontented forest dwellers found a leader in William Beckwith, a man whose status seems to have been on a par with a yeoman. Beckwith's grievance, we are told, was his failure to succeed to a forest office held by a forebear. Indeed a member of his family had been made bailiff of Bilton Park within the forest. For four years, from 1388 until his death at the end of 1391 or early in 1392, he and his followers, which indictments reveal were almost all drawn from the locality, waged a private war against the forest officials, especially the steward and constable of the castle, Sir Robert Rokeley and the chief forester, Robert Doufbyggyng. They were accused of having made an attack on the castle itself and having twice attacked the hunting lodge at Haverah, of lying in wait with intent to murder Sir Thomas Colville and to have ransacked the house of William Nesfield, the escheator of Yorkshire.[27]

Knowledge of Beckwith's activities, documented by commissions of oyer and terminer set up to deal with them, reached Westminster Abbey, where its chronicler recorded what he had heard of them. It was he who picked up the rumour that Beckwith was a disappointed forest official; he told how, when pursued by Sir Robert Rokely, he and his men withdrew into the densest part of the forest for safety, and he added the detail that having escaped his pursuers he was betrayed and murdered by Robert Bland at Barnard Castle, someway to the north. Beckwith was no Robin Hood. Nevertheless the reporting by the Westminster Chronicler of the exploits of this northern forest outlaw suggests that they caught the imagination of Londoners and visitors to Westminster. Not only was the story exceptional enough to be worth telling, but also it was told in such a way as to suggest an element of heroic resistance to authority. Yet his 'betrayer' Robert Bland, pardoned in 1393, was the receiver of Barnard Castle in 1390–1. In 1400, when the earl settled Barnard Castle on his son and heir Richard, included in the grant was land in the lordship earlier conveyed to Earl Thomas by Thomas Bland. It is unlikely that a man with significant local landed connections and the trusted officer of the lord of Barnard Castle 'betrayed' the fugitive brigand in anything other than the popular imagination.[28]

Another gang operating on the Sussex–Surrey borders from before 1417, when it was first indicted, escaped justice for over a dozen years. Led by Robert Stafford, one-time chaplain of Lindfield, it was accused of murders and robberies and poaching from local warrens and chases. As Sir James Holt pointed out, Stafford adopted the alias of Friar Tuck, described as 'newly so-called in the common parlance' in 1417.[29] It seems that his exploits later entered into the popular imagination through the absorption of the character of Friar Tuck into the Robin Hood stories by 1473 at the earliest. The notoriety of Beckwith's gang and the remembrance of Stafford's alias suggest that their exploits were exceptional. Indeed within a decade of the last record of the Stafford gang, the first explicit comparison was made between the behaviour of a riotous company and Robin Hood. In a petition placed before parliament in 1439 the banditry of Piers Venables and his gang of fifteen named yeomen and 'many other unknowyn' in the neighbourhood of Tutbury was likened to that of Robin Hood and his meynie.[30] This was a literary flourish, confidently added, we may suppose, in the knowledge that it would be familiar to its listeners. By the mid-fifteenth century, so unusual had large roving gangs of bandits apparently become that, rather than Robin Hood and his merry men reflecting what one might describe as the 'historical reality', a local disturbance could be construed for rhetorical effect in Robin Hood terms. Life was beginning to imitate art.

There were, however, other kinds of brigands operating in northern England throughout the fifteenth century. The marches with Scotland were plagued by 'highland thieves', whose lawlessness, exacerbated in time of war, was a major threat to life and property. Petitions were presented to parliament in 1410 and 1411 complaining about the collapse of law and order in Northumberland and the activities of gangs of thieves descending on the lowlands from the border dales. Over a century later in 1522, it was reported to the archbishop of York, Thomas Wolsey, that gangs of up to a hundred men from Tynedale were in the habit of descending on Hexham, in his liberty, every market day. Whether the degree of lawlessness implied by these reports was commonplace throughout the intervening years is hard to determine. Cynthia Neville has shown that there was a general breakdown of order in the far north under the early Lancastrians, a lawlessness that revived between 1465 and 1469 when the outlaw Sir Humphrey Neville and his followers harassed the inhabitants of County Durham and Hexhamshire. Humphrey Neville was neither highland thief nor Robin Hood; he was conducting guerrilla warfare against the Yorkist regime. Yet perhaps reports of reivers and partisans gave credibility to the tales of Robin Hood to those living far away.[31]

Like the reivers of later ballad, Robin Hood's gang revelled in violence. There are nine homicides in the early ballads (eleven if we count the killing of the sheriff twice and Robin's own murder), besides the twelve men killed by Robin as he fights his way out of church in Nottingham. This does not compare with the three hundred or more, including the justice, the sheriff, the mayor of Carlisle, constables and catchpoles, bailiffs, serjeants-at-law (judges) and forty foresters of fee killed by William of Cloudesly and his fellows. It does, however, uncannily match the tale told of Andrew Trollope at the second battle of St Albans in 1461 that he killed fifteen men without yielding ground, for which feat he was knighted on the field. There are three battles with the sheriff's men, and there are two single-handed toe-to-toe sword fights, one between Little John and the cook lasting one hour, the other between Robin and Guy of Gisborne a fabulous two hours.[32] Assault, beating people up for the fun of it, is also integral to the outlaws' self-image:

> 'To bydde a man to dyner
> and syth him bete and bynde,
> It is our olde maner', sayd Robyn.[33]

Robin himself has a nightmare in *Guy* in which he dreams that 'they did me bete and bynde'.[34] Yet, curiously, there are very few incidents of actual bodily harm by the outlaws on their victims. Little John, when masquerading as Reynolde Grenelefe in the sheriff's service,

> gave the boteler such a tap
> His backe went nere in two.[35]

Having lured the monk into the forest, Little John turns on him, seizes him by the throat and throws him off his horse:

> John was nothing of hym agast
> He let hym falle on his crown.[36]

But this is the prelude to his murder. The outlaws threaten to assault those they kidnap, but rarely do so. The cowardly sheriff, when he is captured by the outlaws, is in fear of life and limb, but is only made to spend a cold spring night in his shirt and breeches.[37] Indeed in the case of two of their guests, the knight and the king, they honour them. Nevertheless the pervading sense of threat to life and property represented by the outlaws is real. When the outlaws and the king's men ride to Nottingham all dressed in green, the townspeople of Nottingham panic because they think their town is about to be sacked by the outlaws.[38]

The depiction of violence is also casual and matter of fact, nowhere more so than in the murders of the monk and his page:

> *John smote off the Monk's hed*
> *No longer would he dwell;*
> *So did Moch the littul page*
> *For ferd lest he would tell.*[39]

The killing of a little boy is horrific, but a listener/reader might discern a certain black humour in the throwaway line. Even the killing of Guy of Gisborne, though the details are gory (Robin decapitates the body, slashes the face, lifts the head by the hair and rams it on the dead man's bow), is a somewhat cursory description. This act echoes a recorded incident in the early fourteenth century when a poacher, to demonstrate his defiance of the foresters, impaled the head of the killed beast on a stake and left it to be found.[40] The stories revel in violence, but it is a violence taken for granted, ritualised, and sometimes leavened by humour.

As several historians have remarked, Robin Hood is imbued with attitudes to violence that were shared by chivalric values. Peter Coss has suggested that they incorporate a parody of chivalric values, and indeed in some stories, such as the story of

'Little John and the Sheriff', they do make fun of aristocratic etiquette.[41] But more deeply they are imbued with the same fundamental belief that the yeomen outlaws shared the right to practise violence, especially in the protection of honour, as did knights. The violence perpetrated by Robin Hood and his men was not the incidental violence of common or garden crime, but the honourable and virtue-defining violence of chivalry. It is excessive, it is noted in gory detail, and it is celebrated in impossibly long feats of individual prowess. Robin Hood has appropriated much of the virtue of a knight. He is a 'strenuous' yeoman.[42] The infusion of these chivalric values into the persona of the yeoman Robin Hood represents yet another way in which he is made accessible to both gentle and popular audiences: to the gentry for whom chivalric violence is the accepted norm; to prosperous commoners who aspired to gentility; and, let us not forget, to all who just revelled in blood and guts.

One might also assume that violent crime is matter of fact in the stories because it was the common, everyday experience of the century. It is not easy to discern the extent to which the incidents and action in the ballads reflect the general experience and level of violent crime in the fifteenth century; Phillipa Maddern has calculated that in East Anglia between 1422 and 1442 only 6.8 per cent of gaol delivery indictments were for homicide, and a further 5.25 per cent for crime involving assault. Of cases involving violence heard before the King's Bench, only 4.15 per cent concerned homicide, but 15.25 per cent involved assault. Yet over 35 per cent of crimes recorded in the Shropshire peace roll for 1400–14 alleged violence, and in the superior eyre for Shropshire and Staffordshire in 1414 more than half the indictments were for homicide. But the incidence of some of these crimes ran back as early as 1367.[43] Records for northern England provide equally varied data. In nineteen gaol deliveries in Cumberland between 1335 and 1457 only 5.7 per cent of the reported crimes were homicide. In Durham, in fifteen months between 1471 and 1473, 9.5 per cent of cases presented before the justices of the peace and gaol delivery involved homicide, but as many as 46 per cent violent assault. Of the indictments before the King's Bench in the six northern counties of Cumberland, Durham, Lancashire, Northumberland, Westmorland and Yorkshire in the period 1461–85, 17.5 per cent were for homicide and 11 per cent for assault.[44] For the north as well as the Midlands and East Anglia, the evidence is too little and too flawed for one to be able to draw firm conclusions about levels of violent crime.

Not much is revealed by a comparison of case histories with the action in the ballads. There are many cases of ambush with intent to kill or maim. In 1472 three brothers Hedlam, probably of the armigerous family seated at Nunthorpe in the North Riding, with a gang of sixteen or more waylaid Sir Richard Strangways, his brother and two servants with the bungled intent to kill Sir Richard. Another attempted ambush, in a forest, that seems to have been bungled was the subject of an indictment in Shropshire in 1409. Robert of Cotyngham, a mercer of Coventry, lay in wait with six armed men on the highway (alta via) between Bridgnorth and Enddeley in the forest of Morfe to murder Roger Lyney. Richard Weston, one-time forester there, was more successful for he was found guilty early in 1400 of feloniously killing Thomas Knotte in the forest, for which offence he purchased a pardon fourteen years later.[45] Thomas Dennis, an able but shifty East Anglian on the make, lured Walter Ingham into an ambush in January 1454 and inflicted grievous bodily harm on him. Arrested in Norwich, like Robin Hood he made a daring escape. His eventful life came to a sticky end, again like Robin Hood's, when he was himself murdered in 1461. Dennis was on the margins of gentility. In Weardale in County Durham over the winter of 1471–2 there was a spate of murders committed by yeomen. On 8 December 1471 John Redhed of Wotton and four members of the Wilson family, all yeomen, lay in wait at Stanhope and killed John Westwood. A month later Laurence Harper assembled a gang of labourers to attack and murder Richard Ward in Stanhope Park. But there is nothing in these homicides committed by yeomen from Weardale to liken them to the killings committed by the yeomen outlaws of Barnsdale and Sherwood Forest.

There are many known clashes between armed gangs on a scale comparable to those between Robin's outlaws and the sheriff's men. But these were almost always led by rival gentry or lords and they usually derived from disputes over property or were linked to rivalry for local pre-eminence, such as the feud between the Pilkingtons and Savilles which tore apart the royal lordship of Wakefield in the summer of 1478. Such clashes were not usually directed against the king's officers. In 1472, however, sixteen gentlemen, yeomen and labourers led by Robert Vascy of Newland and William Merlay of Weysil in County Durham were indicted before the commission of the peace for attacking the sheriff, John Atherton, who had endeavoured to serve a writ on them at Wolsingham on 15 March. In this confrontation the sheriff, unlike his ballad counterpart, seems to have come out on top.[46]

In many ways the stories in their first written form do not reflect the contemporary pattern of violent crime, homicide and poaching as revealed in legal records, and seem only to relate to the prevalence of highway robbery. How do they relate to the experience of law enforcement and perceptions of justice? As far as the forest law is concerned there appears to have been little correlation. On the ground the protection of the venison lay in the hands of the foresters who patrolled their walks and bailiwicks and presented offenders to the swanimotes and similar forest courts under other names. They were answerable to a chief forester and ultimately the king's justices of the forest, divided between a northern and a southern circuit, the northern circuit encompassing the forests north of the Trent. A Sherwood forester took an oath that he would attach and present any trespassers of the vert and venison.[47] A remarkable feature of the Robin Hood stories is that the working foresters of Sherwood were *not* the enemy. Guy of Gisburne is the possible exception, but he is particularly traduced because he has turned his coat. Only one forester appears in the story on the side of enforcement, and he is presented as a consultant who advises the king that the only way to catch Robin is for him to disguise himself as a monk.[48] In *Adam Bell*, it is true, in the long catalogue of murders that Adam, Clim and William are accused of committing, are 'forty fosters of the fee'. But foresters of fee held hereditary sinecures and were drawn from the ranks of the gentry or aristocracy. One may detect class hostility in this, but not hostility to foresters as such.[49] Roger Manning has provided ample evidence that they became particularly hated in the sixteenth century and there is no reason to believe that they had been particularly beloved before 1340.[50] The point is that Robin and his men *are* the foresters. Little John's retort to the cellarer of St Mary's when Robin Hood is slandered as a common thief is, one may recall, 'Thou liest . . . he is a yeman of the forest'.[51]

The 'high justice' who the knight encounters at the abbot's table in the story of 'Robin Hood and the Knight' contained in the *Gest* could be construed as the chief justice of the forests north of the Trent. But since he is pictured as colluding with the abbot in attempting to defraud the knight of his lands, he is more likely to have been interpreted as the chief justice of common pleas. In other stories the king's judges are found wanting. In *Adam Bell* William of Cloudesly is betrayed to the justice and the sheriff in Carlisle and then is rescued by his fellow yeoman from the scaffold, both the justice and the sheriff being hacked down. In the denouement of *Gamelyn*, the hero comes into court to impose his own justice. His first victim is the presiding justice who, assumed to be corrupt, is literally thrown out of his seat and physically assaulted. The sheriff is allied with the justice in both these stories. In *Gamelyn*, the sheriff is in fact the hero's evil brother, who is brought to justice at the end.[52] It is, of course, the Sheriff of Nottingham who is doomed endlessly to pursue Robin Hood in vain.

In the fifteenth century the sheriff's remit was much reduced from earlier times. The great era of the sheriff as the king's viceroy had been the twelfth and thirteenth centuries. One point of significance is that, as a result of pressure from the ranks of the county elites, from the thirteenth century a sheriff no longer served at the king's pleasure, except in the county palatinate of Durham where the bishop retained the right. In all but three of the counties where the shrievalty was held in fee, a sheriff normally served for just one year and he was appointed or 'pricked' for each county by the king, from a list of three names submitted to him. The office was held in rotation by members of the leading county gentry. They identified themselves as much with their fellow landowners, and sometimes the dominant nobility, as they did with the king. The sheriff's political role as the king's man was thus much reduced. By the fifteenth century his judicial role had also been curtailed by the decline of the county court and the emergence of the justices of the peace.

Yet his duties were still manifold. They included collecting certain royal revenues, presiding over the archaic county courts, including the elections of members of parliament, preparing the business for itinerant justices, holding inquests, summoning defendants and jurors, arresting criminals and keeping them in custody before trial. But he was more the executive and servant of local administration than its author. The fifteenth-century sheriff also had some residual responsibilities towards the forest. It was to him that the king sent writs for the election of verderers in the county court, writs to have inspections (regards) of the forest made or perambulations of the bounds, and writs summoning the forest eyre. He acted as the king's agent in transporting venison or timber from the forest at the king's command and to liaise with the king's hunting establishment. For most of the fifteenth century, when the forest eyres were in abeyance and the administration of the forest somewhat lax, these duties were not onerous, but it was still his responsibility to enforce the common law in the forest, and to pursue fugitives from the common law in it.[53]

It might be thought that attitudes to the office of sheriff displayed in the stories were archaic, echoes of an earlier age, but we should be careful not to play down too much the continuing impact of the sheriff and his office in fifteenth-century society. The first of the three complaints drawn up by the Kentish rebels in 1450 contain clauses which imply that the corruption of sheriffs was, and not just in that county, a cause of resentment. The first clause is a complaint that the sheriffs and under-sheriffs let their offices to farm for such high rates that the holders became extortionate. The point at issue is not the selling of the offices themselves, but the selling at outrageous prices. The under-sheriff, the retained deputy of the serving sheriff for his year in office, was usually a local lawyer, of relatively modest landed means, who carried out the legal duties of the office. He made his living by the profits of his office, fees, sweeteners and bribes. The second is that 'simple people that usith not huntyng' were subject to false indictments by under-sheriffs and bailiffs so as to increase their income. In other words false accusations of poaching were made for the kickback. Another device to raise money was to return names in inquests without summoning or warning the named, so that they were fined for non-attendance. Finally they were accused of levying excessive amercements for personal gain. There was, it seems, if the complainants of 1450 spoke as they claimed for the 'simple people' at large, resentment about the inherent corruption of the sheriff"s office.[54] The sheriff's officers, especially his local bailiffs, had the greatest impact on ordinary men and women; it was against them, not the temporary occupant of the office itself, that complaint was made. In the story of William of Cloudesly, for instance, the outlaws made sure that they massacred all its occupants: constables, catchpoles, bailiffs and beadles. The statute of 1413, which sought to regulate their behaviour and terms of office, recited that the people dared not complain of the extortions and oppressions of the sheriff's under-officers, not the sheriff himself.[55]

In one particular respect, the sheriff, through his officers, was the appropriate representative of royal authority in the stories, for it was he who was responsible for hunting down outlaws in the forest and bringing them to justice. Outlawry was a familiar legal process in the fifteenth century. Anyone accused of committing a crime, either by jury indictment or personal appeal, had to be summoned to appear at four successive county courts. If he failed to appear to answer the charges after the final summons, the accused was outlawed and his goods confiscated. The process normally took from six months to a year. The sheriff was the officer responsible for serving the writs and for pursuing and arresting outlaws by calling out the posse, which the king orders him to do in the *Gest*,[56] though the tasks were usually delegated to hundred or village bailiffs on his behalf. The process was widely believed to be too long and too open to abuse. It was alleged in parliament in 1427 that malicious process all too frequently led to wrongful outlawry. All too often the complex legal process and the arcane technicalities surrounding it were used for personal gain. As in all aspects of the law, delay by the sheriff's officers in executing any of the writs, often in collusion with one of the parties, led to miscarriage of justice. Men were frequently hounded for outlawry when they had no knowledge that they had in fact been outlawed, often in another county.

Perhaps because of the manifest flaws in the procedures, the principal weakness was that outlawry was ineffective in compelling attendance. Originally outlawry was a fearful sentence, for it excluded the accused from society, as by definition he had no protection under the law, and carried the death penalty for the outlaw if he were captured. Yet by the fifteenth century many who were outlawed were able to continue their lives without hindrance; most could, and did, eventually acquire pardons for a financial settlement. Outlawry thus became an empty sanction. To be an outlaw in the fifteenth century was often little more than a technicality; only exceptionally was it to be a fugitive hunted down by the king's officer, the sheriff.[57] Robin Hood and his merry men may have fitted into these exceptional circumstances. Whereas we are informed that Cloudesly was outlawed for poaching and Gamelyn through the vindictiveness of his brother, we are never told why Robin Hood was outlawed. It is implied that he is the victim of malicious litigation by others for personal gain, in which the sheriff has colluded. However, the original reason, even if he were a victim of misjustice, is not relevant. Being an outlaw pursued by the sheriff's officers, as a few documented gang leaders were, seems in itself to have been enough to make him a hero.

In the stories of Robin Hood, however, unlike the story of William Cloudesly, it is very much the man not the office who is significant. He is curiously the Sheriff of Nottingham, not of Nottinghamshire and Derbyshire as he should have been. He has no name. He is, anachronistically, the king's viceroy, occupying the office at the king's pleasure, and in regular communication with him. He resides, it seems permanently, not as a fifteenth-century sheriff would in his manor house, but in the royal castle of Nottingham. He displays many of the characteristics of a great lord. He keeps a great household, under the direction of his steward and butler. He retains on a grand scale, calling out sufficient 'men of armys stronge' to besiege Sir Richard at the Lee in his castle, just as the duke of Norfolk besieged John Paston in Caister. When retaining Reynolde Grenelefe, alias Little John, 'a wight yonge man', he is prepared to pay him 20 marks a year and supply a good horse (more than a leading member of the county gentry might expect). He hunts as a noble man, 'with houndes and horne'.[58] If one were to attempt to find a fifteenth-century equivalent of this great figure it would be Ralph, Lord Cromwell of Tattershall, who in 1434 was granted in fee the royal offices of constable of Nottingham Castle and steward of Sherwood Forest.[59]

The sheriff is moreover given a character, which would not have been particularly flattering to Lord Cromwell: he is an oath-breaker, a coward, a fool and a drunkard. At several levels, therefore, the Sheriff of Nottingham is more than the representative head of the kingdom's fifteenth-century county administration. He can be seen as the personification of the malign exercise of power. He stands for the generically corrupt and repressive agent of the crown, who can be either official, local magnate or court favourite. He stands, as it were, for all the evil ministers of the crown who ever subverted the true order of society and perverted the king's just rule. He consequently meets his deserved violent end twice: once in *Guy of Gisborne*, shot in the back by Little John as he flees; a second time in personal combat with Robin. Robin stands over the body and declares:

'Lye thou there, though proude sheriff
Evil mote thou cheve:
There myght no man to the truste
The whyles thou were a lyve.'[60]

The killing of the sheriff is at one with the receipt of the king's pardon in symbolising the restoration of true justice. His killing also needs to be understood in the context of the inextricable link between violence and the law in fifteenth-century society. Violent self-help in the right cause carried out by the right people was prized in chivalric ideals. The determining factor was motivation. If the motive was just, violence was thereby justified. Violence was not bad in itself; it was bad only if the cause were bad.[61] The legal system itself was based on violence. Authority legitimised right violence; indeed violence was the duty as well as the hallmark of the exercise of legitimate authority. Thus the law was sustained and enforced by violence and public acts of violence, it was believed, could even demonstrate legality. In the same way as just war abroad was believed to lead to true peace, so the king's peace at home was maintained by just violence against lawbreakers. This outlook is exemplified in the stories of Robin Hood. The just order of society is maintained and restored in the stories by the righteous violence of its hero who triumphs over the unrighteous, the sheriff and Guy of Gisborne in particular. Whereas he is godly, courageous, valiant and worthy, they are ungodly, cowardly, treacherous and despicable.[62] The idea of the cleansing violence by which Robin Hood enacts restorative justice is thus germane to the perception of the law in the fifteenth century. The violence is necessary so as to affirm legitimate authority, and this is affirmed in the story of William of Cloudesly and recognised in the *Gest*, by the manner in which the king pardons both men.

The life of crime led by John Belsham of Hadleigh, Suffolk, between 1422 and 1439, including three murders and six assaults, has some similarity to the life of fictional outlaws. Several of his victims were officers of the law, including the constable of Hadleigh, whom he murdered in 1427. Although imprisoned from time to time, and outlawed in 1428–32, he was never condemned for his crimes. Finally brought to trial in 1441 due to the persistence of William Wolf, a kinsman of the woman he had murdered, he was acquitted through the duke of Norfolk's influence. But even here differences are more significant than the similarities. Belsham passed as a gentleman; he was not a masterless man living in the wild; and one of his victims was a woman.[63] In her consideration of the case, Maddern suggests, that unlike the outlaws of fiction he forfeited sympathy. Rather than defend the underlying principles of the law and support its officers, he undermined and defied them. As is revealed in the ceaseless justification of their often violent acts in legal terms, the fifteenth-century gentry had a profound respect for the law. Thus, Maddern argues, far from being admired, as was Robin Hood, he was condemned by local opinion. She may well be right that he lost the sympathy of some of his peers and betters, but does it follow that he was condemned by public opinion at large? Was it the case that 'the murder of a law-enforcer to facilitate criminal behaviour could never be justified by fifteenth-century standards of righteous violence, which demanded the altruistic maintenance of justice and peace'?[64] For this is exactly what Robin Hood celebrates – righteous violence to maintain true justice precisely when the officers of the law have failed. The moral is clear in the story of Robin Hood and Guy of Gisborne. In contrast to the good yeoman Robin, Guy is the bad yeoman. He 'had bene many a mans bane' and, as he himself boasted, like a later melodramatic villain, 'I have done many a curst turne'. He is a bounty hunter, a hit-man who has a contract on Robin. The two meet and fight. He meets a deserved and grisly end.[65] Seen through this prism, Belsham is more like Robin Hood and the man who brought him to justice, William Wolf, more like Guy of Gisborne. One wonders, therefore, whether one should assume that public opinion held an unquestioning or universal respect for enforcers of the law: the Robin Hood stories in which the officers of the law were flouted so openly perhaps appealed to a counter-culture, in which sympathy existed for notorious criminals in their conflict with the law. One is reminded of that group of yeomen and labourers who took to the roads in Norfolk to waylay travellers in 1441 (the same year as Belsham was acquitted), chanting 'We arn Robynhodesmen, war, war, war'.[66] With whom, one might well ask, would they have sympathised, Belsham or Wolf?

5

Religion and the Religious

———•———

It is made abundantly clear to the audience in the early stanzas of
the *Gest* that Robin himself was conventionally pious:

> *A gode maner than had Robyn;*
> *In londe where that he were,*
> *Euery day or he wold dyne*
> *Thre messis wold he here*
>
> *The one in the worship of the fader,*
> *And another of the Holy Ghost*
> *The thirde of Our dere Lady*
> *That he loved all ther most.*[1]

The author of *Dives and Pauper* might have complained in the first
decade of the fifteenth century that people preferred tales or songs
of Robin Hood to hearing mass, but this was not the case with the
hero of the tales himself.[2] Who celebrated the masses for him is
rarely indicated. At the beginning of *Robin Hood and the Monk*, on
a glorious Whitsun morning in May, it grieves him that he may
not hear mass or matins on this 'solem day'. It is a fortnight, he
declares, since he has his saviour seen, and thus resolves to go to
Nottingham. It is while he is praying before the rood, standing at

111

his mass, in St Mary's Church that he is recognised by the monk, who then betrays him to the sheriff.[3]

This is all there is to be found in the surviving texts. However, Walter Bower's continuation of John of Fordun's *Scotichronicon* of *c.*1440, repeats at some length a story that glosses the statement in the first stanza. On a certain day, once in Barnsdale, when Robin was according to his custom most devoutly hearing mass in the usual very secluded place, he was warned by his men that the sheriff had discovered its whereabouts and was coming to seize him. Robin refused to flee, because of his reverence for the sacrament. Trusting in the one whom he worshipped, with those who would stay with him, he completed the mass and then easily routed the sheriff. Having robbed and ransomed the sheriff, he ever after singled out the mass to be held in great respect.[4] Bower presents this as a true story about an actual 'famous robber', Robert Hood, but it has all the hallmarks of a summary of a tale which once circulated, a copy of which he probably had before him, and interpreted for his own purpose. Besides elaborating on the 'gode maner' of hearing mass daily, it reads as if the focus of Robin's devotion was the Eucharist and the story was focused on Robin's celebration of Corpus Christi, a popular cult in the fifteenth century.

There is no need to speculate about Robin's devotion to St Mary, to whom an appeal and dedication is made in every early ballad.

> *Robyn loved Oure dere Lady,*
> *For dout of dydly synne*
> *Wolde he never do compani harm*
> *That any woman was in.*[5]

His devotion is a recurring theme in tune with the prevailing Mariology of the fifteenth and early sixteenth centuries. It need not detain us longer, except to note that all women were protected by his devotion to Our Lady. The Trinity is hinted at in the worship of the Father and the Holy Ghost, and indeed in *Robin Hood and the Monk* he makes a vow to God and to the 'Trenyte'.[6] His desire to see his saviour, and his praying before the rood, may indicate too a devotion to the cult of the name of Jesus, though this is by no means conclusive. More problematic is a further reference to St Mary Magdalene. Towards the end of the *Gest* he tells the king that he had founded a chapel dedicated to her in Barnsdale, to which he wished to return for a seven-day fast.

> *I might never in this seven nyght*
> *No tyme to slepe ne wynke,*
> *Nother all these seven dyes*
> *Nother ete ne drynke.*[7]

In fact he does no such thing: as soon as he arrives, he stalks and kills a great hart and calls up his merry men again. Robin perhaps did not go as far as the eremitic life, though life in the greenwood had something of the quality of a hermit's existence. The hardships are beyond the sheriff, for when he is lured into Robin's hands by Little John, he is forced to spend a cold night, as do the hardy outlaws, sleeping under the greenwood in his underclothes. It is, he complains, a harder order than any hermit or friar.[8] In terms of the cults of saints to which reference is made and the hint of admiration for the eremitic tradition, the stories reflect the devotional practices and interests of parishioners, especially parishioners of yeoman status, in the fifteenth and early sixteenth centuries.[9]

The stories also reflect conventional Christian attitude towards the dignity of manual labour. *Labore est Orare*. Robin's first admonition to his men is:

> *Loke you no husbonde harme*
> *That tylleth with his ploughe.*[10]

Behind this lies a long tradition of social doctrine sanctified by the Church. The idealisation of the honest ploughman was at the heart of late-medieval sermon literature, finding its most poetic outlet in *Piers Plowman*. As Owst put it, 'he is a good and honest worker, contented with his lot, who loves God, whether his fortune is good or bad'. 'To learn and labour truly in the things of his particular calling, resting content therewith, is each man's first duty'. While there are corrupt officials, evil foresters and venal judges to be found in the stories, the honest husbandman, like the good yeomen of the forest, stands for all that is honest and truly Christian.[11] In this context one should place the only reference specifically to the poor, the acknowledgement in the last line of the *Gest* that he 'dyde poor men moch god'.[12] This can be read as a statement of conventional generalised charity, following on as it does to the appeal to Christ to have mercy on his soul.

Whereas, as we have seen, Robin protects hard-working husbandmen and good yeomen and even knights or squires that would be good fellows, he nevertheless makes it absolutely plain to his men that, alongside a bold baron or the Sheriff of Nottingham,

> *These bisshopes and these archebishoppes,*
> *Ye shall them bete and bynde.*[13]

The strong vein of anticlericalism presents an altogether more complex problem. It is thus perhaps strange that not one surviving story, not even one in the compilation which is the *Gest*, actually features an assault on a prelate. Monks and an abbot are humiliated, one is murdered, but never a bishop or archbishop.

The original source for reference at this point to bishops and archbishops is likely to have been the English sermons, homilies and metrical paraphrases which were in wide circulation from the mid-fourteenth century. This corpus of satire and complaint against the evils of the day was to some extent part of a long tradition of Christian writing bemoaning the fallen state of man, especially his falling prey to the seven deadly sins. But they acquired a new prominence in the fourteenth century and a wider dissemination through the vernacular both through the vehicle of preaching and written texts. Familiarity with the ideas they contained was widespread. They can be accessed today particularly through the *Summa Predicantium* compiled by the Dominican friar John Bromyard, which was the core source for Owst's seminal work. We need go no further than this to discover written sources for Robin Hood's declared antipathy to prelates.

Sermon after sermon thundered against the shortcomings of the senior clergy, portrayed as driven by avarice, lust, gluttony and pride, or sinking into sloth. It became a commonplace so to condemn the faults of the leaders of the Church, who should have known better, reflected also in *Piers Plowman* and Chaucer. This is the place neither to ponder on the significance of this outpouring of anticlerical writing, articulated first, it must be stressed, by clergy themselves, nor to consider how accurate a reflection it was of the condition of the late-medieval Church. All one needs to note is that the source of the critical lines at the beginning of the *Gest* is apparent, and that the complaint was repeated throughout the fifteenth and early sixteenth centuries, reinforced by printing and later put to effective use by Protestant propagandists.[14] Bishops and archbishops may not have been assaulted in the pages of the surviving rhymes, but they were murdered by angry crowds in 1381 and 1450. In fact Thomas Gascoigne, commenting shortly after the events of 1450, wrote:

> Nearly everyone was heard crying out 'woe unto the bishops', who grow rich, who wish to be called lords, to be served on bended knee, who ride about with so many and such fine horses, and will do nothing by way of preaching to save men's souls . . . This was common talk about the bishops among clergy and laity.[15]

However, in deeds, rather than words, Robin Hood's victims are monks rather than bishops.

The monks of St Mary's, York, are the villains of the story of the sorry knight. The knight, having mortgaged his lands to the abbot, is rescued by a loan from Robin. When he goes to repay it, he kneels before the abbot dining in great estate, with many lords at his table, begging for charity. Refusing the knight's plea, the abbot haughtily orders him out of the hall. Eventually when the knight in anger reveals he has the money and throws his repayment on the table,

> *The abbot sat styll and ete no more,*
> *For all his ryall fare.*[16]

In this scene it is the abbot's worldliness, avarice and gluttony which is stressed. Later in the plot, when the cellarer is intercepted in the forest, the worldliness of the monks again is emphasised. The cellarer and a companion are on their way to London leading seven pack animals and escorted by 250 men. As Little John comments:

> *There rydeth no bysshop in this londe*
> *So ryally, I understand.*[17]

Faced by three outlaws, threatening to kill the leading monk, the escort and the other monk flee. The monk, who admits to being the cellarer of St Mary's, having been entertained to dinner, is asked to pay for his dinner. He attempts to conceal the fact that he is carrying £800, of which he is promptly relieved. The humiliated monk, twice called a churl by Little John, makes his escape as fast as he can, with the following mocking words echoing in his ear,

'Grete well your abbot', sayd Robyn,
'And your pryour, I you pray,
And byd hym send me such a monke
To dyner every day'.[18]

This penchant of Robin for monks is almost his undoing. For later in the story, the king, being unable to track down the outlaw who has been devastating his forests, finally takes the advice of a forester that the only way to catch him is to disguise himself as a monk and that way be invited to dine. Sure enough the trick works. The king, dressed as an abbot and with five knights as monks, is stopped by Robin in Sherwood Forest, and relieved of the £40 which the king/abbot confesses to be carrying. The story takes a different turn, however, first because the 'abbot' reveals he is in the service of the king, and then eventually that he is the king himself, by which time he has become convinced of Robin's honesty and loyalty. The king/abbot has already revealed that he is no typical monk; he really was carrying only £40. Furthermore the outlaws demonstrate to him their shooting skills in a competition in which failure to hit the target is punished by forfeiting the arrow and receiving a buffet. When Robin fails he asks the abbot/king to deliver the blow. But at first he demurs:

'It falleth not for myn ordre', sayd our kynge,
'Robyn, by thy leve
For to smyte no good yeman,
For doute I sholde hym greve'.[19]

An abbot who respects a yeoman: no ordinary monk is he!

The religious are treated more scornfully in *Robin Hood and the Monk*. In this tale Robin Hood is betrayed by a monk who recognises him at mass in the church at Nottingham. As he explains to the sheriff, Robin robbed him once of £100 and he has been waiting for his chance of revenge. Although the text is incomplete, it is clear that the sheriff then sends the monk with a message to the king concerning Robin's capture. We next pick up the story when Little John, who knows this, falls in with the monk and feigns to be a fellow victim, only suddenly to turn on the monk, drag him from his horse and kill him. He takes on the letter to the king himself. To the king, enquiring what had happened to the monk who was supposed to be carrying the letter, he nonchalantly replies that he died along the way. Later, when he returns to Nottingham with the king's commission, he tells the sheriff that the king was so pleased with the monk that he promptly made him abbot of Westminster.[20] Thus is the monk disposed of, his casual killing a joking matter.

Robin Hood had a particular dislike for monks. The extent to which this is so is stressed by the juxtapositioning of the genuine piety of Robin himself and the hypocrisy of the monks. In *Robin Hood and the Monk*, Robin is described as praying before the rood in a church dedicated to St Mary when recognised by the monk, who promptly informs the sheriff. While the monk is a sworn enemy rather than follower of Robin Hood, a suggestion that his action was akin to the betrayal of Christ by Judas is implicit in the text.[21] In the part of the *Gest* in which the cellarer is robbed of £800, elaborate play is made of the conceit that he has come to repay a debt owed by Our Lady. The scene opens with Robin reluctant to dine:

> For I drede Our lady be wroth with me,
> For she sent me nat my pay.

But along come the cellarer and his companions. For he is of her abbey and she was the 'borowe' of the loan he made to the knight. The pretence is made that the cellarer had come specifically on her instruction.

Thou toldest with thy owne tongue,
Thou may not say nay,
How thou arte her servaunt,
And servest her every day.

And thou art made her messengere,
My money for to pay:
Therefore I cun the more thanke
Thou art come at thy day.

The outlaws find the money the cellarer has attempted to conceal.

Robin declares that one could never find a better lender in all the land than St Mary. He proposes a toast:

And yf she have need to Robyn Hode,
A frende she shall hym fynde.[22]

While this is the reworking of a common fable which might itself have been familiar to the audience, once more it is brought home that Robin and his outlaws are the true servants of Our Lady, who devoutly serve her every day, not the cellarer and monks of the abbey dedicated to her.

Finally, there is the remarkable story of his death, betrayed by the prioress of Kirklees, a nunnery also devoted to St Mary. The early story remains only in fragments, the last six stanzas of the *Gest* being a truncated version. The prioress is his cousin. There he goes to let blood, to receive medical treatment. But there is treachery. She over-bleeds him, and when he is weak, calls in the dastardly 'Red Roger'. Red Roger mortally wounds him, but Robin does not die until he has summoned his last strength to slay Red Roger and has received the last rites from his faithful servant Little John, who has arrived too late to save his life. John proposes to burn down the nunnery, but Robin, true to his principles, forbids him for,

'I should doe any widow hurt, at my latter end,
God,' he said, 'wold blame me'.[23]

The prioress has been transformed into a widow. To some extent it would make more sense if Robin's nemesis had been a widow who had taken a vow of chastity, but broken these with her accomplice. Be that as it may, the short version clearly identifies his betrayer as the prioress. Like Christ he is undone, but not by Judas. His fate is sealed by a servant of his Christ's Virgin Mother, who thereby commits a crime far worse than even the abbot of St Mary's, York.

The critique of the religious orders seems, on the surface, to be devastating. Monks concerned more with maintaining a worldly estate (the cellarer declares as he leaves that he is off to deal with the reeves of the abbey's estates) and, living like lords, have abandoned their true vocation. A nun, who it is hinted has broken her vow of chastity, plots murder. A band of yeoman outlaws living in the woods serve God far more devoutly than they. In this, there is much that comes from the common tradition of complaint and satire. Monks did not escape the barbs of the fourteenth-century preachers. In particular Bromyard drew a sharp distinction between the manner in which the wealthy monastery fawned to the great and powerful, but shunned and humiliated the poor and indigent. And so it is at St Mary's, York. The abbot dines in splendour with the justice, sheriff, lords and his convent rubbing their hands in anticipation of how they will all profit from the knight's ruin. Only the 'prior' expresses misgivings. When the knight himself arrives to dash their hopes, he changes from the good clothes given to him by Robin back into the 'simple weeds' he had been wearing, so as to reinforce the impression of his poverty.[24] 'The habit', it was proverbially said, 'maketh not the religious'.

The same conventional satire of the monk was deployed, more

gently, by Chaucer in his portrait for the *Canterbury Tales*. He was 'An out-rydere, that loved venerye', he did not care to keep the rule of St Benedict too strictly, did not see why he should restrict himself to the cloister. He was a man of the world: 'A fat swan loved he best of any roost'.[25] Yet the literary representation was not entirely critical. Derek Pearsall has pointed out that alongside the image of the fat and greedy monk lay also the idea of the cloister as a haven from all the sins of the world. This was expressed, for instance, by Langland:

> *For yf heven be on this erthe, or eny ese to the soule*
> *Hit is in cloiystre or in scole, by many skills I fynde.*

The contrast was drawn both by Langland and others between the idealised internal world of the monastery, withdrawn from the world, and the corrupted world outside. Worldliness was the consequence for monks, who were as a result,

> *Ledares of lawedays and londes ypurchased*
> *And pryked about on palfrayes from places to maneres,*
> *An hepe of houndes at here ers as he a lord were.*

It was monks outside the monastery who were particularly satirised. Monasteries needed to engage with the world, to be involved in corporate entertainment and maintain good public relations. Indeed, conventional satire notwithstanding, it may well be that many contemporaries accepted this. Certainly there is little condemnation of the worldly monk who features in 'The Shipman's Tale', an obedientiary whose role it is to supervise his monastery's estates; rather, Chaucer implies, an acceptance that this is how the world goes.[26]

Robin Hood's dealings with monks are largely with those who are riding out on the business of their abbey, whether they are met in forest, in the parish church or on the road. It is not the case, however, as Pearsall suggests, that 'there is no particular sense that their [monks'] involvement in the world of business and finance is specially offensive as a violation of their rule'.[27] Rather it is the opposite. The knight's experience of the abbey is not of a cloistered oasis of spirituality. There is no denying that the Robin Hood stories draw upon a long tradition of conventional ridicule and humour at the expense of fat monks, but there seems to be such a level of sustained criticism as to suggest that the ridicule goes beyond the good natured. The juxtapositioning in the narrative of Robin's true devotion to Our Lady and the false dedication of the monks of St Mary's Abbey implies that their worldliness *was* offensive. A vein of particular hostility towards the religious orders running through the stories suggests a more than stereotypical hostility towards them.[28]

However, it is not the religious orders in general who are the target, but the Benedictines in particular and one of their houses, St Mary's, York, specifically. In the *Gest* the identification is of course specific. A degree of verisimilitude is given as first the knight rides from Barnsdale to York, presenting himself the following day to repay the abbot, and later the cellarer and his convoy ride through on their way to London, to attend a high-level meeting with the abbey's estate officers, who have 'done much wrong'. He wryly comments as he departs from his uncomfortable experience in the forest, that it would have been cheaper to have stayed in Blyth or Doncaster.[29] The monk in *Robin Hood and the Monk* is not specifically identified. The compiler would seem to want the reader to think that he is the same man, for he refers to having been robbed himself by Robin (although of rather less than in the *Gest*). He is also described in almost the same terms. Little John recognises him by his 'wide hode' (possibly a mistranscription for 'wide hede'), and he is earlier described as 'gret-heded'. When in the *Gest* we first meet the cellarer, present in the Abbot's Hall when the knight comes to repay his debt, he is described as 'a fat heded monk/the heygh selerer'. Even if this is a common trope, we know the monk is a Benedictine, for, as we have seen, after he has killed him, Little John casually informs the sheriff that the king has made him abbot of Westminster.[30] The Benedictines were the oldest and wealthiest order, which dominated the monastic establishment. 'We are the princes of the priesthood and the masters of the people', declared a preacher to a chapter of the English Benedictines in around 1400.[31] Much of the conventional critique of the monastic orders was specifically directed at them, because they were so much more visible, many of their great houses, notably Westminster and York, being urban.

Not all of these houses enjoyed amicable relationships with their lay neighbours. Monastic boroughs, especially those controlled by Benedictine houses, were on the whole denied self-government. Some, especially the more prosperous, resented subordination. There had been bitter and much publicised conflict between the abbeys of Bury St Edmunds, St Albans and St Mary's and the townsmen on their doorsteps in the thirteenth and fourteenth centuries. In Bury and St Albans, the focal point was the claim of the townspeople for self-government; in York, control of the suburb of Bootham, where the abbey was sited, was at issue. All three disputes, the histories of which run back into the mid-thirteenth century, came to a head in 1326–7. At Bury and St Albans, the townspeople attacked the abbeys, lives were lost and property was pillaged. Conflict in York was a little more muted, primarily because the city, as a fully constituted authority, had considerably more power. In all three the young Edward III stepped in to impose a settlement. At Bury in 1331, he upheld the claim of the monastery imposing compensation on the townspeople. At St Albans in 1327, following a special conference at St Paul's, his council ruled in favour of the townspeople. Within three years, however, the settlement was undermined by the abbey and trailbaston proceedings at Hertford reversed the decision and forced the town to submit. At York in 1334, Edward III confirmed a parliamentary verdict of 1275 which had confirmed the abbey's possession of the liberty of Bootham. But the city never accepted this judgement and succeeded in 1354 in having it reversed. Thereafter, with the exception of Marygate, Bootham was absorbed into the city. Echoes of these conflicts were heard in all three places in 1381, especially in Bury and St Albans, where briefly the townspeople were able to re-establish their independence, but thereafter they subsided. In St Albans a form of civic government was established through the Guild of All Saints. Bury never completely acquiesced in the rule of the abbey. Townsmen, who prospered in the fifteenth century, followed the route of law, taking the abbey to court in a series of suits in the 1480s and 1490s, none of which was successful. In York the abbey accepted that it had lost control of Bootham and relationships thereafter settled down to peaceful coexistence.[32]

These three well-documented conflicts between wealthy Benedictine monasteries and their dependent or neighbouring urban communities reached their climaxes in the early years of Edward III. By the time the Robin Hood stories circulated in writing, they were of the past. But it is possible that the memory of them, recorded in the cases of Bury and St Albans in the highly partisan monastic chronicles, influenced the continuing perception of the Benedictine order long afterwards. It is noticeable too that the Sheriff of Norfolk and Suffolk had been called in to restore order in Bury in 1327. Urban conflicts with local houses in the fourteenth century may have helped shape the attitude to the order in the stories.

However, one has to remember too that other Benedictine houses, and probably the majority, seem to have enjoyed peaceable and largely harmonious relationships with the urban communities outside their gates. Durham and Westminster, to take two prominent examples, for which substantial evidence has survived, were never torn by the strife which afflicted Bury and St Albans.[33] The evidence from Ramsey, where grievances against the abbey were drawn up and resolved (it would appear peaceably) in 1327, is of largely harmonious relationships over the last two centuries of its existence. Town and abbey were closely integrated; indeed, too closely integrated according to two fifteenth-centry visitation reports. Moreover, analysis of the town court leet rolls suggests that divisions within the urban community outside the abbey gates were as significant as conflict between the two.[34] Conflict between local community and abbey in the early fourteenth century is recorded with fewer than a dozen of the over two hundred houses then in existence.[35]

Nevertheless there was a widespread lay perception that the Benedictines were worldly. Zealous bishops drew attention to their shortcomings in visitation reports and satirists made fun of them. Henry V went to the extent of attempting a modest programme of their reform, proposing to a Chapter in 1421 that they tightened the enforcement of their rule, especially to restrict the enjoyment of private property, receipt of individual money allowances and movement outside the cloister.[36] The initiative did not perhaps in the long run make much impact on observance, but royal endorsement of the conventional criticism of the order is itself likely to have been widely reported.

The Benedictines themselves seem to have been conscious of a poor image. As James Clark has shown in the late fourteenth and fifteenth centuries, they undertook a sustained, perhaps even coordinated, campaign to recover the high esteem they had once enjoyed, by explaining in writing, by visual display and by public ritual their positive role in contemporary society. They reached for an audience beyond the clergy. Tabulae, or display boards, were set up in their monastic churches to explain their great achievements to all visitors; the cults of saints popular with the laity were promoted and their shrines advertised; the laity were encouraged to visit their monasteries, to join their confraternities; and the monks went out into the community in ceremonial procession, sometimes dramatised, on key festivals, especially their saints' days. It has been possible partially to reconstruct the nature of this performance as it developed in the Corpus Christi plays in fifteenth-century Durham.[37] By these means an effort was made to reach out to the lay community, to convince it that the Benedictine order had a positive contribution to make to religious life outside the cloister.

The extent to which this sustained public relations exercise was successful, Clark notes, is difficult to judge. If the Robin Hood ballads are anything to go by, it failed lamentably in all but a few places such as Durham. They are represented as uncharitable, greedy, scheming, deceitful, and above all, discourteous. The cellarer is insultingly called a churl twice by Little John. What do you expect ('Thereof no force'), retorts Robin dismissively, he knows not the meaning of courtesy, 'For curteyse can he none'.[38] At the end of the fifteenth century and into the sixteenth the Benedictines were being represented with utter disdain in this corpus of popular lay literature. If the Benedictines did indeed believe so arrogantly that they were the princes of the priesthood and the masters of the people, in these stories they are taken down a peg.

There is one further dimension to explore. The story of the 'Robin Hood and the Knight' focuses on the manner in which the abbot attempted fraudulently to dispossess the knight of his inheritance by means of a mortgage. The circumstantial details of this place it before, or shortly after, the passage of the Statute of Mortmain in 1279. The statute was passed as a result of the pressure from greater landlords, who had witnessed landed wealth and feudal rights being transferred remorselessly into the hands of the religious houses. To them gifts for the salvation of the soul had turned into ecclesiastical rapacity. For the crown a system of licensing ensured that thereafter gifts to monasteries became a source of revenue. While the pressure for the act had come from major landlords, there is evidence to suggest that the lesser landlords, the knightly class, had been particularly vulnerable. Several knightly families who were financially embarrassed are known to have sold their estates to monasteries. This is particularly observable in Yorkshire and the East Midlands. But in her major study of the legislation, Sandra Raban has warned against assuming that rapacious monasteries were taking advantage of defenceless families for motives of naked territorial aggrandisement. In the context of the so-called crisis of the thirteenth century, many families went to the wall. The greater monasteries had the resources to buy them out.[39]

However, before and after the act there were disputed cases and no doubt incidents of fraudulent acquisitions in which impoverished gentry lost their estates, sometimes where a leasehold or mortgage had been involved. In the period after the statute was passed this might have occurred when both parties were anxious to evade it. In one such case in 1315 Crowland Abbey was in dispute with a local freeholder over small parcels of lands which he had mortgaged to it. Sometimes too the king's escheator, who was the royal officer locally responsible for enforcing the act, colluded with abbeys in illicit dealing or was paid off. In 1313, for instance, the chapter of Lincoln made substantial gifts to the escheator and his staff on the occasion of their visit to enquire into mortmain holdings, apparently to good effect since no notifications to the crown were forthcoming.[40]

By 1340, however, the heat had gone out of the issue. In the face of economic and financial strain, the greater monasteries progressively withdrew from the land market. The very cost of buying licences made the transactions even more expensive.

Religious fashions also changed. By the later fourteenth century land was being granted to chantries, secular colleges and hospitals, more directly answerable to the founder, rather than to the old religious houses. The statute of 1391 on enfeoffment recognised the changed circumstances by extending the need for licences to guilds and fraternities. By the mid-fifteenth century little new land was passing into the hands of monasteries.[41]

The context of the story of the knight who mortgaged his lands to St Mary's Abbey is of the late thirteenth and early fourteenth centuries. Little is known that might connect it to a particular incident involving St Mary's Abbey. However, in 1301 the abbey was granted an exceptional general licence by the king to acquire property up to the value of £200 per year. This put the house into a class of its own as far as exemption from the statute was concerned. The privilege was renewed in 1309. By 1315 it appears to have been exceeding the limit, for in that year surreptitious acquisitions were legitimised. Even so, later in the reign of Edward II it had its property confiscated until a royal pardon was confirmed. A few years later, in 1332–5, while the royal chancery was lodged in the abbey itself, the then abbot, Thomas Multon, recorded thirteen loans, among them three to knights. As J. R. Maddicott has commented, it is not known how hard he pressed his creditors, and there is no way of knowing whether this period was typical of his, or his predecessors', engagement in the money market. But St Mary's would appear to have been one of the most active of the great Benedictine monasteries in the land and money market in the early fourteenth century. It may be, and there is no way of knowing this since the records of the abbey itself have been lost, that the story carried in the *Gest* is based on the memory of a particular dispute in the early fourteenth century arising out of a circumstance such as this.[42]

At the heart of the matter stands the memory of circumstances a century or more before the story was committed to writing, a memory which was carried in the pages of the *Gest* right through to the Reformation. This is surely of wider significance to the continuing debate about anticlericalism on the eve of the Reformation. Until the late twentieth century it was a cardinal act of protestant faith that the English people resented the late-medieval catholic clergy. Owst, revising his 1933 text in 1961, felt no need to amend his judgement that the literature of satire and complaint worked deeply into the conscience of the people leading ultimately to the revolt against the Church:

> No society on earth could withstand for ever the continuous shock of such Complaint . . . Spreading from the pulpits into the streets it threatened the very foundations of Holy Church, and helped sweep away the waning respect of many for her ministers and her sacraments.[43]

More recent work has sought to convince us that this was far from the case. Anticlericalism, we are now assured, was *not* a major force in preparing for or shaping the Reformation. Late-medieval lay people had no major or deep-rooted complaint against the clergy as a privileged group. Tensions and conflicts, when they occurred, were on a personal level between parishioners and priests, or focused on unresolved and long-running disputes over particular tithal rights rather than tithes in principle. Very often anticlerical opinions before the arrival of Protestantism in c.1520 turn out, on closer examination, to be Lollard opinions. Most Lollards, that heterogeneous grouping of Wycliffites, sceptics, pagans and atheists, who worried zealous bishops from time to time, came by the early sixteenth century to reject priests on principle. Early-sixteenth-century Lollards were indeed against the clergy, but their antagonism derived largely from doctrine, or what stood for doctrine. Even Richard Hunne, who single-handedly and obsessively challenged the legal rights of the bishop of London and was scandalously murdered for his pains in 1514, was probably a Lollard. While the crown whittled away at clerical immunities, and the common lawyers cast greedy eyes on pleadings reserved to ecclesiastical courts, there was no sustained assault on the ecclesiastical order as such until Henry VIII wanted his divorce.[44]

Robin Hood was no Lollard; he was conventionally orthodox in his doctrine. But the anti-monastic tone of the stories, especially the manner in which audiences are entertained by the assault and humiliation of Benedictine monks, should make us pause for thought. It may be that rich monks, in particular the Benedictines, were resented not because they were monks but because they were rich. St Mary's, York, one of the richest in the land, acted as the crown's northern bank in the early sixteenth century. Here may have lain an additional cause of criticism of wealthy monasteries for straying from their true vocation. Excessive wealth and financial entanglement with the crown were not in themselves reasons to reject monasticism.[45] The recent consensus has been to stress the broad acceptance of monasteries on the eve of their dissolution, their failings tolerated, as fixed elements in the social landscape. Indeed the reading of the Pilgrimage of Grace in 1536 as in part a defence of the lesser monasteries in the north, which had just been dissolved, has led historians to conclude that the dissolution, in the north at least, was not welcomed. Moreover, Robert Aske stated in his examination by the crown in 1537 that they were the ornaments of the commonwealth performing valuable ghostly and social services for northern communities. Twenty years later, Robert Parkyn, a Yorkshire parson and unrepentant catholic, remembered in his memoirs how the monasteries had been furiously trampled under foot by Henry VIII's government. Moreover, it has been argued, only the skilled containment of the threat to the north of the river Don by the duke of Norfolk in the autumn of 1536, not entirely to Henry VIII's liking, stopped the movement sweeping south.[46]

Yet is this testimony so reliable? Aske and Parkyn were deeply conservative, stalwart defenders of the old order. There was in the south no movement in defence of the monasteries, and in the end the greater houses were suppressed with no great opposition. It has been suggested that as institutions they had long lost their true purpose and that by the 1530s they no longer commanded the respect and commitment of the laity as a whole, and the gentry in particular, and were thus not considered institutions worth saving. It may not only have been the greed of local gentlemen, lawyers, yeomen and husbandmen, who saw in their dissolution a golden opportunity to feather their own nests, which encouraged them to participate in sharing the spoils. The lurid stories concerning the superstitious practices, fraudulent relics and sexual misbehaviour of the religious which Cromwell's commissioners uncovered and publicised in 1535 may have been directed at more than the king's ears. It could be that they reflected more widely held views, rather contrary to Robert Aske's, about the worth of monks in the early sixteenth century.[47]

Whether, in the Robin Hood stories, the Benedictine Order stands for all the monastic orders is impossible to say. But the Benedictine houses *were* the richest and the most worldly. They were the most frequently satirised. The repetition of this ridicule in the Robin Hood stories, even if drawing on conventional and stereotypical fun at the expense of the order, could not by the repetition have enhanced the order's reputation. Few, certainly not those familiar with the *Gest*, would have taken seriously the claim made in the preamble to the act dissolving the lesser monasteries that the expelled monks, by joining larger and richer houses, would thereby be corrected and become more dedicated to their vocations. There may therefore have been more cynicism about monks and their lifestyles, which the Robin Hood stories reflected, than recent consideration has recognised. A. G. Dickens reminded us in a late essay that anticlericalism was deeply embedded in public discourse throughout the later middle ages and that the satirical writings of the fourteenth century, as well as Lollard tracts, were recycled in the sixteenth.

When the monasteries fell, local inhabitants quickly joined in the spoliation. In February 1439 one of Cromwell's correspondents, John Marshall, assured him that the commons were saying that the abbeys 'were but the bellimonds and gluttons of the world' and in their dissolution were concerned only for the implication for them of the loss of prayers for the dead.[48] The hostility to Benedictines in the Robin Hood stories may well indicate that the order had failed in its campaign to make itself more valued outside the cloister. It might also suggest, whatever might have been the attitude towards the clergy as a whole, the parochial priesthood and the hierarchy, that one group, monks, even one order, the Benedictines, were not particularly admired, and their passing in 1539–40 not as deeply mourned as later apologists such as Robert Parkyn claimed.

Robin Hood, it may finally be suggested, reflected a particular aspect of lay religiosity and pattern of lay participation in religion in the century or so before the Reformation. Conventional in his devotion to the saints, especially the Virgin Mary, and perhaps fashionable cults such as the name of Jesus, believing deeply in the power of prayer, and actively engaging in worship, he is a model of contemporary lay Christianity. This kind of Christianity links him to the communitarian practice of Christianity of the later middle ages, grounded in the participation and involvement of local elites in the management of their own ecclesiastical affairs as church wardens and as members of parish fraternities. As we shall see later, his devotion to the Virgin Mary and the similarity of his fellowship to such a fraternity connects him with this parochial context. Lay involvement in parochial organisation, extended sometimes to challenging, even as far as disciplining the incumbent and, in the case of guilds, employing their chaplains, was blurring the traditional clear-cut distinction between laity and clergy. By the eve of the Reformation parochial religion represented an approach almost diametrically opposite to monasticism.[49]

Moreover in those parishes where record has survived of the local worthies performing Robin Hood for charitable purposes in May Games, Robin Hood, the disparager of Benedictines, is specifically presented as a devoted Christian. At Yeovil in 1519–20, for instance, the parish clerk recorded on behalf of the wardens that there was 'Received of Richard Hacker, that year being Robin Hood, by his good provision and diligent labours and by the good devotion of the town and country, he presented to God and Holy Church, £6. 8s. 0.1/2d'. One assumes that he did not raise this money by robbing the abbot or cellarer of nearby Sherborne Abbey. Nevertheless, it might be that Hacker and his fellows, stalwarts of the parish and its community, shed few tears for the abbot and his sixteen monks when they surrendered their house on 18 March 1539, and they might have understood why the parishioners there quickly moved to purchase the abbey site a year later.[50] Men like them, devotedly orthodox as most still were, were not, it seems, overly sentimental about their local Benedictine monastery. The disdainful attitude towards monks, especially Benedictine monks, revealed in the Robin Hood stories might help explain why, when it came to it, there was little opposition to the 'voluntary' surrenders of the greater monasteries.[51]

6

Fellowship and Fraternity

———•◆•———

In addition to a ploughman and a good yeoman, Robin Hood instructs his men not to molest a knight or squire that 'wol be a gode felawe'.[1] This exemption is all the more striking because a few stanzas earlier at the beginning of the *Gest*, we have been told that Robin will not sit down to dinner until he has some bold baron, 'that may pay for the best', or some knight or squire to be entertained at their own expense; indeed he goes on to repeat that they can waylay anyone of gentility,

> *Be he erle, or ani baron,*
> *Abbot or ani knight,*
> *Bringhe him to lodge to me*
> *His dyner will be dight.*[2]

Thus a distinction is made between knights and squires in general, who, like any other aristocrat, will have to pay handsomely for the privilege of dining with Robin, and one 'that would be a good fellow', who would not, by implication, be presented with a bill. What did it mean to be 'a good fellow'?

Generally, in so far as comment has been made, a broad distinction between good and bad gentry has been offered as explanation. Good gentry do not oppress the peasantry, or they live up to the chivalric ideal.[3] It is an answer which fits nicely into the perception of the Robin Hood stories being about maintaining the ideal order of society and offering a fiction about restorative justice, and of the ballads as a whole offering an affirmative view of the social norms of the later middle ages. But one needs to note that the future conditional not the present tense is used,[4] and that 'fellow' is not a conventional descriptor of gentility (assuming 'felawe' is more than a convenient rhyme with shawe). Fellowship was extended to social equals. Thus a knight could be a fellow of another knight. There is an implication therefore that the knight or the squire would be prepared to extend his fellowship beyond his own social group, and in particular below his own social group.[5]

The Middle English meanings and uses of the word 'fellow' and phrase 'good fellow' are manifold. Fellow could mean just a man, or a servant, a usage to be found in the Paston Letters. Thus on 24 June 1465, when the dispute over Drayton and Hellesdon was escalating, Margaret Paston informed her husband John that the bailiff of Coshay and 'his fellow' had turned on Richard Calle and his men when they had tried to serve a writ of replevin.[6] It also implies being with a companion, as in the use by John de Trevisa when he described St Augustine coming to England with forty fellows, cited in the *OED*. Likewise in Chaucer one frequently finds the use of the phrase to mean a companion, though usually a singular, personal companion.[7] Good fellow has a more specific meaning as a boon companion, as in a jolly fellow who keeps good company. Chaucer may, or then again may not, have been using it in this sense when he had the Wife of Bath say:

By vertu of my constellacioun
That made me, I could noght withdraw
My chamber of Venus from a good fellow.[8]

He definitely had it in mind of the Shipman, of whom he writes:

> And, certainly, he was a good fellow
> Ful many a draught of wyne had y-drawe
> From Burdeaux ward, whyl that the chapman sleep.[9]

But a sermon text from the mid-fifteenth century presents a disapproving and less tolerant view than Chaucer. 'He that is a ryatour and a grete hawnter of tavernys or of ale howsys, and a grete waster of his goodes, then is he called "a good felaw"'.[10] This is not, I think, the sense in which the phrase is used in the *Gest*.

A more general usage is found in the Paston Letters. John Bocking told an amusing tale, at least one must suppose intended to be amusing to its recipient in 1451, of how Sir Thomas Tuddenham left his Primer at the Tower and sent his man to fetch it: a 'good fellow' thereupon wished that it were rather in Norfolk so that he could go and get it there for Sir Thomas. A droll fellow indeed. Jeffrey Singman has proposed that the phrase, as used in the Robin Hood tales, means just this, being a good sport, someone who will readily join in the feasting, fun and companionability of the greenwood.[11] Yet there could be more to being a good fellow than this. In June 1465 Margaret Paston, having told John II how Richard Calle had been insulted, also recounted how she had sent Richard Charlys, John Seve and three or four other 'god felows', 'for to have done other folks as gode atorne'. More revealingly still in December 1469, after he had surrendered Caister to the duke of Norfolk's men, John Paston III wrote to his brother Sir John that 'thys day ther cam a good felaw, whyche may not be dyscoveryd', who told him that the duke had persuaded the widows of his two men killed during the siege to appeal him of murder. This good fellow, who wished to remain anonymous, clearly informed Paston at some risk to himself.[12] A good fellow in these examples is a reliable servant, one who is true and loyal, or the servant of another prepared to do one a good turn. He is to be distinguished from Pyrs Waryn, 'otherwyse called Sloth', a tenant of Drayton, described in 1465 as a 'flykeryng felowe' who had been 'besy' with the bailiff of Coshay. In the same letter of May 1465, Margaret also recounted how her own servant, John Daubeney, had been insulting called a 'lewde felowe'. One is reminded here of Little John's joke to the monk when he falls with him, pretending also to have been a victim of the outlaws, that Robin Hood had 'many a wilde felow' in his company.[13]

But fellows in other contexts are equals. The best known use of the word fellow is to describe a member of a university college. *Socius* or *sodalis* is translated in English as 'fellow'. A college was, and is, a self-govening society of equals headed by an elected warden, rector or master. By the end of the fifteenth century there were several colleges at Oxford and Cambridge with over forty fellows.[14] It is in this context that the word is used in the English translation of Alain Chartier's *Dialogus Familiaris Amici et Sodalis*, as 'A Familiar Dialogue of the Friend and the Fellow' in the second half of the century. In this short treatise the friend and fellow bemoan the state of France, concluding that the only remedy is for every person to put the common good before private gain. In the dialogue, led by the Friend, the Fellow is presented as an eloquent scholar of 'grete industry of study', not charged with the common weal, but respected for his wisdom among the nobles who are. He is, in short, a leading academic.[15]

The Inns of Court were also societies of fellows. Indeed, as Eric Ives has demonstrated, largely from the records of Lincoln's Inn, they were societies first and only subsequently educational establishments. The members of the Inns were fellows and the whole body was a fellowship. Furnival's Inn, too, described itself as a *societas* and its members as *socii* in 1422, and in the oath taken by the Principal in 1508 as 'this House and the Fellowship of the same'.[16] One would suppose, however, that it was even less likely that Robin Hood was prepared to admit a lawyer to his fellowship than a scholar.

'Fellowship' is, of course, closely linked to the word fellow. A fellowship is both the position of fellow and a collective of fellows, such as having a fellowship of a college or being a member of it. Twice Robin Hood's band is described as a fellowship. In the *Gest* Robin calls up his men:

> *'let blowe a horne', sayd Robin,*
> *'That felaushyp may us know'.*
> *Seven score of wight yemen*
> *Came pricking on a rowe.*[17]

And in *Robin Hood and the Potter*, the potter is offered a fellowship

> *'Y well prey the, good potter,*
> *a fellisschip well thow haffe?'*[18]

In these uses, however, it is clear that the text is not referring to a society of academics or lawyers. This fellowship is a band of armed men.

Fellowship in this sense was a word used in mid-fifteenth-century Norfolk to describe the gangs raised locally from the tenantry and others to enforce the holding of manorial courts and the collections of rents in property disputes. In 1465 both Margaret and Sir John Paston recounted how, at the end of September, they were making an effort to raise a fellowship to counter the fellowship raised on behalf of the duke of Suffolk in their dispute over Drayton and Hellesdon. Indeed Sir John assured his father that he had brought together by raising his tenantry 'ryth a good felawschep' of over 150 men.[19] These fellowships could not compare with the gang raised and maintained by Robert Ledham of Witton-by-Blofield, east of Norwich in 1452. Based at his house there, where he kept a meynie of armed men, he and his principal associates were indicted for at least twenty assaults over nine months from March to February. Operating in groups ranging from just three to over sixty men in what were described as either 'ryottows' or 'mysgoverned' fellowship they allegedly terrorised the well-willers of Osbert Mountford on behalf of Thomas Daniel in pursuit of his claim to the manor of Braystone.[20]

In 1469 the word is also used by the Pastons to describe their beleaguered garrison in Caister. John Paston recruited about thirty men, several veteran soldiers, to defend the castle, which was besieged by the duke of Norfolk from 21 August to 26 September. On 12 September Margaret wrote to Sir John in great agitation that his 'brother and his felesshep stand in grete joperte [jeopardy]' and reported that two of his lieutenants, Daubeney and Berney, had been killed, accurately as far as Daubeney was concerned. Two weeks later, John surrendered. He and his men, his 'fellaship', were given a safe conduct to leave with their goods, horses and harness, but leaving their weapons behind. Nevertheless on 5 October John confided to his brother that 'By Sent George, I and my felawshep stand in fer of my Lord of Norff., for we be thret sore, not withstandyng the save gardeys that my felawshep have'.[21] The small well-equipped fellowship of experienced soldiers raised to garrison and defend Caister from November 1468 to its surrender in the following September was in effect a private army.

The garrison of Calais, on the other hand, was a royal retinue. A jocular letter of 16 September 1473 written by William, Lord Hastings, the absentee captain, is addressed to 'my right hertily beloved frends and felaws, Sir John of Middleton and Sir John Paston, knights'. It thanks them for their good attendance on the king's council at Calais and service to his deputy, Sir John Scott and recommends himself, among others, to the mayor, lieutenant and *fellawship* of the staple and my *felaws*, the soldiers of the garrison. Writing from Nottingham, the captain of the garrison signs himself, 'your felaw, Hastings'.[22]

The word fellowship was regularly used to describe a retinue of war. In January 1463 John Paston III, serving with the earl of Warwick in Northumberland, wrote to his elder brother with news and asked him to assure their mother that he and his fellowship were well.[23] A few years later, the *Chronicle of the Lincolnshire Rebellion* describes how in 1470 Edward IV sent letters into Northumberland and Westmorland to array a certain *felaship* and to the Marquis Montague, with his *felaship*, together to confront the *felaship* raised in Richmondshire by Warwick the Kingmaker.[24] The *Historie of the Arrivall of Edward IV* similarly uses the word to describe the battalions raised by the participants in the civil war of March to May 1471, as, for instance, it is reported how at Leicester there came to the king a 'ryghte-a-fayre felaweshipe of folks'. When the armies drew up for battle on the field of Barnet they were 'hosts'. But, the author stresses, the battle was finally turned in Edward IV's favour not only by his own hardiness and courage, but also through 'the fathefull, welbovyd, and mighty assistance of his felawshipe', who fought valiantly by his side 'so that nothing might stand in the syght of hym and the well asswred felowshipe that attendyd trewly upon hym'.[25] Even when the fighting was over, in the autumn of 1471, according to Sir John Paston, Sir Thomas Fulford escaped sanctuary and quickly gathered a great fellowship of diehard Lancastrians within five miles of London, which, rumour had it, numbered 200 men.[26] It is not surprising to find therefore that in Malory's almost exactly contemporary eyes, King Arthur campaigned with a 'felyship', addressed his companions in arms as 'felowys', or that his queen was always accompanied by a 'grete felyship of men of armys about her', the most part of whom were 'yonge men', known as the 'Queen's Knyghts'.[27]

Andrew Ayton has stressed the military characteristics of Robin

Hood's outlaw band as such a fellowship. The legend, as he sees it, was

> affected, indeed stimulated by the experience of war in a number of ways: by the prominent role of archery in the English military machine, by the impact of the demobilised soldiery on the character of the greenwood community – and also, in all probability, by the active encouragement of the military community itself.

It is the idea that the character of the greenwood community is shaped by the model of the military retinue, or fellowship of this kind, which is germane here. As Ayton points out, the outlaws not only are skilled archers, but also fight the sheriff in skirmishes which are reminiscent of actions of war. Furthermore Kelly DeVries has noted that mounted archers, yeomen who had the resources to provide their own horses and swords, as well as bows, became a feature of English armies after 1330 and remained a prominent element for a century.[28] The prominence given to Robin's men as archers, the notion that as foresters they are the best shooters, and thus the best military reservists in the realm, the stress on Robin himself being the best archer in the land, and the frequency with which archery contests are held, all suggest a military milieu.

This is made explicit in the case of the knight's retinue of war. After he has recovered his lands and collected sufficient rent to repay Robin, he buys a hundred bows and sheaves of arrows of the best quality, retains a hundred men whom he dresses in his livery of white and red, and leads them, lance in hand, to Barnsdale. Later, reinforced by Robin's men, this retinue defends his castle against the siege laid by the sheriff.[29] Here, as one would expect, the full military retinue is to be found.[30] Robin Hood is the head of a band of irregulars and auxiliaries, exactly as one would expect of foresters. In this capacity he and his men serve, appropriately, under the command of the knight. The knight does not serve under Robin. There can be little doubt that the words fellow and fellowship evoke the atmosphere of the military retinue. But they do so in a context in which the proper social and military hierarchy is maintained. To this extent the company of outlaws is modelled on an Arthurian fellowship.

Linked to the notion of the fellowship as a band of men in arms is the idea of a meyny, or following. The knight arrives at St Mary's Abbey to repay his mortgage accompanied by his' meyne'. The abbot too is surrounded by his meyny.[31] On two and possibly three occasions the outlaw band is described as a 'merry meyne/maney'. When the knight returns to Barnsdale to honour his pledge, 'he founde there Robyn Hode/And all his merry meyne'.[32] At the beginning of *Robin Hood and the Potter*, Robin is described as follows:

Bot as the god yeman stod on a day,
Among hes mery maney.[33]

In stanza 335 of the *Gest*, they are 'his fayre mene'. In other places they are the merry men, not the merry meyny. Is there more than assonance? Might it be that the closeness of the words has led to some confusion, if not for the late-medieval reader or listener, then for the modern, between two close, but separate ideas? The interchangeability of the words is suggested in the Derbyshire petition of 1439 complaining about the misdeeds of Piers Venables and his followers, which likened them to 'Robin Hood and his meyne'. In 1465 John Payn recollected that in 1450 Cade had sent 'certeyn of his meyny' to ransack his lodgings in Southwark.[34] How close the words were is revealed in the indictment of the 'principall menealle men of the seyd Robert ledham ys hous' for their misdeeds in East Anglia in 1453.[35]

There are powerful reasons, therefore, for supposing that a 'gode felawe' is one who was willing to serve truly under Robin Hood as one of his meyny, his fellowship of yeomen in arms. This idea seems to lie behind the recruitment of the cook to Robin Hood's service in the *Gest*. Having proved his valour in combat with Little John, he is offered, one assumes jokingly, alternative household service: livery twice a year and fee from Robin Hood of twenty marks a year. He accepts

> *'put up thy swerde,' saide the coke,*
> *'And felowes woll we be'.*[36]

Here is one who will be a good fellow. The idea that a good fellow is understood to be a true and trusted member of the fellowship becomes clear in *Robin Hood and the Potter*. The opening twenty-eight stanzas portray an admission ritual to the fellowship. The postulant in this version is, of course, an artisan, not a knight or squire. He is described to begin with as a proud potter, one who is always travelling through the forest without paying a toll (pavage) to Robin. In fact he has already had the better of Little John, who once tried to levy it. As the action begins, Robin lays a wager that he can outdo him. But in the confrontation the potter gets the better of Robin as well, who has to be rescued by his men (watching to see who would win). Robin concedes he has lost his wager. The potter now complains that this is no way to treat a poor yeoman going about his honest trade.[37] Robin admits he 'seys god yemenrey' and agrees that he will never be hindered again. He continues:

> *'Y well prey the, god potter,*
> *A ffelischepe well thow haffe?*
> *Geffe me they clothing, and thow schalte hafe myne;*
> *Y well go to Notynggam'*

143

'Y grant thereto', seyde the potter,
'Thow schalt ffeynde me a ffelowe gode,
Bot thw can sell mey pottys well,
Come ayen as thow yede'.[38]

In this whole passage the word fellow is used no fewer than six times: twice by the potter in the initial confrontation to show that he is the match and equal to Robin – 'Ffelow let mey hors go', three times to describe Robin's men (or meyny?) – 'Leytyll John to hes ffelows he seyde', 'Than spake Leytell John,/And all hes ffelohes heynd' and Robin addresses them, 'Ffelowhes, let me a lone', and finally by the potter promising that he will be a good fellow, a fellow true to the fellowship: 'thou schalt ffeynde me a ffelowe gode'.[39]

What constitutes good fellowship is also demonstrated in the story of *Robin Hood and the Monk*, in which Little John refuses any longer to be Robin's subordinate. Robin declares at the beginning that he is to go to Nottingham and will take only Little John with him as his bowbearer. Little John refuses to go as servant, you bear yours and I will bear mine, he retorts. To demonstrate his equality of status he challenges Robin to an archery contest, which Robin loses with ill grace. They come almost to blows.[40] In the event Little John holds back,

'Were thou not my maister', seid Litull John,
'Thou shouldis by hit ful sore,
Get the a man where thou wilt,
For thou getis me no more'.[41]

And off he stalks. Robin goes to Nottingham alone, where, having been recognised by a monk, he is captured by the sheriff. Little John, despite the rift, despite his having left Robin's service, comes to the rescue. He kills the monk and helps Robin escape. At the end of the tale, Robin and John are reconciled. Little John has proved his loyalty when tested to its limit. 'I have done the a gode turn for an evil', he wryly remarks.[42] A chastened and wiser Robin offers to stand down, for Little John has shown himself to be a better fellow than he:

> *'I make the maister', seid Robyn Hode,*
> *Of alle my men and me'*

> *'Nay, be my trouth', seid Litull John,*
> *'So shalle hit never be;*
> *But let me be a felow', seid Litull John,*
> *'No noder kepe I be'.*[43]

Thus harmony is restored to the fellowship. Little John is content just to be a good fellow.

Both good fellows, the potter and Little John, are yeomen. This is made explicit in *Robin Hood and the Potter* by his complaint that it is not courteous of Robin Hood to prevent a poor yeoman going about his lawful business, and at the end of *Robin Hood and the Monk* by the king, on hearing of Little John's exploits declaring that he is one of the finest three yeomen in his land.[44] Little John is the model of a good fellow; the potter, another yeoman, is accepted as a potential good fellow. The fellows are yeomen, and the fellowship to which they belong is a fellowship of yeomen. It is worth recalling that these fellows are yeomen foresters. Like the fifteenth-century forester of Sherwood he is imagined to be, Little John is bound by his oath to be true to the master forester and his fellows.[45]

How is it, therefore, that a knight can also be a good fellow? Does he have to show that he is prepared to give up his rank and subordinate himself to the yeoman Robin Hood as his master? This would seem hardly likely. As we have seen, in the narrative of the *Gest* the knight commands his own company and Robin, the yeoman, as is proper, serves under him in war.

An answer can be found if one identifies a different kind of fellowship. This solution is suggested in the first part of the story of 'Robin Hood and the Knight', with which the *Gest* opens, and for which Robin's exhortation to his men not to harm a knight or squire 'that wol be a gode felawe' is the preamble. This story is, among other things, a story of how a knight does indeed become a good fellow. It too, like *Robin Hood and the Potter*, is a story of initiation into the fellowship.

The prologue to the *Gest* can be read as the prologue to a particular story of how a knight became a good fellow.[46] It opens, appropriately, with an address to a gentle audience,

> *Lythe and listin, gentilmen,*
> *That be of frebore blode,*

which leads up to the admonition to Little John, Will Scarlock and Much not to molest one who would be a good fellow. The three then immediately go over to the Sayles, where they waylay a knight who is invited to dine. Unfortunately he is impoverished: 'all dreri was his semblaunce', he rode his horse sloppily and he was unsuitably dressed, for 'A soriar man than he was one/Rode never in somer day'.[47] Yet, he knows of Robin Hood – a good yeoman of whom he has heard much good – and is pathetically grateful for the opportunity to dine with him and his brethren. He is welcomed to a lavish feast. When it is discovered that he cannot indeed 'pay for the best', having but 10 shillings on him, he tells the sad tale of how he fell on hard times, how he has mortgaged his lands to the abbey of St Mary's, York, and how his friends, who were many when he was rich, have deserted him now that he is poor. Robin, however, is prepared to assist him. He is fitted out with livery, horse and saddle and lent £400 from the common treasury: for 'it is alms to help a gentyll knight, that is fall in poverty'. The only surety that the knight can give is that of Our

Dear Lady, which of course is good enough for Robin, and the knight is bound by his solemn oath to repay the loan in a year's time. And so off he rides escorted by Little John.

The next scene takes place at the abbey, where the knight has arrived to redeem his mortgage. Here he finds no welcome; the abbot has plotted with the chief justice to defraud him of his land. Another feast is in progress, but from this the knight is discourteously excluded – he is made to kneel as a supplicant to beg for the term of his mortgage to be extended while the abbot, justice and their guests continue to eat. Here is no kindness, no charity, no fellowship. He is summarily dismissed. However, he then reveals, to their amazement, that he actually happens to have £400 about his person and is able to recover his land. Off he goes home, raises another £400 to repay Robin and sets out a year later to settle his debt. On the way he is able to reciprocate the good turn to another yeoman, one wronged in a wrestling match, and this makes him late. His good turn is recognised by Robin: 'What man that helpeth a a good yeman/His frrendde than wyll I be'.[48]

In the meantime, in scene three as it were, Robin has waylaid the cellarer of St Mary's Abbey, who, unlike the knight, declares that he thinks no good of Robin, a common thief. The cellarer is, however, welcomed to dine. The fellowship is summoned in their best livery. The honoured guest is formally welcomed to the table and served with the best wine. Robin declares that, since Our Lady gave surety for the loan of £400 he had made to the knight, and since the cellarer is the servant of Our Lady, he assumes that the cellarer has come on her behalf to honour the surety she gave. But the guest dishonourably abuses the hospitality. He falsely claims that he has only marks on him, but he is found to be carrying £800, of which he is promptly relieved. After the monk has left, his tail between his legs, the knight arrives to repay his debt. But Robin has no need; instead he gives the knight the additional

£400 recovered from the cellarer. The knight has proved himself to be a 'gode felaw', the cellarer a 'lewde fellow'.

That the knight does not become himself a full member of the outlaw fellowship, as do the potter and the cook, becomes fully apparent as the story develops. The unlikelihood of it is made manifest early on. When first the knight is entertained in the forest and it becomes apparent that he cannot pay for his dinner, Robin comments:

> *It was never the maner, by dere worthi God,*
> *A yoman to pay for a knight.*[49]

It would simply be against the divinely ordained order for a knight to serve in a fellowship under a yeoman. In time, when the knight is preparing to repay his loan (and pay for his dinner), as we have seen, he gathers together his own retinue of a hundred archers, well harnessed and kitted out in his livery of white and red, and himself rides out at the head with a lance in his hand. Later, when Robin Hood is fleeing from the sheriff, he is given shelter by the knight, now named as Sir Richard at the Lee, in his 'fayre castell' for forty days and there withstand the sheriff's siege.[50] The knight had explicitly declared that he would repay the help that was given to him by Robin when he was in need, and now he does. Just as Robin accepted the knight as an honorary member of his fellowship, now he and his men reinforce the knight's retinue to garrison the castle and defend its walls:

> *'Shyt the gates, and draw the bridge,*
> *And let no man come in,*
> *And arme you well, and make you redy,*
> *And to the walles ye wynne.'*[51]

And then they feast.

Bordes were layde, and clothes were spredde,
Redely and anone:
Robyn Hood and his merry men
To mete can they gone.[52]

Hospitality is returned in the great hall of the castle. It is clear, however, that the fellowship of the outlaw band is not only separate from, but also different in kind from the fellowship that is the knight's retinue.

The story of 'Robin Hood and the Knight' interwoven into the *Gest* has many perspectives to it, not least the anticlericalism, explored earlier. But it is in essence a story that juxtaposes true and false fellowship, true and false brotherhood, and true and false charity. True fellowship, brotherhood and charity are to be found in Robin Hood's band – explicitly described as a fellowship of 140 wight yeomen that Robin summons to dine with the cellarer when he arrives. The false brotherhood is in the monastery, where a gentle knight is made to grovel while the abbot and his cronies eat. Central to the meaning is the feast, as a ritual of inclusive brotherly love in the forest and in the castle; and of exclusivity, selfishness and gluttony in the monastery. The outlaw band, or fellowship, is represented in short as an idealisation of a lay fraternity, to which the knight is admitted as an honorary brother.

Fraternities, or guilds as they were alternatively styled, were many things to many men. They were collective chantries, dedicated to particular saints, most popularly to the Blessed Virgin Mary, which offered prayers for dead brothers and sisters, and which played many roles in supporting parochial activities. They were friendly societies, especially to help brethren and sisters fallen on hard times. They were communal associations in which the shared identity, social solidarity and harmonious relationships of all the members were continuously renewed and reinforced, especially by means of the annual patronal mass and feast. Yet they were selective. Members, who paid small subscriptions, were chosen, were ritually admitted, and had to take an oath to abide by the rules of the brotherhood. Membership was not usually determined by wealth, but by personal worth. Brothers needed to be able to demonstrate that they were respectable and of good repute. Fraternities were hierarchical and oligarchic, being ruled by a master, but they espoused an ideology of internal equality bringing people of different social backgrounds together in virtuous common purpose. They frequently had subgroups, being divided into occupational, gender or age groups, which were often associated with the maintenance of particular lights in the parish church or guild chapel, and for which they raised funds. They were of many sizes: some were large and took on town-governing roles, as at Coventry, Luton, Wells, Westminster or Wisbech; others were also the local club for the great and the good, as was the Corpus Christi Guild at York and the Guild of St George at Norwich. Yet others were much more modest, such as the Guild of St James at Northallerton, or even tiny, perhaps even fleeting in existence.

Most fraternities acted as a point of contact for town and country. People from the surrounding countryside joined fraternities in their nearby town, just as they came into its market. The large, prestigious fraternities, such as the Corpus Christi Guild at York, admitted the county gentry. All in all there was a very large number in late-medieval England; many thousands according to Gervase Rosser. Virginia Bainbridge found 350 in Cambridgeshire, David Crouch unearthed reference to approximately 350 of one sort or another in Yorkshire, Ken Farnhill calculated almost 500 in Suffolk and over 500 in Norfolk, and Joanna Mattingly identified approximately 150 in Cornwall. Merging religious and secular functions, the fraternity or guild was ubiquitous and arguably the most important social institution beyond the family of late-medieval England. Audiences in the parishes of Cambridgeshire, Cornwall, East Anglia, Yorkshire and all the counties of England would have had no difficulty in recognising that the story of 'Robin Hood and the Knight' was about the knight being admitted to a fellowship remarkably like the fraternity or guild to which they themselves belonged, and to the more prestigious of which knights and squires were admitted. Indeed one can easily picture the same story being told at their own fraternity feasts, no doubt with a suitably reworked introit.[53]

The argument that Robin Hood's outlaw band shares many of the characteristics of a fraternity is not new.[54] There are 140 members who wear a common livery; they maintain a common fund from which they help the deserving who have fallen on hard times; feasting and conviviality are central to their rituals; when joined by the king they process in livery to Nottingham; as a brotherhood they are dedicated to a patron saint, especially to St Mary; they have a master, Robin Hood himself. In short, the outlaw band is a forest fraternity, a fraternity of yeomen foresters.

There nevertheless remains the substantial objection that the words 'fellow' and 'fellowship' are not the normal vocabulary of fraternities; 'brother' and 'brotherhood' are. The admission oath of the Guild of St George at Norwich required the new member to swear 'to susteyne, lawfully mayntene and defende . . . the prosperites, wurshipp, profites . . . of the ffraternite and gild'. It is described consistently in its ordinances as the 'fraternite and gild' of 'the bretheren and sisteren of Seynt George'. Thus, if a brother or sister fell into poverty he or she should be relieved and helped by 'the bretheren and sisteren of the ffraternite' to the tune of 8d a week.[55] At Coventry the master of the Trinity Guild undertook to be 'gode and true to the Bretheren and Systen'. Letters to the guild were addressed to 'Your worshipfull (or reverend, or full honourable) mayster' and 'worshipfull (or worthy) brethren'.[56] Yet the gap between fellowship and fraternity was not wide.

Let us take the great companies of London, later to be known as the livery companies. They were constitutionally fraternities, but they came to style themselves as fellowships. In the early sixteenth century Robert Fabyan, himself a leading Draper, referred in the *Great Chronicle of London* to all the livery companies as fellowships. No friend of the Tailors, he wrote, for instance, of how around 1500 'the fellyshipp of Taylours being grievously dyscontentyd, had many Riottous and heinous wordys by the ffelyshipp of the drapers', as a result of which 'malice . . . of those ij ffelyshyppys grewe'. More snidely, under the year 1503–4, he remarked how 'thys felyshypp of the Taylors . . . thinking that the name of taylours was not correspondent to theyr worship . . . laboured . . . to be namyd . . . marchaunt taylours'.[57] Perhaps all the great companies of London considered themselves to be grander than mere fraternities and thus appropriated for themselves the style of fellowship.

Thus they continued in their ordinances to combine the language of fraternity and fellowship. In 1490 it was ordained by the maligned Merchant Tailors themselves, a fraternity dedicated to St John the Baptist, that:

> Where as in tyme past it hath been used and accustomed that the brethren of this ffraternitie yerely the morne after mydsomer day shuld pay ther duettie for ther mete and almes in the cloystre . . . the brethren of this felaship from hensforth shall pay . . . in this place (probably the parlour).[58]

The Mercers were the same. On 19 December 1497 Sir William York was admitted as a 'brother' of 'oure feliship': 'the said felishipp ben right glad and they hooly and by oon assent do amytte youe a brother with them'.[59] Not surprisingly perhaps, given its close links, the same mixed terminology was used in respect of the Company of the Staple. On 20 September John Pasmer, a skinner and prominent merchant adventurer, wrote to George Cely at Calais to remind him of his promised support.

> Sir, please it you to understond that as touching the matter wherof I commoned with your maistership at your last beyng in London for myn entry and admission into the right worshpfull and honourable Felaship of the staple at Caleys, I am fully appointed and condescended in my mynde, and wold be right gladde to be a pore Brother of the same.

Would Cely, therefore, broach them on his behalf to accept him as 'a Brother of their said worshipfull Felaship'?[60] The tendency to perceive their organisations as fellowships was not confined to the great mercantile companies of London. The more humble craft guild of Smiths in Coventry ordained that their new officers should be chosen by twelve of 'the eldest and discredtest of the feliship'. The Butchers' Guild of Durham decreed in 1403 that 'every brother of the sayd ffellowsip' should perform in their play at Corpus Christi.[61] Fraternity and fellowship were interchangeable words in the vocabulary of guilds great and small.

The Order of the Garter, which one would be inclined to perceive as a fellowship (and its historians have described as such), was constitutionally a fraternity. So too were all military orders, established with statutes, dedicated to a patron saint and celebrating the saint's day with solemn mass before proceeding to a lavish feast. The statutes of the Garter specifically refer to the Order as a company as well as a fraternity. The twenty-six companions, as brothers in arms, entered into solemn obligations of mutual assistance and loyal service to their sovereign. Contemporaries, who were exercised by the niceties of such things, found it necessary carefully to distinguish a military order, as a form of brotherhood, from a permanent retinue, or meyny, such as that bound by contract to John of Gaunt in the later fourteenth century, as a form of fellowship. But historians of the Garter and military orders, following Malory, who described Arthur's mythical brotherhood as 'the noble felyship of the Rounde Table', recognise in their use of the word fellowship that there was fundamentally little to distinguish the two.[62]

Robin Hood's band was represented in the fifteenth-century stories in a similarly ambiguous way. Just as the great London companies were fraternities which called themselves fellowships, and the Order of the Garter was a military fellowship formally constituted as a fraternity, so Robin and his merry men are fellows in a fellowship which shares many of the characteristics of a fraternity. Indeed early in the *Gest* the knight, when first welcomed to the greenwood by Little John, Will Scarlock and Much, agrees to join Robin Hood at his table with the words:

> 'I graunte', he saide, 'with you to wende,
> My bretherne, all in fere [company]'.[63]

The outlaws are instinctively recognised by the knight as his brothers and he will gladly accept the invitation to the feast.

It might be objected that the forest fellowship as described in the stories is, like the military fellowship, a much less formally structured body than a fraternity. This is undeniable. The parish fraternity is not literally transposed to the forest in all its functions and regulations. The resemblance is generic. Like the civilian fellowship, but unlike the military, the forest fellowship is inclusive. It brings together, as does the fellowship in the forest, people from different walks of life and of different social status. It can include a potter and it can include a knight or squire that would be, in its terms, a good fellow. The values and ideals of Robin Hood's fellowship reflect the essential communitarianism, common purpose and conviviality of late-medieval fraternities.

Finally, it is part of the wide appeal of the Robin Hood stories that the fellowship of the outlaws evokes different associations, none of which is mutually exclusive. It can mean what the reader and listener want it to mean. Fellowship in the stories has resonance with military retinues and chivalric romance, with its obvious appeal to the more gentle, or would-be gentility. Its appeal could have extended to the greater fraternities, as it has been argued, such as the London mercantile companies. There may well also be an undercurrent of mockery of fellowships, such as in the scene in the *Gest* in which Little John fools around with the measurement of cloth, which might have been directed at Merchant Tailors.[64] One can also find parody of the military orders, of household etiquette and of hunting rituals, as well as parody of chivalry itself, which could just as easily entertain an aristocratic gathering in a great hall as a gathering of town and country people in a market place. Elements in the *Gest* can be seen as all these things, and plausibly were seen on different occasions and in different contexts as all these things.

Thus there are many different layers of meaning of one who 'wold be a gode felawe'. It can mean a boon companion, one who would give loyal service, a worthy colleague in a society of equals, and a reliable comrade in arms. But there is one meaning that is all inclusive, and this is in the sense of a fellow member of a guild or fraternity. The most fitting context in which one might understand the admonition not to molest a knight or a squire who would be a 'good fellow', and with which the story of 'Robin and the Knight' begins, is that generically of the late-medieval fraternity to which gentlemen were admitted. Here the outlaw band is represented as a forest fraternity and the narrative tells how a knight can become, as it were, an honorary member of this idealised fellowship.

7

Authority and the Social Order

———•———

Dr Max, the media don in Julian Barnes' novel *England, England* with whom we began, presents a research report to Sir Jack Pitman on the significance of the Robin Hood story. It is, he argues, in his politically correct learned way, the legend of the ur-freedom fighter, pursuing liberationist actions and redistributive economic policy. The outlaws are a group of marginalised men led by an equal-opportunity employer, who was, whether he knew it or not, one of the first implementers of an affirmative rights programme. And so Robin Hood is set up as a major attraction. Eventually, however, the actors playing Robin Hood and his Merrie Men, disenchanted with their conditions of work and enforced 'period' lifestyle, rebel against the establishment. They go native, take the law into their own hands, and start poaching from the neighbouring farms: as one character exasperatedly remarks, 'the bastards seem to be killing everything they can hit with those arrows'. After a farcical 'cross-epoch' event in which the Merrie Men get the better of an SAS (Special Air Service) team, the actors are sacked and a new cast is hired to bring 'respectability back to outlawry'.[1]

Dr Max's interpretation of the Robin Hood legend, drawing heavily on the work of twentieth-century historians, sums up the conventional view that the stories of Robin Hood reflect dissent and subversion in late-medieval England. However, the resolution of conflict with a new team of obedient and subservient actors who bring respectability back to outlawry, also reflects an alternative perception which has gained ground that the stories were in their first written and published form essentially affirmative of authority. It is a debate about the social and political significance of the stories that continues.

A useful starting point is Eric Hobsbawm's *Bandits*, a brilliant essay first published in 1970, when Che Guevara was still a name on the lips of the romantic left. In this wide-ranging comparative study of social banditry, the phenomenon of peasant outlaws who were regarded as common criminals by the authorities, but heroes by their own people, Hobsbawm identified Robin Hood as the archetype of one of his three types, 'the noble robber'. Robin Hood, the most famous and popular type of bandit, Hobsbawm argued, is what all peasant bandits should be. Displaying total solidarity with the peasantry, he is the righter of wrongs, the restorer of justice and the champion of social equity. Among the common attributes are his taking from the rich to give to the poor, his refusal to kill except in self-defence and just revenge, the admiration in which he is held by his people, his invisibility and invulnerability until his death by betrayal, and his unswerving loyalty to the king but relentless opposition to those who misgovern and oppress in his name. It is important to stress that the noble robber is not in conflict with the fount of justice, which is incorruptible, but only with those who pervert justice. And this is recognised by the ruler, who pardons him and takes him into his service. Robin Hood, the noble robber, is not therefore a social revolutionary, he seeks restorative justice, the re-establishment of things as they used to be and ought to be. Thus he 'represents an extremely primitive form of social protest, perhaps the most primitive there is'. He does not abolish oppression, but he does demonstrate that poor men need not be passive, helpless or meek. He is a continual reminder that without justice, as St Augustine observed, kingdoms are nothing but robbery.[2]

Two characteristics are worth stressing. The first is that Hobsbawm clearly placed Robin Hood in the world of fiction or myth. His is the quintessential bandit legend. He never really existed. From the moment when the stories were first recorded, they dealt with a bandit who flourished in an era that had passed. While he dies in the stories, he never dies in memory. He cannot die, for he is invented. He represents a dream of justice. The second is that Hobsbawm's Robin Hood, the noble robber, is a bandit who belongs to the peasantry and to no other social group. His story is a universal phenomenon wherever societies are based on agriculture. He cannot exist except in the context of peasant society and his myth is incomprehensible in urbanised countries.[3] The first is largely uncontroversial. No historian, even the most ardent seeker of an original outlaw around whom the legends were later woven, would disagree. The second lay at the heart of debate for forty years. Was the outlaw ballad an expression of peasant discontent?

Hobsbawm was himself a party to this debate, which first emerged in the late 1950s. A similar interpretation was forcefully argued by Rodney Hilton in a ground-breaking article in 1958. Robin Hood was conceived as a free peasant representing peasant ideology for a peasant audience. The ballad audience was for the most part plebeian. The social milieu was one in which peasants and landowners faced each other in mutual antagonism, at a time when townsmen were regarded with suspicion by both. That social milieu is to be identified as of the thirteenth and fourteenth centuries, when agrarian discontent was endemic.[4] The same view was taken up by Maurice Keen in 1961. Focusing especially on links with the Peasants' Revolt of 1381, he stressed the common man's demand for social justice, which found its fullest political expression in that rising. In a chapter which seems to have influenced Hobsbawm, Keen argued that the protest is not against an unjust social system, but against unjust social superiors; indeed outlaw justice is exacted as pitilessly and violently as was royal justice.[5]

The strict correlation between the stories and a peasant society has not, however, stood up to scrutiny. Very soon after Hilton published his essay, Sir James Holt answered with a counterblast arguing that the stories originated in the context of aristocratic households. The tales of Robin Hood were nurtured in the halls of castle and manor, and were not designed for peasant ears. In so far as they expressed resistance to authority they reflected the resentments of the gentry and aristocracy against the crown in the thirteenth century.[6] Keen later retreated from his original position and conceded that the close association of Robin Hood with the peasantry was not ultimately sustained by the texts. They appeal, he conceded, more than he once thought to the glamour which attaches to the activities of a 'gentleman bandit', and the emphasis, he suggested, should be switched from class conflict to a more general concern for the proper administration of justice.[7]

Few would now argue that there was such a direct correlation between the stories of Robin Hood and peasant outlooks as that initially advanced in the late 1950s. It is not easy to sustain the argument from the texts and it is also to be questioned, as we have seen previously,[8] whether England was a peasant society in the later middle ages. The Robin Hood stories, as they took their first recorded form, did not belong to a peasantry and cannot in any meaningful sense be said to be an expression of *peasant* discontent. But they could still have been an expression of *popular* discontent.

The tales have been interpreted as reflecting social tensions and unease in other ways. A specifically urban context has been proposed. Richard Tardiff focuses on what he describes as the late-fourteenth-century yeoman fraternity movement in London and elsewhere in which journeymen associated together for collective bargaining and to challenge the domination of master craftsmen in their guilds. This model of association is reflected in the Robin Hood ballads, in which the fellowship of 140 merry men represents the journeymen yeomanry, a suppressed guild which has become an outlawed criminal band. Many urban issues are echoed in the stories. In fine, he suggests that they were composed for an urban audience who saw refracted in them their own social protest.[9]

Thomas Ohlgren takes it a stage further and shifts the emphasis. Yes, urban, though not (he argues) reflecting the world of these journeymen associations, but essentially the world of the great livery companies of London themselves. The stories are as relevant for the masters as they are for the servants; this relevance is detailed in respect of six different aspects of the stories as well as the evidence of the language of performance in the *Gest*. Moreover, picking up a passage in the *Gest* in which measuring and selling of cloth are parodied, he goes as far as to suggest that this famous composite work was commissioned by the Merchant Tailors or the Drapers. The stories of Robin Hood, he concludes, should be seen not in the context of conflict within urban society, but the larger transition from feudalism to capitalism, in which it is the great guilds who are both appropriating for themselves and challenging the mores of knightly society.[10]

In respect of the urbanity of the tales, the point is well made that the dual foci are the town of Nottingham and the forest of Sherwood/Barnsdale. York features, Doncaster is mentioned as is Blyth, but villages and villagers do not loom large in the medieval versions of the stories. A sheriff, monks, a knight, a king, a potter, the inhabitants of Nottingham all feature, but not one husbandman or cottager; only Much the Miller's son, who is himself an outlaw. In so far as the setting is concerned we switch from forest to town and back from town to forest; as for the stream of people passing through the forest, and the hands of the outlaws, none is a peasant, even by the limited definition of a largely self-sufficient smallholder. But the world to which these stories relate does not need to be exclusively urban. There were guilds and fraternities in villages and small market towns all over England.[11] The great London companies, upon which Tardiff and Ohlgren focus, were far from typical. Moreover the trades upon which their theses concentrate, tailoring and pottery, were rural occupations as well as urban.

Let us take medieval pottery for example. Tardiff argues that the issue at the heart of the ballad of *Robin Hood and the Potter* is payment of pavage, or tolls, which was bitterly resented by towns people, exemplified by the potter. Yet the medieval pottery industry by the later middle ages was largely rural, located in semi-industrialised villages concentrated in particular districts such as Northamptonshire and Leicestershire. Many villages had come to specialise in pottery because of the abundant supplies of clay and fuel; the names of some, such as Potters Marston in Leicestershire, changed because they became so well known. Two pottery manufacturing centres were actually in the heart of a forest: Brill and Boarstall, where pottery which was sold widely in the south Midlands was produced from the late twelfth century, were within the forest of Bernwood. Brill potters presumably travelled through the forest on their way to sell their wares in markets outside its bounds. Some potters, such as George Bayly of Nuneaton, who served as constable of the town and was taxed on goods worth £12 in 1524–5, were substantial husbandmen, if not yeomen in status.[12]

In the light of our knowledge of the commercialised character of fifteenth-century economy and society, it is unnecessary and misleading to draw a sharp distinction between town and country. We should perhaps focus more broadly on the 'commons', on all those lacking gentility. Colin Richmond has done just that. He has identified an appeal to yeomanliness in the ballads that echoes the aspirations and anxieties of a middling group of townspeople and country-dwellers, which he characterised as caught between declining feudalism and advancing capitalism in the fifteenth century. The Robin of the tales, he argues, distances himself from both the knightly and the mercantile. He is frugal but he is not accumulative. He is polite and courteous, but he is bound to no man. He is non-aspirant and asocial. His place and his popularity reflect a particular moment in time when a middling group existed in a society, which, as we have described, was no longer peasant, but on the other hand was not yet fully commercialised.[13]

These recent interpretations move a long way from identification with 'peasant discontent', towards a more diffuse critique of corrupt authority and the perversion of justice in contemporary society, or a more general expression of social unease and tension. Does this amount to a more general subversiveness? The ballads do after all celebrate an outlaw band that gets away with murder, poaching and theft and make a hero of a leader who continually humiliates the representatives of the wealthiest religious order in the realm and the king's local officer. Thus Stephen Knight, reluctant to identify a particular social context, has concluded that through the ages they have always represented resistance to authority, but, even though it is the central idea and strongest value, offering nothing more concrete than a dream of resistance.[14] Peter Coss too has suggested of the *Gest* that there is 'something subversive about it', partly through parody, partly through its mocking tone and partly through its blurring of status distinctions. On these grounds, as did Maurice Keen in his study of outlaw legends, he tentatively reconnects the genesis of the text with the disturbed conditions and social relations of the last three decades of the fourteenth century.[15] Are the texts subversive or do they affirm the social order?

We need at this point to remind ourselves that attitudes to the 'rymes' of Robin Hood were not uniform throughout the century and a half preceding the Reformation. There was sustained disapproval in certain clerical quarters throughout the late fourteenth, fifteenth and early sixteenth centuries. One early-fifteenth-century sermon, in the tradition of castigating the laity for preferring the ribaldry of certain secular writings to the word of God, remarked that 'they take more hede to these wanton proficiis, as Thomas of Asildowne and Robyn Hoode'. Prophecy was frequently used as a covert form of political discourse, either to promote or to undermine a regime, as Henry IV well knew. The prophecy of Thomas of Erceldoune, widely disseminated in the fifteenth century, did just that. By associating Robin Hood with that tradition, by describing it as a prophecy, the preacher revealed that he at least considered the tales not just lewd and worthless entertainment, but also subversive.[16]

But equally outlaw stories, and outlaw games, were enjoyed by the gentry, aristocracy and even the crown from the mid-fourteenth century, when a pageant was laid on for King John of France, to the early sixteenth century, when Henry VIII was delighted to play the king to his servant's Robin. The very act of printing the *Gest* at the end of the fifteenth century (and reprinting at least four times by 1560),[17] and the presumed existence of a market and continuing demand for it in literate circles, suggest that the stories were, certainly at the end of the fifteenth century, enjoyed as much in educated as in lewd lay circles. The deliberate appeal to a gentle audience by the compiler suggests that he was aware that there was an audience among the respectable classes. It is quite possible that the sole surviving text of *Robin Hood and the Potter* is in a collection once owned by Richard Calle, Margaret Paston's bailiff, who was ostracised by the family after he married Margery, his employer's daughter, in 1469. Calle was a lesser landholder and also a grocer who traded in Framlingham. While the Pastons were scathing about his social origins and refused to countenance the marriage between an upstart servant and one of their own blood, he was himself a man of substance in his own right and unimpeachable respectability. Margery had married below her station, but she had descended only to the middling sort. This might not have been a story with quite the same elevating social message as contained within the *Gest*, but its dedication to all good yeomanry might be just as germane for a man of Calle's rank.[18]

Sir John Paston may have been scandalised by Calle's marriage, but he nevertheless shared his taste in Robin Hood stories. In 1473 he complained that the servant he had retained in 1469 to play *Robin Hood and the Sheriff*, as well as St George, had abandoned his service. Paston wrote to his brother in jocular vein that

> W. Wode which promised yow and Dawbeney, God have hys sowle, at Castre, that yff ye wolde take hym in to be ageyn with me, that then he wold never goo from me, and ther upon I have kepyd him thys iij yer to plaeye Seynt Jorge and Robyn Hod and the Shryff of Notyngham, and now when I would have good horse he is goon into Bernysdale, and I without a keeper.[19]

It has been plausibly argued by John Marshall that the play Wode performed was the surviving text fragment of *Robin Hood and the Sheriff*, which may well have originally been among the Paston Papers. This play is a reworking of *Guy of Gisborne*, though here the villain is a knight, not a forester as he is in the ballad text.[20] It may be that Paston knew the *Gest* well enough to identify himself with Sir Richard at the Lee. Did Sir John find consolation in hearing how the sheriff fails in his siege of his castle and the king eventually restores the knight to all his property? We may speculate, but Paston knew the Robin Hood stories and possibly owned a copy of a play text.

The Robin Hood stories in the later middle ages were controversial and their content divided opinion. Fraternities too had once been controversial. In the late fourteenth century these associations were treated with some suspicion by those in authority. Although the large civic guilds, such as those at Cambridge or Lynn, had been well integrated into civic government, many smaller and newer guilds which had emerged since the mid-fourteenth century were feared as possible centres of dissent, driven by 'wicked intention of confederacy', a concern which perhaps gave rise to the great survey of 1389.[21] The context of the late fourteenth century is important, for these are the decades not only of popular unrest and religious dissent, but also of wide-ranging legislation to control employment, dress, sports and hunting – legislation that was constantly renewed and elaborated thereafter.[22]

The process of change by which such suspect fraternities themselves became acceptable is nicely illustrated by the case of the yeoman, or bachelor, fraternities attached to the great London livery companies. These associations of wage-earners emerged in the early fourteenth century, but grew in number and militancy after 1350 as combinations seeking to increase wages and improve conditions of work for journeymen. They possibly formed themselves into religious organisations, as guilds attached to a parish church, for legal protection, for they were perceived as a threat by the masters, who sought to ban them. However, during the fifteenth century they changed in character. Eventually accepted and recognised by the companies, they became associations for young men on their way up and for the lesser independent craftsmen who never quite made it. They were integrated into the companies and by the early sixteenth century had taken on the role of small business associations, the 'Lions', as it were, to the 'Rotary' of the great twelve.[23]

The move towards greater respectability of the guilds is also reflected in the growth of gentle membership. Prestigious associations such as the Corpus Christi Guild at York, or the Guild of St George at Norwich, as we have seen, found the local gentry knocking on their doors, and were only too pleased to open them.[24] Within the guilds themselves care was taken in the later fifteenth century to maintain their enhanced status. The Guild of St Mary, Lichfield adopted new statutes in 1487 following the advice ('high consideration') of Sir Humphrey Stanley. Concern was specifically shown to keep unity and good fellowship among the members and to regulate behaviour. They were not to associate with 'persons that suspiciously walketh by night' (presumably female), or those keeping 'alehouses in ryott and mysdoing in trobeling there neighbours'. They were also to be well ruled themselves and maintain perfect love and harmony. The worshipful brethren of the guild had standards to maintain so that they were clearly differentiated from the riff-raff.[25] The same outlook is to be found in the code of social control imposed in manorial courts by local elites to regulate personal behaviour, especially sexual, disorderly ale-houses, loose living and gaming. By the last third of the fifteenth century the middling sorts had enthusiastically embraced for themselves the values underlying the social legislation of the late fourteenth century.[26] The transformation of fraternities over a century or more from seemingly potential threats to pillars of established authority is perhaps echoed in the conflicting perceptions of the Robin Hood stories in contemporary minds. Thus, while the fictional forest fellowship continued to represent to some a challenge to authority, to others, perhaps, it reflected the most ubiquitous local agency of order, conformity, probity and respectability – the fraternity itself.

Affirmation of hierarchy and the social order is revealed in the subplot of *Robin Hood and the Monk*, which concerns the rebellion of Little John against the authority of his master. Little John refuses to bear Robin's bow; that is, as has already been discussed, he refuses to play the part of servant to the chief forester. As a consequence of this rift Robin is captured by the sheriff. Eventually the repentant John rescues his master and the rift is repaired, the king having also appeared on the scene. At the end Robin offers to stand down as master. John now demurs and accepts his subservient role. As the oath of the bowbearer of Sherwood Forest required, he was henceforth to be 'trewe man' to the 'maister forster of the forest'.[27] In the story the restoration of the proper order and correct relationship between master and servant is then blessed by the king, who, addressing the sheriff, remarks:

> *He is true to his maister,*
> *He loves better Robin Hode,*
> *Then he does us ychen.*[28]

Little John has recognised that society properly ordained depends on hierarchy and the servant obeying his master.

The records of the city of Wells reveal a remarkable case of life imitating this art. Wells was governed through the Trinity Guild of which every burgess was a member. The master of the guild was the de facto mayor. For a year in 1500–1 the guild was split by a conflict between the master, Nicholas Trappe, and a prominent burgess, John Welshot. Welshot refused to take up the post of rent-collector to which Trappe had nominated him. In one meeting he shouted: 'I sette not a pynne by the mayster', banging the table with his fist. Trappe, whom the official record presented as a model of tact and patience, rode out the rebellion, eventually persuading the recalcitrant Welshot to submit, humbly to acknowledge his master's authority and to take up the office.[29] He too learnt to be true to his master. To challenge the authority of the master was a petty treason which threatened the ideal of the fraternity. Whether in the fictional forest fraternity, or the governing body of the city of Wells, brethren are required to accept their place in a properly ordered society. In the fiction the king gives endorsement; in town government he expected no less.

Performing Robin Hood in parochial May Games was another manifestation of order. There are a large number of surviving references to Robin Hood activities from the last quarter of the fifteenth century through to the 1580s in surviving churchwardens' accounts. It is difficult to interpret them. They were, it is clear, an integral part of May Games (held around Whitsun from 10 May to 13 June) in some parts of southern England, noticeably the West Country and the Thames valley, but not apparently in other parts, for example East Anglia. Even where they were common, only selected parishes performed Robin Hood. Chagford and Chudleigh in Devon did, Morebath did not. Thus the opportunity existed for the Kingston-upon-Thames performers to take their show to Croydon and other neighbouring parishes in 1515, or for Robin Hood of Henley and his company to descend on Reading in 1505, or later, between 1553 and 1570 for the Yeovil performers to tour neighbouring villages, thereby swelling their parochial incomes.[30] Only rarely does information survive from the side of the audience. Evidence given at a visitation of the Hospital of St Mary in the Newarke at Leicester in 1525, however, reveals that it was customary every year for the parishioners of St Margaret's to bring their May Games, stage plays and spectacles, including twelve pageants of the months, and playings of Robin Hood and of St George for the entertainment of the canons and the hundred poor folk in the almshouse. They presented their shows ('ostensions'), Bishop Longland was assured, for the profit and wealth of the church.[31]

The form of the 'ostension' varied. Some were gatherings, or reckonings, which it seems were like twentieth-century undergraduate rag-stunts in which locals impersonating Robin

Hood and his merry men held people to ransom for charitable purposes. These were similar to the Hock-Tide game, earlier in the season, when young men would capture young girls and ransom them, in a 'merrie way'. Some were archery contests. Special arrows, some of silver, were treasured as trophies for the winner of the annual contest at Chagford and Exeter St John. Some were plays: Thatcham in Berkshire, which had a 'King play', invested one year in elms for bushing Robin Hood's bower. This strongly suggests a performance of 'Robin Hood and the King', similar to that put on for Henry VIII at the same time. Whatever the activity, special costumes were maintained at the parish expense for Robin Hood and his men. In some parishes a group of Robin Hood's Men was permanently maintained; in others there were Young Men's Guilds, which might have performed Robin Hood as they did at Chagford, but did not at Morebath. In some parishes a Robin Hood game was played every year, in others not. All of this playmaking was for charity, especially church funds, sponsored and performed by members of parochial fraternities. The money so raised belonged to the community and was carefully audited.[32] Around 1500 the Guild of St Cuthbert, Wells commissioned Nicholas Trappe to inquire into who had pocketed the goods and monies collected recently for the commonalty from the '"Robinhode", the dancing girls, the common church ale and the like'.[33]

Analysis of the churchwardens' accounts of Croscombe in Somerset, just a few miles from Wells, has revealed more fully how one such custom worked for the common good. Here Robin Hood revels were customary, but not held regularly. Between 1475 and 1478 there were two intense periods of activity, one from 1481 to1485, another from 1505 to 1511 in which large sums were raised by the revels, in the first period for the building of a new church house and the second for the construction of a chapel of St George, at the east end of the northern aisle of the church.

Robin Hood came in to 'rob from the rich' to pay for improvements to the property for which the parishioners were responsible. Moreover the principal participants in the revels in these years were drawn from the ranks of the leading parochial families. All the men who played Robin, with the possible exception of one, were, had been, or would become churchwardens. Several were craftsmen employed in the textile industry, one or two clothiers; one Robin Hood (in 1481), Roger Morris, a fuller, left generous bequests to the church in 1519, including 20 shillings to the chantry of Croscombe, perhaps in the chapel of St George which later performances of Robin had helped build. Croscombe was at the centre of a prosperous textile district in the early sixteenth century and typified the new proto-capitalist economy of pre-Reformation England. At Croscombe Robin Hood was, as it were, adopted as a local worthy.[34]

It would seem, therefore, that in parochial entertainment Robin Hood, far from being the subversive figure imagined by strait-laced clerics and protestant reformers, was representative of deference, communal solidarity and fraternal virtues. The performers, churchwardens and other worthy parishioners, by appropriating some of Robin Hood's heroic and noble characteristics, enhanced their social standing. Richard Robinson in 1583 recalled of his Oxfordshire/Berkshire youth in the reign of Queen Mary:

> *A May game was of Robyn Hood and of his train that time*
> *To train up young men, striplings and each younge childe*
> *In shooting, yearly this with solepmne feast was by Guilde*
> *Or brotherhood of Townsmen done, with sport, with joy, with love.*[35]

No doubt nostalgic, Robinson's memory encapsulates the way in which the stories of Robin were assimilated into the rituals of respectable society in the century before the Reformation in order to inculcate a sense of responsibility and to reinforce authority. What once in the troubled later fourteenth century may have been subversive had become, by the mid-sixteenth century in parish society, affirmative of the social order.

Yet these May Games were also periods of carnival and licensed misrule, in which the world was turned upside down. Carnival, in the modern sense, is a time when authority is both reaffirmed and subverted. It is on one level a safety valve, an occasion in which tensions can be released and channelled into harmless sport, with joy, with love. It is on another level an occasion on which authority is challenged and threatened. Through it an alternative perception of order can be maintained and the established hierarchy denied. This is the interpretation of the revels at Croscombe advanced by Katherine French. She detects irony in the churchwarden taking the role of the outlaw, as the performer was turned from an upstanding member of the community into a bandit. Authority is parodied.[36] In the ritual, one might add, parishioners are reminded, and can remind their leaders, that local government without justice is but licensed robbery.

The symbolism of the ballads, in which normal boundaries are trangressed and hierarchy is inverted, is the symbolism of carnival. A particular aspect of this is the manner in which Robin is a trickster, like 'Robin Goodfellow', especially in his dealings with the sheriff, of whom he continually makes a fool. The same is true of the story of 'Little John and the Sheriff' included in the *Gest*, in which John, disguised as Reynolde Grenelefe, impersonates the disloyal servant. He pretends to abandon his current master, the knight, for better conditions, but confides to the audience:

I shall be the worst servaunt to him
That ever yet had he.[37]

He proceeds to demand to be served dinner by the steward, assaults the butler for being discourteous, helps himself at his lord's board, and finally attacks the cook. After a long fight, the cook is persuaded to abandon his master and join Robin Hood in the forest. The two then decamp to the greenwood taking the household silver and £300.[38] Later, after he has returned to the forest, Little John comes across the sheriff out hunting and leads him into a trap. In answer to the sheriff's complaint that he has betrayed him, he declares:

> *'I make myn avowe to God,' sayde Litell John,*
> *'Mayster, ye be to blame,*
> *I was mysserved of my dynere*
> *When I was with you at home'.*[39]

The whole story is a parody of household etiquette, which can be found elaborately set out, no doubt with the nouveau riche particularly in mind, in contemporary books of courtesy and guides to the proper serving of meals. These set out the carefully delineated roles of the yeomen ushers of the hall and the chamber, the yeomen of the chamber and the hall, and the yeoman cook. It is hard not to believe that contemporary audiences would not have understood this lampoon. In fact it can be read as parody of the *Book of Nurture*, in which a masterless young man is instructed in all the arts of service and finer points of etiquette so that he can enter and prosper in household service.[40] Little John, masquerading as a masterless man, turns the sheriff's household upside down. Where the conventional book of courtesy celebrates service, this rejects it.

The audience can appreciate the distinction between good and bad master, and good and bad servant, and can also enjoy the jest at the expense of service, and subservience at large. Its retelling is all the more ambiguous since it is specifically addressed to a gentle

172

audience. 'Lythe and listen gentilmen/All nowe be here' calls the storyteller as he is about to begin, 'Of Litell John, that was the knightes man,/ Good myrth ye shall here'.[41] A gentle audience might enjoy a joke at its own expense; at the same time a non-gentle listener or reader cannot be prevented from enjoying the implied rejection of all social order. In a society ordered on the principle of hierarchy, domestic rebellion was petty treason. It is the very antithesis of the subplot of *Robin Hood and the Monk* in which true service is affirmed.

Knockabout comedy undermines authority. It is for this reason that disapproval of Robin Hood and his ribaldry continued in certain clerical and official circles throughout the fifteenth and sixteenth centuries.[42] In lowland Scotland, where the stories of Robin Hood were equally popular, the same ideas surfaced. Walter Bower, who as we have seen, unusually stressed Robin's devotion to mother church at some length, did so to correct the customary disapproval of 'the famous murderer', of 'whom the foolish populace are so inordinately fond' and 'about whom they are delighted to hear the jesters and minstrels sing above all other ballads'. But come the Reformation there, too, Robin was suppressed. In the northern kingdom the threat to order seems to have been taken more seriously than in England. There, in Aberdeen, Ayr, Edinburgh, Dumfries and many other towns, Robin Hood was often the focus of a civic parade, in which the outlaw and his men led the jocular celebration frequently alongside an abbot of unreason. The Scottish parliament ultimately decreed in 1555 that Robin Hood should be banned and anyone electing him arrested and imprisoned. The ban proved difficult to enforce. In 1561 a riot took place in Edinburgh in which a tailor was 'elected' Robin Hood, naming him 'Lord of Inobedience', and after the old wicked manner, the mob seized the city gates and released all the prisoners. In the 1580s several reformed town authorities still had difficulty in suppressing the profane plays.[43] The description of an event in 1561 which unfolded in the old way suggests that in Scotland Robin had been associated with carnival as a feast of misrule in a much more explicit manner than in England. Were guilds of *homo ludens*, as in Rabelaisian France, more common in Scotland than in England?

But it is clear that in England too matters could run out of control. The city council at Exeter was sufficiently concerned in 1509–10 to ban any 'riot kept in any parish by the yong man of the same parish called Robyun hode, but oonle the Churche holyday'.[44] The association in some parishes between Robin Hood performances and young men's groups, and the masquerade of Little John as an unruly servant in the *Gest*, draws one's attention particularly to the boisterous pranks and rebelliousness of youth. Should the disturbances leading up to Willenhall Fair on Trinity Sunday 1498 be interpreted in this light? Gangs from Wolverhampton (under the leadership of the 'Abbot of Marram') and Wednesbury (led by Robin Hood) were accused by the mayor of Walsall of threatening the men of Walsall. But Robin Hood's defence (alias Roger Marshall of Wednesbury) was that it was customary for the men of the three towns to come to Willenhall Fair in disguisings and there to gather money with their disports to the profits of the said churches; and that moreover on the day they met with the men of Walsall with as good cheer as they should do to their loving neighbours. What seems to have happened is that earlier in the week a brawl had occurred in Walsall between a man of Wednesbury and a man of Walsall in which the Walsall man was beaten up and as a result of which the Wednesbury man had been arrested. Whereupon Marshall had raised a gang to release their man, only to be stopped by the justices of the peace, who had also placed an order on them not to attend as customary the Willenhall Fair. All this appears to have happened during the week of May Games. No doubt drink played its part. Unless Marshall's testimony that it was all good sport is to be believed, under its guise old scores were being settled. Certainly the event was perceived by the local authorities as a serious disturbance of the peace.[45]

Whether or not Marshall and his fellows were young men, such as, according to their elders in Exeter, 'kept riot', rebellious adolescents were a perceived problem in the fifteenth century. Hoccleve commented that 'for the moste paart youthe is rebel'. There was a body of didactic literature which sought to inculcate respect for authority, obedience and loyalty, both by positive and negative exempla. Ungoverned youths too often succumbed, it was believed, to the temptations of loose women and drink, and were exhorted to avoid taverns where 'wilde felaws to-gider draw'. In their contracts some apprentices were required to undertake not to fornicate, drink or gamble. The Mercers sought to prevent the 'misorder' of those apprentices who spent money on harlots, unsuitable games and fancy clothes. May Day celebrations in London in 1517, like those earlier in Exeter (and perhaps Willenhall), were marred by a general riot of apprentices, when high spirits ran out of control.[46]

A more clear-cut example of May Day revelry leading to lawlessness is an incident in 1503 reported in the *Great Chronicle of London*:

> This yere also was quyk & common talking of a man which excercysid many pagents after the comon ffame of the people, of Robin hood, But among he Robbyd and did sundry ffelonys to the grete hurt of sundry of the kynges subgectis, The which soo contynuyng lastly abowth midsomyr he was takyn and his company scalid, This was namyd Greneleff, but what becam of hym the certynte was not opynly knowyn, albe It that sundry tales were told of hym which as uncertain I over passe.[47]

Here it seems was a performer and his company, from the Thames valley, who transgressed from play to actual robbery during the season of May Games. His pseudonym of 'Greneleff' is exactly that which Little John adopts in the *Gest* when he enters the sheriff's service. The passing notoriety of this felon it seems caught the imagination because he became a 'real-life' Robin Hood.

This fellow may well have been a haunter of ale-houses, such as worthy members of the Guild of St Mary, Lichfield and London apprentices were enjoined to avoid. Here we come to an overtly subversive gloss on what it might mean to be a member of Robin Hood's fellowship, as likely to be disapproved by Sir John Paston, Richard Calle, the grocer of Framlingham, and Roger Morris, the fuller of Croscombe, as by Robert Fabyan or Hugh Latimer. Ale-houses were believed to be the haunts of vagabonds, cut-throats and whores. When one passes through their doors one enters a world largely hidden from history. We know what local worthies, the respectable and opinion formers thought of them, but we do not know much about who their habitués were, or what they thought of their betters, although we might guess. Is it not possible that stories of Robin Hood were known and told with a somewhat different slant behind their doors? As the mid-fifteenth-century Gloucester sermon declared, 'he that is a ryatour and a great haunter of tavernys or of ale howsys and a grete waster of hys goodes, then is he callyd a good felaw'.[48]

Rodney Hilton argued in 1973 that the phrase *magna societas* which crops up in Walsingham, Knighton and the indictments following the Peasants' Revolt of 1381 meant a large company or big gang of rebels. It could also be translated as large fellowship, a word, as we have seen, frequently used later to describe just such a rebellious gathering.[49] In October 1450, a few months after the suppression of Cade's Revolt, an eavesdropper in a Sussex ale-house reported to the authorities that a rebellious husbandman, John Merfeld of Brightling, had proclaimed so that all could hear one Sunday morning that he and his fellowship would rise again, and when they were up 'they wolde leve no gentilmen alyve, but such as theym list to have'.[50] At Beauchamp Roding in Essex, forty-three years later, a stand-up row in church between the vicar and one of his parishioners occurred. Insults flew: 'A woyd out of my churche and walke among your fellows'; 'What felaws have I & what know yow wha felaws I have?' 'A meny of fals harlotts and theffs'.[51] Could it therefore also be that the band of yeomen and labourers (also spilling out of an ale-house?) who waylaid travellers in Norfolk in 1441 chanting 'We are Robin Hood's men, war, war, war' (as one can imagine did Roger Marshall and his Wednesbury lads when they weighed into the Walsall boys with such good cheer in 1498) came from the same disreputable world?[52]

It is possible, then, that among the disaffected, including rebellious youth, disgruntled yeomen and husbandmen, the dispossessed and the marginalised, of whom there were not a few in late-medieval England, Robin Hood represented something altogether more subversive than he did to the worthies of town and parish. This world is difficult to penetrate, not least because the language of subversion itself, as the letters of Jack Miller, Jack Carter and Jack Trueman recorded by monks during the Peasants' Revolt reveal, were often deliberately cryptic.[53] Whereas to the respectable middling sorts the outlaw could be seen as standing for the maintenance of justice and the idealised social order in which their own local place was preserved, to others he might have represented the desire for an alternative social order and a society without orders, one that to them was personified by the outlaws in the freedom of the greenwood.

Even so there never was a clear-cut distinction between obedience and dissent in fifteenth-century England according to social status. For popular unrest was not restricted to the disenfranchised, dispossessed or marginalised. That there was discontent from time to time in the ranks of the worthy and respectable men of town and country is not in any doubt. From the Rising of 1381, through Cade's Revolt of 1450, the Western Rising of 1497, to the Pilgrimage of Grace in 1536 and the Rebellions of 1549, encompassing many lesser rebellions, demonstrations and localised actions, they objected to unjust taxation, they protested about the abuse of power, aired social and economic grievances and gave vent to religious dissent. One shared characteristic of these many manifestations of popular challenges to authority is that a prominent part was played in them by the local elites, the more substantial villagers and manorial, parish and guild office holders. They were the very people who had gained most from economic and social amelioration, the leaders of their communities in normal times, many of whom enjoyed the parliamentary franchise and several of whom served as churchwardens, bailiffs, constables, local jurors and tax collectors, and some of whom, as representatives of small boroughs, even sat in the house of commons. Even though they had the most to lose, as the record of prosecutions, enquiries and pardons reveal, they also led their communities in protest against government action when they were driven to it. Just as in happier times they were the persons on whom crown, lords and church relied to transmit their views, rally support, enforce common and customary law locally, and collect taxes, so in less happy times they were the ones who articulated grievances and led protest in defence of the proper order of society when they believed it to be threatened by bad government.[54] It is a mistake to assume that there was no popular, in the sense of non-elite, participation in late-medieval politics. On the contrary ordinary men, and to some extent women, were continuously engaged as, in the words of Ethan Shagan, 'the audience for, or interlocutors with political action'. To which one might add that they were actors as well.[55]

The commons, moreover, shared a political ideology with the

ruling elites: the concept of the common weal, the common good, or *res publica*. An old notion, that the kingdom should be governed for the benefit of all, this became more widely deployed, and in English, during the fifteenth century. It was specifically articulated in protest against misgovernment in the mid-fifteenth century and rapidly became a central and contested element of political discourse.[56] Both the crown and opponents of the crown justified their actions in terms of the common good. Oppositions, whether aristocratic or popular, claimed that they represented the true public interest and that violent action for the greater good could be taken in the name of the common weal. It has even been argued that this amounted to a programme, and that a movement of reform, led by great aristocrats, especially the earl of Warwick, developed in the 1450s and saw its last flourish in the brief reign of Richard III.[57] The crown, from 1459, responded that the public interest could not be served through rebellion but could be guaranteed only through absolute obedience. Being above the fray, it was the only institution capable of ensuring the common good. It has further been suggested that an influential group of royal councillors, including Sir John Fortescue and Bishop John Russell, promoted under successive kings from 1471 the development of a conciliar form of government through which the responsibility of the crown to promote the common weal was exercised. This came to underpin early Tudor government. It was an approach, John Watts has proposed, which implicitly recognised what he described as the democratic implications of England's parliamentary system and the interaction between government and people.[58]

Thus the common weal was invoked in rebellion. The commons rose in its name, claiming to be the true subjects of the crown, acting in the king's best interest against his evil councillors who were perverting justice or overburdening the people. As the Kentish protesters expressed it in 1450:

> They . . . calle us risers and treytors and the kynges
> enemys, but we schaalle be ffounde his trew lege mene
> and his best freendus with the helpe of Jesu, to whome we
> crye dayly and nyztly, with mony thousan more, that
> God of his riztwysnesse schall take venganuse on the false
> treytours of his ryalle realme that have brouzt us in this
> myschieff and myserie.[59]

They called upon a powerful rhetoric of protest. When the earl of
Warwick sought to raise the same commons in 1459 against the
government of Henry VI, the first article of his proclamation
declared that 'the commone wele and good politik lawes
hereaforne notably and virtuously used' had been 'piteously
ovurturned'; the fourth blamed the king's covetousness and
selfishness of those about the king. The same refrain was repeated
in 1460, and ten years later when Warwick next rose against
Edward IV.[60] The local elders and notables, the leaders of village
society, to whom Warwick appealed in these years, had a deep
concern for the proper order of society and the impartial
administration of justice.

It is no surprise, therefore, to discover that men who had served
as churchwardens at Croscombe, and had played Robin Hood in
Maytime, came out with the western rebels in June 1497. John
Halse and Roger Morris, the churchwarden in 1481–2, jointly led
the Robin Hood revels that year and raised just over £2. Halse,
who died in 1500–1 leaving bequests to Our Lady, the Rood and
the bells, was fined £4 for his participation. Morris, his fellow, an
altogether more successful man, began his career as a fuller, but so
prospered that he became a clothier and was buried in 1519 in the
chancel of the church. He was fined £20. John Carter,
churchwarden in 1486–7 and again in 1513–14, was another local
clothier who was fined £23 and his son John, warden of the Young
Men, £4. Another son (and brother) William, himself dying in

office as churchwarden in 1513–14 when his father stepped in, was Robin Hood in 1505–6 when he delivered £2 13s 4d (4 marks exactly) 'of the sport of Robarte Hode and hys company'. Finally John Stevyn, alias Sadler, warden three times in 1537–8, 1542–3 and 1544–5, who played Robin Hood in 1511–12, was also fined, when still a young man, for his participation in 1497. There may well have been other Robin Hoods implicated, for the accounts do not always identify who the player was.[61]

In Wells, too, many members of the Trinity Guild were later fined for their participation. Lord Audley had briefly come to the city in early June and had raised men before marching on to Blackheath. At the end of September, when Henry VII descended in strength, led by their new master, Nicholas Trappe, the whole body of the guild humbly submitted to him. It was of little avail. Three years later all those implicated in June were heavily fined, the city itself being second only to Taunton in the scale of the punishment meted out. Prominent among those fined was Nicholas Trappe, whose penalty of £10 was levied at the beginning of his subsequent term of office as master, the term of office during which he himself faced rebellion in the ranks of the guild. His king was not as forgiving as Robin Hood's.[62]

Trappe, Halse, Morris, Carter and Stevyn rose in rebellion specifically in protest against supplying men, material and money to support a war against the Scots, in circumstances in which they were still smarting from the consequences of Henry VII's recent trade embargo with Flanders. They believed that it was justifiable to take direct action in defence of what they perceived to be not just their own interests, but the well-being of the West Country, dependent as it was on cloth manufacturing and exports. They may well have believed, as Perkin Warbeck's backers that year expressed it (and opponents of the crown for generations had articulated), that Henry VII was being misled by 'caitiffs and villains of simple birth'.[63] One does not find the same particular issues articulated in the Robin Hood stories, but the outlaw hero articulated a similar philosophy, and a similar conviction that rebellion in defence of the public good was justified. He was, to this extent, the personification of a loyal rebel, who by being outside the law defends the law and by being disorderly restores order. Underpinning the stories, and connecting them with all ranks of lay society, is the late-medieval tradition of loyal protest designed to help the king put right wrongs which have been supposedly executed in his name without his knowledge. They gave expression to a tradition of protest against a corrupt government in defence of the social order and a society of orders. In the world of the storytelling Robin Hood is rewarded and is taken into the king's service for speaking truthfully to his monarch. In the harsh world of popular protest and uprising, unfortunately, rulers were not so magnanimous: village Robin Hoods were either hanged by the neck or, as in 1497, hanged by the purse.[64]

The early stories of Robin Hood thus both subverted and affirmed the social order depending on who one was and from what perspective one viewed them, and according to the time and circumstances in which one engaged in them; or, to put it into late-twentieth-century jargon, there were contested meanings which were being continuously negotiated. There is no reason why they could not even have been enjoyed at one and the same time by one member of an audience, or participant, as subversive and by another as affirmative. It might further be suggested that they carried different meanings for different social groups. For those about the king and at court in the early reign of Henry VIII, one might reasonably assume they carried no subversive meaning. Some gentry, such as the Pastons in their struggles in the 1460s and 1470s, beside entertainment might have found solace in Robin Hood's support for a knight wronged by those greater than themselves. For the respectable middling sorts, town and village worthies, the stories were perhaps double edged. In local matters, in good times, in parochial revels, they tended to affirm the proper order; in times of discontent the message they contained could be deployed to articulate and justify action against authority in the name of restoring the proper order. Finally, in the hidden and largely silent world of the displaced and dispossessed, they might for all we know have carried an altogether less ambiguously subversive meaning. Politically, too, by the early sixteenth century Robin Hood was all things to all men.

8

History and Memory

———•◆•———

Audiences listening to or reading the *Gest* when it was first compiled were emphatically reminded that Robin Hood had been a living person, with the implication that the adventures to be recounted had actually happened.

> *Robyn was a prude outlaw,*
> *Whyles he walked on grounde*
> *So curteyse an outlawe as he was one*
> *Was never none founde.*[1]

The *Gest* is constructed as a tale of his deeds, just as the *Gesta Henrici Quinti* was the tale of Henry V's deeds. It is, however, unlike *Henrici Quinti* (we suppose) a fiction, and one would be surprised if listeners or readers thought it other than a fiction. One would similarly be amazed if late-fifteenth-century readers of Malory's *Morte D'Arthur* took literally as historical facts the stories he told of the exploits of the knights of the round table. Robin Hood comes no closer to ever having actually walked on ground than a Romano-British leader who defeated the Saxons and briefly rallied the British peoples in the fifth century AD, and possibly as close as Brutus of Troy, the great-grandson of Aeneas, who came to Britain in 1170 BC to be its first king. But just as the compiler of *The Brut* and Geoffrey of Monmouth fixed these stories as historical fictions of a supposed past, so also the anonymous authors of the Robin Hood stories created a fiction about an English past which not only entertained their audiences, but also recounted for them a history. That history was not what the twenty-first century understands to be history, but the stories derived some of their relevance from the notion that they were indeed about a past that had once existed 'while he walked on ground'. Scholars try to track down an 'ur' Robin Hood, just as they do a King Arthur, and there is an undeniable fascination in the quest, but the more pertinent question concerns what collective memory of which past the setting and incidental detail of the stories woven around the hero reveal.

Some historians have treated the rymes of Robin Hood, and especially the *Gest*, as quasi-historical sources, seeking to demonstrate that they are grounded in events that actually happened and are thus accounts of them. John Bellamy ingeniously sought to identify the models for Robin Hood, Little John, Will Scarlock, the Sheriff of Nottingham and Sir Richard at the Lee in the 1320s and argued that the *Gest*, commissioned by a later Lee, was a genuine account of the exploits of an outlaw band led by a man named Robin Hood.[2] In an article published seven years earlier J. R. Maddicott more cautiously proposed that the *Gest* was composed in the mid-fourteenth century, drawing upon events and people active between 1334 and 1338. He suggested that the Sheriff of Nottingham was modelled on the notorious John de Oxenford, who held that office from 1334 to 1339, the abbot of St Mary's based on Thomas de Multon, abbot 1332–59, and the 'high justice' on Sir Geoffrey le Scrope, chief justice of the King's Bench, 1324–38. Much of the action took place in and around York because in that decade the king's government was frequently based there.[3]

While not going as far as Maddicott in specifically identifying persons with the events in the 1330s, Ohlgren and Ayton have suggested a specific military context in the same decade in which the figure of the sorry knight/Sir Richard at the Lee and the outlaw band can be set. The knight goes off to fight the wars 'in Englonde ryght' in Brabant, or Flanders, or Brittany after 1337, and returns enriched to repay his loan to the abbot. 'England's right' was, as Ohlgren points out, Edward III's rallying cry at the beginning of the Hundred Years War. This argument depends, however, on an ambiguous line in the text.[4] Ayton similarly has looked to the late 1330s, inspired by the remarkable manner in which a member of the royal garrison on the Isle of Wight in 1338 gave his name to the musterer as Robin Hood, as a starting point for his suggestion that Robin Hood's 'meyny' is modelled on one of the many gangs of discharged soldiers who for a while plagued England in that decade.[5] One can add to this the copious evidence of social conflict in the royal forests in the early fourteenth century, the tensions between lesser landowners and religious corporations which still echoed after the passing of the Statute of Mortmain, and the conflicts between some urban communities and their neighbouring Benedictine monasteries in 1327.[6] If not the story of an actual outlaw band, a powerful argument can be made that the *Gest* drew upon knowledge of circumstances, people and events that happened in the early fourteenth century.

It is, however, difficult to sustain the argument, as both Bellamy and Maddicott did, that the *Gest* itself, as a complete work in the form we now have, was compiled almost immediately after the events it thus describes. The *Gest* was not itself a primary text. Its pre-eminence depends on a combination of having been printed and of being the first known attempt to create one Robin Hood story. The text itself is clearly a later compilation of different stories, coming from different traditions and in different tones into one loose narrative. It also has more than the one plot; it incorporates subplots of a completely different tone. One might argue that the central narrative of 'Robin Hood and the Knight', their dealing with the abbot of St Mary's, their brush with the sheriff and reconciliation with the king, did in fact draw upon such a specific milieu, but an immediate or even later composition of the *Gest* in the precise form in which it later came to be written down is, to say the least, unlikely. It is even more difficult to identify the other surviving stories, including the story of 'Little John and the Sheriff' interpolated in the *Gest*, as historical evidence of events of the first part of the reign of Edward III.

Historians are agreed, however, and this consensus needs no further elaboration, that the setting of the stories is, at its widest, the era encompassing the reigns of the first three Edwards up to c.1340. Whether or not the legend of Robin Hood, as opposed to articulated stories about him, already existed is impossible to tell. 'It may well have been in the 1320s and 1330s', Barrie Dobson wrote in 2000, 'that the legend began to expand, to explode indeed, and to be adapted to narrative form and to take on many of what we regard as its critical defining features'.[7] But then again it may not have been. One might agree that one can go further than the earlier more cautious proposition that the tales 'may be at their most historically revealing in exposing, if through a glass darkly, social attitudes to authority and disorder during the reigns of Edward II and Edward III rather than earlier or later'.[8] But as Maddicott, Ohlgren and Ayton have suggested, more than attitudes to authority and disorder is revealed.

That there was an outlaw persona, possibly based on a person or persons who had once existed, called Robehod or variations of that name, known fairly widely by the 1260s, is not in doubt. But we do not know when or by whom stories about this persona were first created, let alone when and by whom some of them were brought together as a narrative recognisably set in the early fourteenth century. Do we possess early-fourteenth-century storytelling about Robin Hood, which has been reworked over the generations, or do we have later storytelling about Robin Hood consciously set in an earlier period?[9] Since no texts earlier than those of the fifteenth century survive, we cannot know. However, since attitudes to the past are as much to do with the present as with the past itself, arguably the more important question is what that past meant to audiences and listeners when the first surviving written versions of the stories were in circulation. History is a process by which the present makes sense of the past and gives it contemporary meaning. And since the present itself is endlessly (one hopes) and remorselessly (one knows only too well) moving into the past, so the interpretation of the past is itself ever changing. What is true of the twenty-first-century present was surely broadly true of the fifteenth-century present as contemporaries then reflected on an earlier age. The stories may first have come into shape in the early fourteenth century (or even earlier), but they need not then have contained the same detail, or carried the same interpretation, as they did when first written down.

This principle can be illustrated vividly by reference to the changes over the centuries since 1500.[10] Four features stand out in the story as it exists at the beginning of the twenty-first century: Robin Hood robs to give to the poor; Robin, himself a dispossessed Anglo-Saxon earl, is a freedom fighter resisting the Norman occupation; the sheriff is an agent of the evil Prince John and is restored by Richard I returning from the crusades; Robin has a romantic attachment to Maid Marian. None of these featured in the stories in circulation before 1550; all entered into the stories from the later sixteenth century, reflecting the growth of modern class consciousness, the development of the myth of the Norman Yoke, the emergence of the Whig interpretation of Magna Carta, and the displacement of Catholicism by Protestantism as the established religion. It is of no moment that most recent historians are sceptical about the Norman Yoke and question the traditional interpretation of the reign of King John, or even class consciousness, for interpretation of the past has always been contested. What matters is that these elements were, and in some quarters still are, believed to be 'historical' and integral to our 'national story'. They thus carried, and still carry, a set of political values germane to the English-speaking peoples. The mythology of the Norman Yoke had a long and influential pedigree influencing radical thought in the seventeenth and nineteenth centuries. It is thus of particular note that to accommodate these ideological transformations the pre-Reformation tales were altered. The identity of the king changed from an Edward to Richard I and the setting moved back more than a century, while Robin's divine love for Our Lady, the Blessed Virgin Mary, is replaced by his romantic love for Maid Marian, herself an aristocrat of Anglo-Saxon descent.

It follows that if such important details changed in the age of print culture, it is not less likely that other details might have changed before the stories were set down in the earliest form we now possess. By the very nature of things we cannot know how. But we can be reasonably certain that the earliest surviving texts, set down in the fifteenth century and little changed before the Reformation, had resonance for that particular present. In so far as they contain history we can thus focus on the history as it was understood and had relevance for that time, and no earlier time. What follows seeks to identify what was historical in the stories in the late fifteenth and early sixteenth centuries and to assess the significance of that history to that present. The endeavour will involve identifying absences as well as presences, and evaluating the significance of those absences, potentially as revealing as the presences themselves. The focus will be on the *Gest*. But first one needs to consider the mechanism of how knowledge of the past might have been transmitted into the written text.

It is now acknowledged that oral tradition and written texts have always interacted. It is not the case, as is sometimes supposed, that literary cultures supplanted oral cultures. Thus in grappling with the question of how history was transmitted through to the written texts of Robin Hood it is not to be assumed that a purely oral tradition of storytelling, passed on from generation to generation was, at a defined point in the fifteenth century, committed to writing. Rather the earliest surviving written texts will reflect the interchange over previous decades, if not centuries, of written and oral traditions, the one infusing and transforming the other. Adam Fox has amply demonstrated the way in which orality and literacy constantly intersected and interacted in the sixteenth and seventeenth centuries. Oral culture drew on and elaborated literary culture. Literate culture was not above inventing tradition and fabricating myths to enhance venerability or authenticity. These inventions could then be enshrined in oral tradition. Illiteracy was no barrier. Reading aloud transmitted the written to the oral; dictating to an amanuensis transferred the oral to the written.[11]

Fox concluded that written culture was probably more culpable than oral in the fabrication of distorted, exaggerated and spurious versions of the past. He observed that it was the very popularity and widespread distribution of the written versions of the stories in the sixteenth century that led to the proliferation of Robin Hood place names, and identifications of the tombs of Maid Marian and Little John, neither of which are recorded before 1540.[12] One might also trace the conversion of the king from Edward to Richard during the sixteenth century through Scottish influence. The first identification of the king as Richard I is to be found in John Mair's history of Britain in which 'the most famous' and 'humanest' robber is located in the late twelfth century.[13] It may be that sixteenth-century Scots found it more comfortable to associate the heroic outlaw with Richard I, who had acknowledged Scottish independence, than with any of the Edwards who, to say the least, had not. How this was then transmitted back to England is not so apparent, but it may be no coincidence that Henry II granted Malcolm IV of Scotland the title of earl of Huntingdon and that his younger son, David, Richard I's contemporary, inherited that title. By the end of the sixteenth century Robin Hood had been transformed in Anthony Munday's plays into the disinherited earl of Huntingdon.[14] Thus we might be able to discern a process of transmission in the sixteenth century, via Scotland, whereby Robin Hood becomes an outlawed noble in the reign of Richard I.

It is surely no less likely that what happened in the second half of the sixteenth century might also have occurred in the fourteenth and fifteenth centuries. The intersection of the written and the oral did not depend on printing for reproduction and circulation. In the century and a half before Caxton set up his press there were many English language texts in circulation; the homilies and metrical paraphrases which have already been discussed; popular political poems; Lollard texts and writings; royal proclamations; rebel manifestos; and in approximately 200 surviving copies, the popular history of England known as *The Brut* after the mythical founder of Britain, Brutus. Significantly, perhaps, these vernacular texts proliferated from the beginning of the fourteenth century. Robert Mannyng of Brunne stated in the opening lines of his *Handling Synne* in 1303 that,

For lewde men y undertok
On englyssh tunge to make this boke.[15]

Lewd originally meant lay, not clerical, and thus unlearned in Latin, and in the early fourteenth century still held this meaning. Not until the later part of the century had it begun to develop a social dimension characterising the uncultured, vulgar lower orders. But the fact is that once in English, texts such as this were accessible as well. We inadvertently get a glimpse of one way in which a text might be subversively disseminated, even in the early fourteenth century, from the last stanza of The *Outlaw's Song of Trailbaston*. The *Outlaw's Song* was undoubtedly composed for a gentle audience (its language is French) and is a complaint against the then recently instituted commissions of trailbaston. Yet it adopts the form of being a popular protest. The last stanza reads (in translation):

> *This rhyme was made in the wood, beneath a laurel tree.*
> *There sing the blackbird and nightingale, and there hovers the hawk.*
> *It was written on parchment to be better remembered,*
> *And thrown on the highway so that people should find it.* [16]

It is hardly likely that subversive verse written in Anglo-Norman French and distributed in this way would have much impact. But the author's literary device reveals how songs of popular protest in the lewd tongue could be circulated; how leafleting, as it were, was believed to be done in the early fourteenth century.

The *Outlaw's Song of Trailbaston*, albeit originating in French, might have been an influence on the Robin Hood stories, or equally might have been a variation on the same common tradition. It represents the outlaw band sympathetically and as unjustly pursued. It identifies the green forest as a Utopia where there is no bad law or deceit, to which men flee to escape miscarriages of justice and where they can join an outlaw band, become skilled in archery and live by poaching and highway robbery. While the Song accuses named early-fourteenth-century justices of corruption (who do not subsequently feature in the Robin Hood stories), it nevertheless identifies sheriffs as typically corrupt officers of the crown. One line, 'Nor was I wicked robber to do people harm', is remarkably close to the last two lines of the

Gest: 'For he was a good outlawe,/And dyde pore men moch god'.[17]

Equally striking is the contrast in tone between the *Outlaw's Song* and the rhetoric deployed by the crown in the commissions of trailbaston themselves, of oyer and terminer, and of the peace of the early fourteenth century, which conjured up an image of outlaws roaming all over England, gathering in the woods, ambushing honest wayfarers whom they robbed and sometimes slayed, aided and abetted by the rebellious common people.[18] Of course Robin and his men ambush honest wayfarers (the knight, the potter) as well as dishonest ones (monks) and they also rob, assault and sometimes kill their victims. Yet they are constructed as good, not evil, outlaws who deserve the support of the common people. It almost certainly was, as Barbara Hanawalt has shown, that early-fourteenth-century highwaymen and outlaws lived a miserable existence, preyed most frequently on ordinary people like themselves, and terrorised whole districts. Just as the burgesses of Nottingham feared the outlaw rout that was apparently descending on them after the king had taken Robin Hood into his service, so Scarborough and Whitby were on occasion in the early fourteenth century seized by local bandits.[19]

Yet several texts transformed such bandits into heroes. These texts can be linked with the publicity given later to the activities of the Cotteril and Folville gangs, and the emergence of the idea of Folville's laws, whereby the outlaw was seen to put right the wrongs suffered by the weak at the hands of the powerful. They interacted with and helped shape a whole body of outlaw tales, which include *Gamelyn* and *Adam Bell* as well as of Robin Hood. Some elements were clearly in place by 1357 when Edward III devised a mock ambush of his prisoner King John of France as he journeyed from Winchester to London, probably at the notorious Pass of Alton. Household men, dressed in green, it was reported, imitated outlawed foresters who waylaid travellers. The story was taken up and repeated by the author of the *Anonimalle Chronicle*, probably a monk of St Mary's, York, compiling his text at the end of Edward III's reign. If, as it has been suggested, the incident of the mock ambush were taken from a contemporary newsletter, one would have early evidence of the widespread circulation of this central trope of the outlaw gang of foresters dressed all in green. The idea was already commonplace; the royal household enacted it; a newsletter recorded it; the idea became even more deeply embedded in popular imagination.[20] In the matter of the forest outlaw, the interpenetration of orality and literacy is readily apparent.

One can also see how the scene in the *Gest* in which the chief justice conspires with the abbot of St Mary's to deprive the knight of his lands is derived from stock complaint against venal judges found in the same or similar texts. The high justice's retort to the knight, 'I am holde with the abbot, both with cloth and fee', can be placed in a specific early-fourteenth-century context too. From the late thirteenth century judges tended to be retained by nobles, corporations and religious institutions, a circumstance which led to frequent complaint and occasional purges. In 1346, however, Edward III in his Ordinance of Justices took more radical action by requiring all his judges to take an oath not to receive robes or fees. While this was difficult to enforce, leading to its restatement in 1384, circumstances in the later fourteenth century did combine to bring the regular taking of fees as retainers to an end.[21] Antagonism towards the king's officers is more strongly developed in the mid-to-late-fourteenth century *Gamelyn* in which the hero, himself the youngest son of a knight, is unjustly dispossessed by his wicked eldest brother of the lands left to him by his father.[22]

Much incidental detail in *Gamelyn*, as we have seen, tallies with detail in the *Gest*. The outlaw band of yeomen live by poaching and highway robbery, especially of monks. His principal enemy is the sheriff, although in this version also his brother. He too meets a sticky end. But this is the story of a wronged younger son of the gentry, who becomes the 'king of the outlaws' to avenge himself and secure the restoration of his lands. It is in effect a version of the story of the sorry knight. But its date of composition, set variously between 1340 and 1370, clearly establishes that several of the conventions concerning Robin Hood's milieu were in circulation long before the *Gest* itself was compiled.[23] The Robin Hood stories, as did the story of William of Cloudesly, drew upon and reworked this established textual tradition. The earliest fragment of the text of the story of William of Cloudesly dates from 1536, but it is almost certainly an older tale in circulation at the same time as the first written Robin Hood tales.[24] Other literary influences on the texts can be discerned. The story of 'Little John and the Sheriff', in which John vows to be a bad servant, draws upon and inverts homilies criticising disloyal servants. Maurice Keen has shown how many incidents such as the disguise of the hero as a potter, or the robbing of a monk who would not tell the truth about the amount of money he was carrying, have long literary pedigrees. Peter Coss has drawn attention to a degree of crossover from chivalric romances.[25] Many different written sources influenced and shaped the early stories of Robin Hood.

It is not always possible, of course, to detect a written source. There might, for instance, have been enshrined in the Robin Hood stories a memory, transmitted orally or textually, of the notorious Pass of Alton as a haunt of highwaymen. The pass was, as we have seen, almost proverbial for William Langland. The king's own household was ambushed there in 1261. It was a place, the justices of eyre recorded in 1269, where foresters and shepherds who used the neighbouring woods, committed heinous crimes against innocent travellers. It might well have been the refuge of Adam de Gurdon, one of Simon de Montfort's prominent followers, who fled there after the battle of Evesham and lived for a while by highway robbery and plundering the local countryside. He was brought to account by Henry III's son, the Lord Edward, the future Edward I, was pardoned and rehabilitated in 1267, being granted property in Alton. A fictional account by Nicholas Trivet had the two engage in personal combat with the prince, who being impressed by his foe's prowess pardoned him forthwith. There are enough echoes here to make one wonder whether the story did not find its way into the *Gest*.[26] It may be too that there is a link with Walter Bower's assertion that the famous robbers Robin Hood and Little John 'arose' 'from among the disinherited', i.e. Simon de Montfort's followers in 1266, although in Barnsdale not Alton, and were remembered to his own day by the commons who loved to sing of their deeds.[27]

But there are some elements for which we have virtually nothing to go on. The story of the foreclosing of a mortgage, by which a grasping abbot endeavours to swindle an honourable knight fallen on hard times, does not appear to have an immediate written source. The scene in which the knight presents himself as poverty stricken at the abbey gate echoes a passage in the early-fourteenth-century *Simony*. This contrasts the cold reception given to a poor man seeking alms from a monastery and the warm welcome given to a person of influence.[28] But the mortgage story itself is not to be found in fourteenth-century songs of protest or homilies. It appears not to have been part of the stock complaint against clergy. The detail may reflect a memory of the behaviour of a particular abbot of St Mary's, but if so it would seem to have been carried by oral tradition.[29] More broadly, too, the ambience reflects the 'crisis' of the gentry in the thirteenth century when some lesser gentry families were forced to sell and mortgage lands, often to monasteries.[30] This too might draw on oral tradition and memory rather than texts then in circulation, which are now lost.

It is possible that the antagonism towards the Benedictine Order found in the stories drew on memories of the conflicts between certain abbeys and their urban communities that came to a head in the early fourteenth century.[31] Memory is probably even more important as far as poaching and conflict in the king's forests is concerned. Whereas there are many texts concerning outlawry, there are few to be found concerning poaching and the long-running conflict over the rights to game, which was particularly intense in the late thirteenth and early fourteenth centuries. The records of forest eyres reveal innumerable local Robin Hoods living off the king's deer in the royal forests of England at that time. The legal documents themselves, in Latin and not circulated beyond the courts, carry the detail of local poaching in the royal forests by ordinary men and women, who believed they had an equal right to game. But again early-fourteenth-century songs of protest, such as *The Simony* and especially *The Song of the Husbandman*, are notably silent about this grievance. By the mid-fifteenth century, like large outlaw bands roaming the land, conflict over the right to game in royal and seigneurial forests were distant memories. As we have seen, the poaching of deer was not perceived to be a major problem by crown or lords. Only when large gangs took systematically to poaching, as did Robert Stafford, alias Friar Tuck, and his men in the Weald in the 1420s, was it of any concern to the crown. As Stafford's pseudonym indicates, and as the likening of another riotous gang fifteen years later to Robin Hood's meyny also suggests, conflict over rights to game and the outrages of outlaw bands had by this time become memories of the past more familiar through storytelling than current experience.[32] Life was beginning to imitate art.

It is therefore possible, but impossible to demonstrate, that the Robin Hood stories drew on oral traditions alone for the memory of some of their historical detail. Memory was long. The *Libelle of English Policy*, written in the 1430s, claimed that there were old knights living who participated in Edward III's victories and still, like Falstaff and Justice Shallow, recalled the days they had seen.[33] It was common practice in manorial courts and parochial administration for jurors and churchwardens to call upon the memory of their elders to elucidate custom and to establish precedent. The churchwardens of Yeovil, for instance, when faced at the beginning of the seventeenth century with a dispute over seating in the church sought the advice of old men.[34] The most cited example of this process, yet still the most vivid, is John Smyth of Nibley's reminiscence that in the late sixteenth century he often heard old men and women of the neighbourhood, who had been born in the reign of Henry VII, relate the reports of their parents, kinfolk and neighbours, who as children had witnessed the 'battle' of Nibley Green in 1470.[35] Such oral transmission might perhaps explain the way in which very particular and precise geographical locations as Sayles near Wentbridge found their way into the stories, which may have drawn upon incidents of which there is some record in the late thirteenth and early fourteenth centuries.[36] It is therefore conceivable that memories of the era before the Black Death were transmitted, by ordinary men and women in town and country, over two or three generations.

On the other hand, not all the potentially relevant memories of that era carried either orally or in writing found their way into the stories of Robin Hood. The modern story of Robin Hood makes much of his resisting the exploitation of the peasantry by the Anglo-Norman aristocracy. This is not prominent in the earliest texts. Although it was once the subject of considerable debate among twentieth-century historians, it is now accepted that the early texts have little to say about the condition of husbandmen, serfs and agricultural labourers. This is to some extent surprising in that there was a well-established literary discourse, from the early fourteenth century, on this theme. In the *Song of the Husbandman*, the poet/narrator laments the manner in which, on top of the bad weather which has destroyed his harvest, he is harassed by the officials of the lord of the manor and subjected to incessant taxation by the king to the point that he is driven off the land. It is a complaint that can be specifically placed in the context of Edward II's reign. It was later echoed, almost summarised, in the complaints of the shepherds, driven to the point of despair by exploitation, in the opening of the *Wakefield Second Shepherd's Play*. The Wakefield play is contemporaneous with the Robin Hood tales.[37] Yet there is little reflection of the same complaint. Robin was a good outlaw who did poor men much good and he charged his men not to molest a husbandman. But that is it. He did not even rob the rich to give to the poor. It was John Mair, once more, who first established this leitmotif ('nor would he despoil the poor, but rather enriched them from the plunder taken from the abbots').[38] The past suffering of the peasantry, intense in the early fourteenth century, and it *was* in the past in the later fifteenth and early sixteenth centuries, was not part of the historical memory in the Robin Hood stories.

Even more remarkable, given its later prominence, is the absence of the notion of the Norman Yoke, in the Robin Hood stories. In the late thirteenth century Robert of Gloucester developed in his English verse history of England, followed by Robert Manning in 1338, the elaborate and ingenious idea that the English people were subjected after the conquest to Norman servitude. Thus the present feudal system, 'the thraldom that now in England is / through Normans it came, bondage and distress',[39] was a consequence of the occupation of England by a foreign power and the subjugation of the Anglo-Saxon people. The history of England in the two centuries following the conquest that they tell, especially Robert of Gloucester, focuses on the effort of the English to recover their lost liberties. It may well be specious and tendentious, but it highlights the wickedness of King John and links the oppression of the English people with the rule of an alien aristocracy.[40] The myth of the Norman Yoke has had a long and venerable part to play in English history, and has become embedded in the modern story of Robin Hood, but it was entirely absent from the pre-Reformation versions. One possible reason may be that their principal reference point lay not in circumstances before the early fourteenth century, but in the still vivid memory of the reign of Edward III.

Attention has recently been drawn to the political poetry of Laurence Minot, himself a minstrel or ribauldrer, whose rhymes commemorating English victories against the Scots and French, between 1333 and 1352, were drawn together as a continuous narrative shortly after 1352. One poem in particular, written about 1339, remarks how

> *Edward oure cumly king*
> *In Brabant has his woning*
> *With mani cumly knight.*

As Thomas Ohlgren has suggested, a direct link can be proposed between this passage and the description of 'Edwarde oure comly kynge' in the *Gest*. Furthermore the story of that comely king in disguise is remarkably similar in content to two other mid-fourteenth-century ballads, *King Edward and the Shepherd* and *King Edward and the Hermit* which deal with the king, clearly identified in the texts as Edward III, engaging in disguise with his outlawed subjects in their sports, listening to their complaints and finally revealing himself and pardoning the outlaw who has proved his loyalty. The similarities do not end here. In *King Edward and the Hermit* the setting is Sherwood Forest, and the king, in disguise, is enticed into the forest by a forester's promise of a great-headed deer, gets lost and finally meets a hermit-friar who makes his living by poaching. Thomas Hoccleve in his *Regement of Princes*, written in 1411–12, knew them, for he advised the future

Henry V to find out what his subjects thought of him and whether his officials were oppressing them by moving in disguise among them like the 'benyngne Edward the laste'.[41] Later, of course, William Shakespeare had Henry V carry out this advice on the eve of Agincourt, while the whole plot of *Measure for Measure* hangs on the same trope. The story of the king in disguise was commonplace (surely not restricted to Edward III), but was repeated about that monarch, and appeared in several different texts, not just in the *Gest*. There is thus good reason to suppose that 'Edwarde oure comly kynge' is Edward III. This identification provides the key to understanding the historical significance of the main narrative of the *Gest* and the broad significance of the early-fourteenth-century historical context of the stories for the late-fifteenth century present.[42]

'Here lies the glory of the English, the flower of kings past, the pattern of kings to come, a merciful king, the bringer of peace to his people'. So ran part of the epitaph displayed on a tablet near Edward III's tomb in Westminster Abbey, written in both Latin and English so that all could understand.[43] Very shortly after his death he was being remembered in such glowing terms that the word comely seems but faint praise. The continuation of *The Brut* covering his reign, completed before 1399, ends with this peroration to his eulogy:

> And ther sprang and shone so muche grace of hym that, what maner man had byhold his face, or had dremd of hym, he hoped that day that all shold hap to hym joyful and lykyng . . . and that in no land under heven had be brought forth so noble a kyng, so gentyll and so blessyd, or myghte reyse such another when he were dede.[44]

He was incomparable. This may be set alongside the words of the recognition scene in the *Gest*:

Robyn behelde our comly kynge
Wystly in the face
So dyd Syr Richard at the Lee

And so did all the wylde outlaws
Whan they se them knele
My Lorde the kynge of Englonde,
Now I knowe you well.[45]

There follows Robin's pardon and his welcoming into the king's service. Is not the king in the *Gest* the same as the king in *The Brut*?

By 1400 Edward III was already established in the imagination as the king who had restored justice and social peace to an England torn apart during the reign of his father. He was not only the great warrior king, but also a merciful and loving king, whose concern for his subjects was close to his heart. Hence the spread of stories of him moving in disguise among them so that he could discover their true complaints and root out those servants of his who were perverting the course of justice in his name. The extent to which this king became associated with the restoration of true justice and the proper order of society is revealed in the preamble to a private petition probably presented to the parliament of 1472–5. 'Revolve chroniques', the petitioner begged Edward IV, 'serche tymes passed, remember the dayes and blessed acts of your most noble progenitors (when the laws were obeyed), and especially the immortal fame of Edward III', consider how chaos consumes kingdoms if the law fails and note how in *these* times, 'owte of venymose rotes and kursed simony and perjury greweth al maner exorbitant myscheves . . . Whereby in your realm peas hath ben exyled and law subverted, without thextirpation of which', prosperity cannot be restored.

He then moves to his main purpose, to suggest some rather radical reforms of the administration of the law that in fact stood little chance of enactment. It is the preamble which is significant.[46] The petitioner no doubt knew that Edward IV had already launched an appeal to his subjects for support for war in France on the grounds that outward war brought inward peace. He was no doubt also aware that Edward IV himself was self-consciously presenting himself as the heir to Edward III. But his appeal nevertheless suggests that the image of Edward III as the restorer of law and order was deeply etched in general memory. Moreover, the reference to simony, conjures up an immediate historical comparison with the evil days of Edward II, and suggests familiarity with *The Simony* which blamed the failure of the law in his reign on the covetousness and simony of the knights, justices, merchants and above all the clergy.

One does not need, therefore, as Bellamy and Maddicott proposed, to match incidents in the stories of Robin Hood closely with people and events to place the action of the stories in the first four decades of the early fourteenth century, including the young Edward III's own difficult apprenticeship. One should not rule out altogether the possibility that a particular sheriff or a particular abbot was the inspiration for a character in the later stories of Robin Hood, but the historical significance does not depend on it. While the *Gest* contains no reference to the political history of the years 1300 to 1340 available by the late fourteenth century in English through the pages of *The Brut*, it reflects some aspects of the social history of that era and draws on the notion that Edward III, the benign king of blessed memory, brought decades of injustice and corruption to an end. The *Gest* contains a set of memories of what that 'corruption' had been; a mixture in fact of specific grievances with which Edward III dealt, as in the instance of the high justice taking robe and fee from the abbot, of knowledge that outlaw gangs had been a much publicised problem, and of more general complaints about the state of the kingdom. Moreover it builds on the widely held belief that Edward III emerged in the 1340s as a king who guaranteed the rights of all his subjects, supervised his judicial agents scrupulously, and tempered the severity of the law through the prerogative of mercy, all for the common good.[47] It is not a question of whether Edward III did in fact personify this ideal; it is that he was widely represented as having done so. As history, therefore, the Robin Hood stories remind their audiences of how Edward III, 'pereless of alle princis that regnyd over England',[48] restored good government after a period of misgovernment.

What did this past mean for the pre-Reformation present? As we have seen in 1472–5, the notion that Edward III was a king to be emulated because through outward war he had secured inward peace was being given very heavy emphasis. We might link this to Edward IV's dynastic propaganda, that the kingdom had recently fallen into disorder and lawlessness because of the Lancastrian usurpation, a theme recycled and recalibrated to meet the needs successively of both Richard III and Henry VII. But there is more to it than a reflection of the aspirations of Yorkist and early Tudor kings. We must bear in mind that in the *Gest* Robin Hood abandons the court after fifteen months. Most of his merry men, whom he took with him into royal service, have left. He misses the freedom of the outlaw life and regrets his failing skills at archery. His true worth and virtue are being undermined; 'My welthe', as he puts it, 'is went away'. Moreover he finds the cost of keeping up with court life is crippling. 'Alas and well a woo', he bemoans,

> *'Yf I dwele longer with the kynge,*
> *Sorowe wyll me sloo'.*[49]

There is contained here a conventional critique of the court and courtiers, the caterpillars of the common weal. It is worth stressing, however, that Robin is not forced to leave the court. He is not an innocent victim of court intrigue. He breaks his bond with the king. To do so he deceives him. He seeks and is given permission to go on pilgrimage to a chapel he had founded in Barnsdale. He is given leave of absence for a week, but never returns. And thus the narrator concludes,

> *Robyn dwelled in grene wode*
> *Twenty yere and two;*
> *For all drede of Edwarde our kynge,*
> *Agayne wolde he not goo.*[50]

Robin deserts his comely king. It is a deliberate act of defiance and rebellion.

There is underlying the action an implicit message that no king, not even Edward III, of whom it was said

> That in no land under heven had be brought forth so noble a king, so gentyl and so blessyd, or might reyse such another when he were dede

could in fact match the ideal of kingship. Indeed, as audiences were just as likely to know, even Edward III in the end revealed he had feet of clay. For, as the eulogy in *The Brut* continues sadly to recall, 'moving of his flesh' was the undoing of him.

> In his age, drawing down his lechery and other sins, little by little all the joyfull and blessed things, good fortune and prosperity decreased and misshaped. And infortunate things and unprofitable harmes, with much evil began for to spring and, *the more harme is, continued long after time.* (my italics)[51]

Ultimately, no king is perfect.

This eulogy was composed during the reign of Richard II. By implication it is a criticism of his rule. The 'harmes and evils' continued well into the fifteenth century, one might even argue became far worse by mid-century. While Henry V briefly restored the confidence and optimism of the high point of Edward III's reign, disorder and misgovernment were perceived to return thereafter. The stories of Robin Hood, and especially the *Gest*, had continued resonance in the later fifteenth and early sixteenth centuries. Both Edward IV, after 1471, and, at the beginning of his reign in 1509, Henry VIII raised hopes of the restoration of just government. In his games of Robin Hood, Henry might self-consciously have seen himself as the comely king Edward, bringing in a new golden era, just as he fabricated himself as a new Henry V abroad. But if Edward III, memorialised in the *Gest* as *our* comely king, fell from the supreme standard attributed to him, how could any other later and lesser king, an Edward IV, a Henry VII or Henry VIII or whoever might be raised when he were dead, surpass him?

In this respect it is particularly germane that after a year and three months at court, Robin Hood took to the woods again. He, and with him the audience, understand that there can be no lasting restoration of good government. It is but an illusion. Covetousness and simony will always return. History repeats itself. Robin's abandonment of the court and his return to his life are thus ultimately more significant than his pardon by the king. In the other outlaw stories the restored hero, whether it is Gamelyn or William of Cloudesly, prospers for the rest of his life at court. William becomes the king's bowbearer and chief riding forester of the northern forests, is made a 'gentleman of clothing and of fee' (an esquire of the body?) and his brothers yeomen of the chamber. They came to court and died contentedly still in service, 'good men all thre'.[52] Only Robin Hood rejects the court, promotion and prosperity. His rejection declares that there will always be a need for the outlaw, who stands as a reminder to all rulers that the court glows like rotten wood and that justice is never administered fairly for the true good of the common weal.

It is sometimes suggested that the outlaw stories, by dealing with restorative justice, are essentially conservative. They end, it has been argued, with 'a resounding restoration of the status quo' and that all it does through the reconciliation of the outlaw with the king is merely legitimise royal authority.[53] This may be true of *Gamelyn*, or of the story of William of Cloudesly, which does indeed end with an affirmation of the proper order. But it is certainly not true of the *Gest*. Robin Hood, until his betrayal and death, remains at large in the greenwood, a threat and a warning to his king. The *Gest* does not merely represent wishful thinking about an ideal order either. By being placed in a specific and recognisable English past, and by invoking the collective memory of England's most heroic king, it carries an explicit historical interpretation. While the audience 'knew' that Edward III had been a king who once restored a just society, they also were aware that that restoration did not last. The *Gest*, as history, not only reminded the audience that there had once been a time when a king ruled justly, but also reminded it that his just rule was short lived. It ends by emphasising that a remedy always lies at hand against any king, any regime, which neglected the common good. Robin Hood defied Edward *our* king, who was both the king who had reigned as the third of that name in the fourteenth century and his successor of any name occupying the throne at any time. The outlaw hero, who flouted authority, and reminded a king where his duty lay, is a perpetual reminder to all kings that their authority can be flouted again.[54] Men who played Robin Hood in their parish fund-raising games were men, too, who risked outlawry by flouting the king.[55]

There is moreover an underlying intimation running through the texts in the confrontations which take place with the king that Robin, loyal as he is, will never bow to royal authority. In the action of the *Monk*, Little John is pardoned and taken into the king's service as a yeoman of the crown. But he dupes the king as well as the sheriff in rescuing Robin Hood. The king is not pleased with John's treachery.

> *Then bespake oure cumly kyng,*
> *In an angur hye;*
> *'Little John has begyled the schereff,*
> *in faith so hase he me'.*[56]

For which crime, he continues, Little John should be hanged. But the crime is condoned, for he has proved his greater truth to his own master, Robin Hood, whom he loves better than either the king or the sheriff. Thus it ends, abruptly, with the king declaring:

> *'Speke no more of this mater', seid oure kyng,*
> *'But John has beguiled us alle'.*[57]

The king gives way, accepting and endorsing Robin Hood as an alternative and equal authority.

In the *Gest* Robin behaves in much the same way. When the king in disguise as the abbot produces a letter sealed with the privy seal, Robin kneels before him. The seal itself is as sacred as the king in person.[58] But thereafter, when Robin summons his men to attend, they all then kneel before him. As the king wryly observes:

> *'Here is a wonder seemly syght*
> *Me thinketh, by Godddes pyne,*
> *His men are more of his byddyng*
> *Then my men be at myn'.*[59]

As in the *Monk*, the equal status of the outlaw is acknowledged. The reconciliation between king and outlaw that then ensues is itself conditional. Robin agrees to join the king's service with seven score and three of his men, but adds,

But me lyke well your servyse,
I will come agayne full soone,
And shote at the donne dere
As I am wonte to done.[60]

A royal pardon is not conditional. No outlaw being readmitted to the king's grace negotiated the terms of his pardon. These are the words of an equal concluding a treaty with a king, not of a subject submitting to his authority. And in time he duly carries out his threat. He returns to his kingdom and summons again his seven score men to his side:

And fayre dyde of theyr hodes,
And set them on theyr kne:
'Welcome', they sayd, 'our mayster,
Under this grene wode tre'.[61]

They do fealty to their returning lord under his trystel tree. Thus Robin remained at large for a further 'twenty yere and two' and 'for all drede of Edwarde our kynge' would not return to court. He defies him. The warning of the sheriff to the king earlier in the narrative concerning Sir Richard at the Lee that:

He will be lorde, and set you at nought
In all the northe londe[62]

proves all too prescient in the case of Robin Hood himself.

The ambivalence in this relationship is clear. Robin recognises and respects royal authority. He shows all deference to it. But he challenges it, negotiates with it and in the end defies it. The greenwood offers an alternative kingdom, an alternative social order, and an alternative 'popular' law. In this respect the Sheriff of Nottingham, who loyally serves his king in seeking to bring the outlaws to justice is *not* the personification of the king's evil minister, but the representative of his constituted authority. The alternative *regnum* is founded on an awareness that kings never live up to their rhetoric, or reach the ideals of monarchy set out in the 'Mirrors for Princes' literature, not even the peerless prince, King Edward III. It recognises, too, that all new governments fail in their promise to put right the evils of the past. A Henry V, an Edward IV or Henry VIII may claim that a new age is dawning, but it never does. Everything is changed, but everything remains the same. Robin Hood is deeply distrustful of the exercise of power, and of people in power. He is not unlike Raphael Hythlodaeus, Thomas More's proponent of Utopia, who, adapting St Augustine, commented:

> when I consider and turn over in my mind the state of all commonwealths flourishing anywhere today, so help me God, I can see nothing else than a kind of conspiracy of the rich, who are aiming at their own interests under the name and title of commonwealth.[63]

In this respect the *Gest* is fundamentally subversive, for no government is to be trusted to maintain the common weal. When Robin walked on ground things were different, in an alternative greenwood kingdom. But then, of course, so courteous an outlaw was never found.

9

Farewell to Merry England

———•———

It has been a recurring refrain in these pages that Robin Hood at the end of the fifteenth and in the early sixteenth centuries was all things to all men. The differing figuration of his persona, the varied tone of the stories addressed to audiences from different social backgrounds, the evident enjoyment of them from king to commoner, the range of media from the printed story to the dramatic performance, and the continuing controversy over the morality of the tales reveal that Robin Hood was at the heart of English popular culture. They were seen by some contemporaries, a vocal minority perhaps, as lewd ribaldries, low-taste comic stories that led people astray, by others simply as harmless entertainment. During the century before the Reformation they were brought together in a narrative compilation that had pretensions to something more highbrow, and more self-consciously literary.

It is essential for our understanding and interpretation of what Robin Hood meant to contemporaries to recognise that the stories were told on different occasions, in different places, at different levels and to different audiences. They were not fixed but were infinitely variable. There was a continuously changing relationship between texts and contexts and, thus, reflected in the tales, continually changing social relationships and social messages. They were texts, in the jargon, which were being constantly renegotiated and contested. Thus they appealed to the gentry because Robin was courteous and respectful of those that lived up to the values of that status and rank. On the other hand, they also appealed to the non-gentry because the hero, and more particularly his lieutenant, Little John, could be a prankster who mocked aristocratic values and flouted the authority of the sheriff. Robin was a conventionally pious and devoted son of the Church who loved the Virgin Mary. On the other hand he despised Benedictine monks. These differences and contradictions should be neither ignored nor reconciled in one composite figure. They are the consequence of the kaleidoscopic character of the texts.

However, it is possible to find a set of dominant motifs, especially as they emerge in the *Gest*, which, after it established itself as the central narrative of the story of Robin Hood at the end of the fifteenth century, became the basis of all later developments of it. As we have seen, there are certain significant differences between the narrative as it emerged then and what it later became. It is this version, in its printed form, that received the widest circulation and became best known to audiences of all ranks. In it, more than any other working of the stories, a mirror is held up to Merry England.

First, it is crucial to our understanding that in all the stories, not just the *Gest*, Robin Hood and all his merry men are yeomen. He is not a gentleman, but he is not a peasant either. He is in between. The 'in-between' is a much contested area. It is part of the argument of this work that he, and all his men, are something altogether more precise than the generalised representation of a particular intermediate status group in late-medieval English society. He is figured as a particular type of yeoman – a yeoman of the forest, or a forester. He is also a 'strenuous' yeoman, who exercises great prowess in combat, for foresters as we have seen were believed to make some of the best archers in English armies. As a diligent and well-informed forester, he also knows the codes and skills not only of woodcraft, appropriate to a working man, but also of venery appropriate to a gentleman. This positions him as a figure not just intermediary but straddling the worlds of the gentry and non-gentry. It is one reason why it is possible to hang on him adventures of different sorts that appealed to one or the other, or sometimes both audiences. Nevertheless, he is quintessentially of the middling sort. He is, in fifteenth-century context, most closely linked in social standing to those men in town and village who carried the local government of the kingdom at the lowest level, who led parish or ward communities and frequently represented them in their dealings with higher authority, especially in legal and fiscal matters. The relationship between middling sort and higher authority was ambiguous. These men accepted their place in the social order and willingly acted as agents for royal government. But they were also independently minded and when they were so moved were not afraid to remonstrate and protest against the abuses of royal authority. Robin Hood can thus be located in a specific social space from which particular historical significance arises.

The forest bathing in perpetual springtime, which his fellow outlawed foresters inhabit, and he rules, is a paradigm of a just and well-ordered society. Being northern it is distanced from many of the audience. While it is a wilderness, as the north was stereotypically imagined in the south to be, it is benign. It is not, by any stretch of the imagination, a 'real' setting. Yet neither does it represent mere escapism; nor is it an elegy for a lost world of liberty; nor is it a utopian dream of a world which will never be. In the relationship with the action of the story, the greenwood represents something with a far sharper edge: awareness that the dreams and aspirations of spring always end in the disappointment of autumn. It thus grounds the stories psychologically in that human contradiction between optimism and pessimism, between recurring hope that things can be made better and a realisation that this never happens.

The greenwood is home to a fellowship of the forest outlaws. The words 'fellow' and 'fellowship' are key words in the texts, not only of the *Gest*. In encounters with Robin, even within the band itself, men have to prove themselves 'good fellows'. There are many different shades of meaning of this term, and the ambiguity not insignificant. A duality of association is evoked. One connotation is the fellowship of men in arms with its Arthurian overtones and its association with aristocratic affinities and retinues of war, of the kind in which it would be no surprise to find these outlawed yeomen. But another mirrored in the texts is the late medieval fraternity or guild, of which there were thousands of different types and sizes in England on the eve of the Reformation. Fraternities were societies of respectable men and women bound together in virtuous common purpose, for religious, charitable, economic and, in some cases, administrative ends. In earlier days distrusted by the authorities, they were by 1500 the characteristic social organisation of the middling and lesser sorts of society in town and country, defining their ideal, at popular and communal level, of how society should be ordered. It is the evocation of this kind of fellowship rather more than the military fellowship which links the outlaw band to the world of the middling sort with which yeomen of all kinds, including foresters, were associated. Paradoxically, Robin Hood and his fellowship, exiles in the greenwood who violently live by theft like an irregular military fellowship, also maintain the true values of such peaceful, respectable and law-abiding associations.

A contrast is drawn between the true fellowship to be found in the forest fraternity and the false fellowship to be found in a great monastery. The outlaw feasting in the forest represents true conviviality and hospitality, the celebration of inclusive brotherly love and charity, while the feast in the hall at St Mary's, York, is exclusive, selfish and lacking in charity. Robin has a true devotion to St Mary; the monks in an abbey dedicated to her do not. No doubt, as in so much in these stories, there is much that is stereotypical and humorous. However, one cannot escape the conclusion that there is also a significant strain of anti-monasticism, and specifically anti-Benedictine feeling, in them. The repetition of ridicule tends to undermine the standing of the ridiculed. In the great debate about anticlericalism on the eve of the Reformation this needs to be taken into account. It suggests not a general distrust of the clergy, but a particular cynicism about the richest and most worldly of the religious orders. As such it may reflect growing lay involvement in religious practice and, in certain contexts, control over ecclesiastical affairs discernible among the gentry and at parochial level in the later middle ages. Tensions may have existed between the assertive and more independent laity and the old orders who still considered themselves the princes of the Church, especially where urban societies and religious communities rubbed shoulder to shoulder. If so, and we ultimately do not know how the stories were read or heard, it may have contributed to the willingness of the laity in general to accept the dissolution of the greater monasteries, including all the Benedictine Orders, between 1538 and 1540.

Just as Robin and his fellowship might be seen to embody more sincerely than a great Benedictine monastery the true Christian ideals, so also he is an outlaw who maintains justice more impartially than the chief justice of the realm. He was a good outlaw while he walked on ground, which is fundamentally a contradiction in terms: a thief, a murderer and a renegade upholding the law? The pattern of his crime does not entirely fit the pattern of crime in England in the fifteenth and early sixteenth centuries. Poaching was not a matter of serious concern or site of social conflict in the fifteenth century, though it became more so during the sixteenth. Highway robbery was a continuing problem. But it does not matter so much whether the crime he commits is characteristic of the period; its purpose is to signify that a fellowship living beyond the law does more to uphold true justice than the enforcers of the law themselves. Moreover Robin is an outlaw who does not hesitate to use extreme violence, even to take life, in the cause of true justice. Violence is 'valorised' for two reasons; one is that, in imitation of chivalric values, it is a demonstration of his prowess and a sign of his honour; the other is that the just use of violence is what underpins all enforcement of law. In the inverted world of Robin Hood in which an outlaw defends the law, the violence of a just outlaw is likewise justified.

Robin Hood is apparently in legitimate rebellion against a regime that is undermined by an evil and corrupt minister, the Sheriff of Nottingham, who has prevented the king from fulfilling his true vocation of protecting and serving the common weal. Self-seeking officials and venal ecclesiastics are legitimate targets, for these are the people who have failed the king and corrupted society. The outlaws in this reading are thus not in rebellion against the king, but against the misdoers and misleaders in his service. They are perpetually in such loyal rebellion. This is an ideology very much in tune with the ideology of loyal rebellion to be found articulated, justified and practised in England from 1450 to 1550. It is to be found in the manifestos produced during Cade's rebellion, was taken up by York and Warwick, and remained a standard call right through to the Pilgrimage of Grace in 1536 and the risings of 1549. Those who rebelled in these years, whether following a dissident nobleman or, more spontaneously, to air their own grievances, were led at the local level by the same middling sorts who were the agents of local government. The appeal was to gentlemen as well as to commoners. They shared the conventional ideal about justice and due order, but in rebellion sought to enforce it, violently.

The crown, however, insisted that no rebellion could be justified; that only through complete obedience can the true interest of the common weal be served. Yet this was a contested principle in the years between 1450 and 1550, in both high and not so high circles. The *Gest* of Robin Hood engaged in this debate, for it implied through its hero's defiance of the king that rebellion can be justified if it is undertaken in the true interest of the common weal. An alternative ideology can be discerned that the common weal cannot ultimately be guaranteed by the unfettered authority of the crown, but only by the action of subjects. The story elaborated in the *Gest* is thus implicitly political. It uses history by referring back to Edward III, the paradigm of kingship. Its avowed and apparent line is that Robin Hood stands for the perfection of the desired order, and in this respect is intensely conservative: in line with loyal rebellion to reform and make perfect that which should be. Yet there is also something beyond the conventional rhetoric of loyal rebellion: an underlying subversiveness contained in the denouement of the story. It implies that all kings fail, even the best; that society can never work as it is meant to and that there will always need to be rebellion to assert the rights of the ruled. Robin Hood treats with the king; he does not submit. While he recognises the king's sovereignty and overlordship, he is an independent ruler of his own forest lordship, where the ideal of the perfect commonwealth is sustained. In so doing he represents independence of mind and independence of action in a social order that abhorred such independence. There is something in this reminiscent of more modern theories of anarchy, an ideal of a society with no rule, as well as the long-standing English tradition of independent thinking. This ideal commonwealth was Merry England.

In *Henry VI, Part* 2 Shakespeare entertains his audience with a parody of this perception. Jack Cade addresses his fellowship of comic handicraftmen who have risen in rebellion. He promises a realm in which all shall be in common and it will be a felony to drink small beer. And he shall be king and 'apparel them all in one livery, that they may agree like brothers, and worship me their lord'. As John Holland, one of the fellowship, declares, 'Well, I say it was never merry world in England since gentlemen came up'.[1] The Robin Hood stories did not advocate overturning the social order, but in many respects they located a Merry England in the communitarian ideals of the era before the Reformation. The texts are self-consciously aware of this Merry England. The outlaws are merry men, who we meet on merry mornings in the merry greenwood.[2] When Robin tires of the court he watches yeomen shooting and regrets that he gave up that life.

> *Somtyme I was an archere good,*
> *A styffe and eke a stronge;*
> *I was comted the best archere*
> *That was in mery Englonde.*[3]

The king proclaims Little John's pardon through all 'mery Englond'.[4] When Little John is wounded in the fight with the sheriff's men, he begs Robin to kill him rather than let him fall into his enemy's hands. But Robin refuses to abandon him:

> *'I wolde not that,' said Robyn,*
> *'Johan, that I were slawe,*
> *For all the golde in mery Englonde'.*[5]

The same oath is sworn by the sheriff after his uncomfortable night in the forest:

> *For all the golde in mery Englonde*
> *I would not longe dwel her.*[6]

The king proclaims that he will reward any man who kills the good knight, Sir Richard at the Lee, with all his lands

> *To have and hold for ever more*
> *In all mery Englonde.*[7]

There is, however, a subtle difference between the phrase in Robin's mouth and in the mouths of the sheriff and king. When used by Robin, it represents the ideal world; by the sheriff and the king, the unjust world as it is. The sheriff turns his back on the forest; as far as he is concerned Merry England is not there. The king punishes the honest knight in the name of Merry England. Robin Hood abandons the court because it weakens the sinews of Merry England. Merry England was not associated with the king or his authority: it was to be found at a distance from the throne.

This Merry England was orthodoxly Christian; it was communitarian on the model of fraternities, and justice could be enforced by direct action. It was rooted in a contemporary view of the common weal. Merry England was not just a construct of a later era looking back nostalgically to a perfect world before the break with Rome. Yet Merry England was swept away by the political and religious revolution of the mid-sixteenth century. Among the casualties were the fraternities and guilds that were so central to pre-Reformation local society. An alliance of crown and Protestants (holy or unholy depending on one's standpoint) removed one of the principal elements of the popular culture in which the Robin Hood stories had flourished. Ethan Shagan has drawn attention to the puzzle of the uncontested abolition of intercessory prayers, and of the dissolution of the instititutions which had sustained them, so apparently important in the century or so before the Reformation. How come, he asks, that the chantries folded so easily after 1547? His answer is that in many different ways, including a desire to share in the spoils, men and women, who could have done more to resist, willingly collaborated with the regime.[8] The same question can be asked, even more pressingly, abut the fraternities and guilds which were so much more than collective chantries and were even more embedded in communal life.

It is difficult to comprehend the completeness and relative ease with which thousands of fraternities and guilds, which for a century and more had played such a significant secular as well as religious role in local society, were swept away. To say the least, it makes one wonder whether they really were so important. It raises serious questions about the depth of the roots of fraternities and guilds, and the validity of a conclusion that suggests that Robin Hood tapped into popular involvement in secular and religious affairs at the local level. Perhaps we do not fully grasp the revolutionary nature of events in the mid-sixteenth century. Men and women had for centuries grown accustomed to dual allegiances: one to the crown and the other to the Church. Now they had been merged into one. The Church became an arm of the state and not a separate focus. The power of the crown was immense. There was little choice but to accept and obey, especially after the collapse of Mary's counter-revolution. We should not belittle the bewilderment and powerlessness of local communities in the face of a government and local magistracy determined to carry out reform, especially as it occurred incrementally, small step by small step, backwards as well as forwards, over a period of thirty years or more.[9] Second, the Protestant Reformation did offer, in alternative ways, a continuation, indeed in some respects an enhancement of lay involvement in and control over religion and the clergy, and reinforced the code of respectable behaviour. But there was a price to pay, and that price was the old guild and fraternity structure, which had been one of the mainstays of local communal association and promoters of the stories in May Games and related rituals.

Even so May Games and ales did not disappear as rapidly as intercessory prayers for the dead. Only after 1560 was the process of closing down the plays and gatherings begun, at a quickening pace after 1570. They held on at Chagford until 1588. In 1607 a complaint was raised in Weston Zoyland against the vicar there, Mr Wolfall, that he encouraged his parishioners on a Sunday in Whitsuntide to leave church and, according to custom, follow Robin Hood to the ale. In Yeovil in the same year some parishioners complained to the justices of similar sports in the name of Robin Hood, which, shamefully, included the churchwardens keeping the church house open until midnight and allowing the youth to dance and drink.[10] There were to be no more cakes and ale and the Robin Hood performances at local level were expunged in both England and Scotland, though not finally until the end of the seventeenth century.[11]

Robin Hood performances were removed along with the fraternities and parochial rituals. But the stories survived in different media in the new social and political order. The view of the crown that it alone could maintain the common weal was ruthlessly enforced in order to protect Henry VIII's dynastic settlement and the unchallenged right of his descendants to the throne. Absolute and unquestioning obedience was demanded. There could be no loyal opposition. The break with Rome, the gathering threat from religious dissidents and the growing gulf between rich and poor, all put greater stress on obedience to the crown as the only hope of maintaining order and of advancing the common good. A yeoman hero, who defied the crown in maintaining justice, was no longer politically correct. Other forces were at work too. A commercial theatre in London and its suburbs, backed by aristocratic patronage, supplanted parochial playing. A significant increase in literacy speeded up the transition from the spoken to the written word. The Robin Hood stories changed to match these contexts. A new, more aristocratic and affirmative story version emerged, encapsulated at the end of the century in Anthony Munday's plays. When Duke Senior took refuge in the forest of Arden he was likened, we should note, to the Robin Hood *of old*. Respectability was put back into outlawry.

However, the radical Robin Hood refused to lie down; a new popular ballad literature, in single-sheet broadside form, emerged, which in the seventeenth century sustained the old traditions. The commercial broadside, as Dobson and Taylor have stressed, became the main vehicle for the transmission of the stories of Robin Hood in the seventeenth century. Subsequently they were collected together and sold in 'garlands'. In the process the content and form tended to fossilise as traditional entertainment.[12] In the revolutionary and romantic decades of the late eighteenth and early nineteenth centuries, the Robin Hood of old was revived and rediscovered in literary circles, later adapted to music hall entertainment, and transferred to film. And so, it eventually came to pass that the 'Hood Myth' was given priority rating in a project to turn the Isle of Wight into a heritage theme park. For it was:

> A primal myth, better still, a primal English myth. One of freedom and rebellion – justified rebellion, of course. Wise, if ad hoc principles of taxation and redistribution of income. Individualism deployed to temper the excesses of the free market. The brotherhood of man. A Christian myth, too, despite certain anti-clerical features. The pastoral monastery of Sherwood Forest. The triumph of the virtuous yet seemingly outgunned over the epitomic robber baron.[13]

NOTES

1 Texts and Context

1 Julian Barnes, *England, England* (London: Picador, 1999), p. 148.

2 Ibid., pp. 83, 146–51, 221–5, 227–32.

3 Maurice Keen, *The Outlaws of Medieval Legend*, 2nd edn (London: Routledge, 1977), p. 177. The same passage is translated by Stephen Knight and Thomas Ohlgren, eds, *Robin Hood and Other Outlaw Tales* (Kalamazoo, MI: Western Michigan University Press, 1997), p. 26, as 'whom the foolish populace are so inordinately fond of celebrating both in tragedies and comedies, and about whom they are delighted to hear the jesters and minstrels sing above all other ballads.' See also p. 112.

4 Chaucer, *Complete Works*, vol. 4, pp. 645–67 (*Gamelyn*) and Dobson and Taylor, *Rymes*, pp. 258–73 (*Adam Bell*). While the hero of the story is William of Cloudesly, it has always been known as *Adam Bell, Clim of the Clough and William of Cloudesly*. All references to the text are therefore to *Adam Bell*.

5 *Gest*, stanza 315.

6 For a recent discussion of the problem of dating see R. B. Dobson, 'Robin Hood: The Genesis of a Popular Hero', in Thomas Hahn, ed., *Robin Hood in Popular Culture* (Cambridge: D. S. Brewer, 2000), pp. 64–70. Linguistic analysis by Douglas Gray, 'The Robin Hood Poems', *Poetica*, 18 (1984), 1–18, indicates *c.*1400 and possibly earlier as the date of composition of parts of the text of the *Gest*. Stephen Knight, *Robin Hood: A Complete Study of the English Outlaw* (Oxford: Basil Blackwell, 1994), pp. 47–9, has proposed a date of recording as late as *c.*1450, but this does not preclude earlier oral composition. Thomas Ohlgren has suggested in a private communication that the text was brought together from lost manuscripts by its first printer in the 1490s. In their surviving versions, the other 'early' ballads (*Robin Hood and Guy of Gisborne, Robin Hood and the Monk* and *Robin Hood and the Potter*) seem to date from before or shortly after 1500.

7 Dobson and Taylor, *Rymes*, pp. 113–22; Knight and Ohlgren, *Robin Hood*, pp. 31–4.

8 Dobson and Taylor, *Rymes*, pp. 123–32; Knight and Ohlgren, *Robin Hood*, pp. 57–9; Thomas Ohlgren, 'Richard Call, the Pastons and the Manuscript

Context of Robin Hood and the Potter (Cambridge, University Library Ee.4.35.1)', *Nottingham Medieval Studies*, 45 (2001), 210–33.

9 Dobson and Taylor, *Rymes*, pp. 140–5; Knight and Ohlgren, *Robin Hood*, pp. 169–71; John Marshall, 'Playing the Game: Reconstructing *Robin Hood and the Sheriff of Nottingham*', in Hahn, ed., *Robin Hood in Popular Culture*, pp. 161–74.

10 Dobson and Taylor, *Rymes*, pp. 146–64. Stephen Knight, *Robin Hood: A Mythic Biography* (Ithaca, NY: Cornell University Press, 2003), pp. 14–33 suggests that the *Gest*, more self-consciously heroic in tone than the three free-standing stories, transforms what had been similarly more down-to-earth tales into a format for a more socially elevated audience, and thus represents a stage in the growth of the respectability of the hero.

11 *Gest*, stanzas 1, 144 and 317. The second occasion, addressed to 'All that nowe be here', is at the beginning of the third fytte introducing the story of 'Little John and the Sheriff' and promises them 'Goode myrth'.

12 *Gest*, stanza 456.

13 *Potter*, stanzas 2 and 83. The yeomen audience is addressed as 'Comley, cortessey and god'.

14 Ibid., stanza 83; *Gest*, stanzas 71–4. Little John is described as the 'devil's draper'. The mercantile theme has attracted recent attention. Knight and Ohlgren, *Robin Hood*, pp. 58–9, while noting the wide appeal of the tale, stress the mocking of 'mercantile' values in *Potter*. On the other hand, Ohlgren, 'The "Marchaunt" of Sherwood: Mercantile Ideology in *A Gest of Robyn Hode*', in Hahn, ed., *Robin Hood in Popular Culture*, pp. 175–90, suggests that the narrative reflects them.

15 G. R. Owst, *Literature and Pulpit in Late Medieval England*, 2nd edn (Oxford: Basil Blackwell, 1961), pp. 10–11. For minstrels and their role in the dissemination of the Robin Hood stores, see Holt, *Robin Hood*, pp. 110–13; 128–41.

16 T. H. Jamieson, ed., *The Shyp of Folys of the Worlde*, (London, 1874), vol. 2, p. 155. Was Barclay making a specific reference to the *Gest* by consciously playing on the meaning of the word, for a jest, after all, is both a story and a joke, and a jester is both a storyteller and a joker?

17 G. E. Duffield, ed., *The Work of William Tyndale* (Appleford, Berks.: Marcham Manor Press, 1964), p. 164; E. Arber, ed., *Hugh Latimer, Seven Sermons before Edward VI* (London: Murray, 1869), pp. 173–4.

18 Dobson and Taylor, *Rymes*, pp. 1–4.

19 Adam Fox, *Oral and Literate Culture in England, 1500–1700* (Oxford: Clarendon Press, 2000), *passim*.

20 Dobson and Taylor, *Rymes*, p.3.

21 Ibid., 38–42; David Wiles, *The Early Plays of Robin Hood* (Cambridge: D. S. Brewer, 1981), *passim*; Knight, *Complete Study*, pp. 98–108; Jeffrey L. Singman, *Robin Hood: The Shaping of a Legend* (Westport, CT: Greenwood, 1998), pp. 62–103. See also note 9 and pp. 168–71.

22 John Marshall, '"goon in-to Bernysdale": The Trail of the Paston Robin Hood Play', *Leeds Studies in English*, 29 (1998), 185–217.

23 *Monk*, stanza 17.

24 *Monk*, stanza 84.

25 Dobson and Taylor, *Rymes*, pp. 260–77.

26 Chaucer, *Complete Works*, vol. 4, pp. 645–67; Keen, *Outlaws*, pp. 78–94; Richard W. Kaeuper, 'An Historian's Reading of the Tale of Gamelyn', *Medium Aevium*, 52 (1983), 51–62. For a version in modern English see Stephen Knight, 'The Tale of Gamelyn', in Thomas H. Ohlgren, ed., *Medieval Outlaws: Ten Tales in Modern English* (Stroud: Sutton, 1998), pp. 168–86.

27 Keen, *Outlaws*, pp. 1–8.

28 Dobson and Taylor, *Rymes*, pp. 41–6; Singman, *Robin Hood*, pp. 84–5; Knight, *Complete Study*, pp. 115–34; Knight, *Mythic Biography*, pp. 49–65. It is possible that the introduction of Maid Marian into the story drew upon 'The Nut Brown Maid', another late medieval story concerning a maiden who proved her love by enduring the privation of the forest.

28 Dobson and Taylor, *Rymes*, pp. 53–8; Knight, *Complete Study*, pp. 153–217.

30 D. Crook, 'Some Further Evidence Concerning the Dating of the Origins of the Legend of Robin Hood', *EHR*, 99 (1984), 530–4; D. Crook, 'The Sheriff of Nottingham and the Robin Hood Stories: The Genesis of the Legend?', in P. R. Coss and S. D. Lloyd, eds, *Thirteenth Century England*, vol. 2 (Woodbridge: Boydell & Brewer, 1988); J. C. Holt, 'The Origins of the Legend', in K. Carpenter, ed., *Robin Hood: The Many Faces of that Celebrated English Outlaw* (Oldenberg: BIS, 1995), pp. 27–34; R. B. Dobson and J. Taylor, 'Robin Hood of Barnsdale: A Fellow Thou has Long Sought', *Northern History*, 19 (1983), 210–20; Dobson, 'Genesis', pp. 70–7.

31 Dobson and Taylor, *Rymes*, pp. xxi–xxii, xxx–xxxii, 10–17.

32 For the texts of Wyntoun and Bower in translation, see Knight and Ohlgren, *Robin Hood*, pp. 24–6.

33 S. Schama, *Landscape and Memory* (London: HarperCollins,1995), p. 149; N. Davies, *The Isles: A History of Britain* (London: Macmillan, 1999), pp. 437–8; A. J. Pollard, *Late Medieval England, 1399–1509* (London: Longman, 2000), pp. 1–11.

34 A. J. Pollard, *The Wars of the Roses*, 2nd edn (Basingstoke: Palgrave, 2000), pp. 19–40, 65–80.

35 For this and the following paragraphs see R. H. Britnell, *The Commercialisation of English Society, 1000–1500*, 2nd edn (Manchester: Manchester University Press, 1996), pp. 155–237; Christopher Dyer, *Making a Living in the Middle Ages: The People of Britain, 850–1520* (New Haven, CT: Yale University Press, 2002), pp. 265–365; Mark Ormrod and Philip Lindley, eds, *The Black Death in England* (Stamford, Lincs.: Paul Watkins, 1996); Pollard, *Late Medieval England*, pp. 169–203.

36 Durham, Dean and Chapter Records, Halmote Rolls, Billingham, Summer 1477.

37 A. McFarlane, *The Origins of English Individualism* (Oxford: Blackwell, 1976), *passim*.

38 J. Fortescue, *On the Laws and Governance of England*, ed. S. J. Lockwood (Cambridge: Cambridge University Press, 1997), pp. 42–3.

39 J. Whittle, *The Development of Agrarian Capitalism: Land and Labour in Norfolk, 1440–1580* (Oxford: Clarendon Press, 2000), p. 11; P. R. Schofield, *Peasant and Community in Medieval England, 1200–1500* (Basingstoke: Palgrave, 2003), pp. 1–10.

40 Dyer, *Making a Living*, pp. 163–8; Whittle, *Agrarian Capitalism*, pp. 5–16.

41 See in particular the argument of Britnell, *Commercialisation of English Society*, esp. pp. 228–237.

42 C. C. Dyer, 'Were There any Capitalists in Fifteenth-Century England?', in Jennifer Kermode, ed., *Enterprise and Individuals in Fifteenth-Century England* (Stroud: Sutton, 1991), pp. 10–16, 19, 21. For Keith Wrightson, *Earthly Necessities: Economic Lives in Early Modern Britain, 1470–1750* (Harmondsworth: Penguin, 2000), p. 29, the key point, at the beginning of the sixteenth century, is that there was no 'concept of a market order as a self-regulating system of economic relationships' (p. 29); see also Britnell, *Commercialisation of English Society*, pp. 233–7, and the comments of L. R. Poos, *A Rural Society after the Black Death: Essex, 1350–1525* (Cambridge: Cambridge University Press, 1991), pp. 291–3, concerning the economic and cultural differentiation of northern and central Essex where a 'proto-yeomanry' dominated the countryside, which had a predominance of wage-earners and a distinctive industrial sector. Others might have said 'proto-capitalist'.

43 John Hatcher, 'The Great Slump of the Mid-Fifteenth Century', in R. H. Britnell and J. Hatcher, eds, *Progress and Problems in Medieval England* (Cambridge: Cambridge University Press, 1996), pp. 237–72.

44 R. H. Britnell, *The Closing of the Middle Ages? England 1471–1529* (Oxford: Blackwell, 1995), 208–47, esp. pp. 241.

45 *Gest*, stanza 437.

46 See especially Gray, 'The Robin Hood Poems', *passim*; Knight, *Complete Study*, pp. 44–81; Knight, *Mythic Biography*, pp. 1–32; Ohlgren, 'Richard Call', *passim*, and Marshall, 'Playing the Game'. Knight, *Mythic Biography*, pp. 193–202, offers a selective discussion of the writings of twentieth-century historians, in which he remarks that some 'have produced some of the most limited and intellectually self-centred of the accounts of the hero's biography' (p. 201). While one is not sure what he is driving at, one hopes, since it is not a 'biography', that this work will escape such censure.

47 *Potter*, stanzas 76–9.

48 *Gest*, stanzas 126–7, 334–9.

49 *Gest*, stanzas 451–5. In *Death*, a fuller though not complete version of the story which was perhaps the source, she is first the prioress and then a widow (Dobson and Taylor, *Rymes*, pp. 134–7).

50 *Gest*, stanzas 1–18.

2 *Yeomanry*

1 *Potter*, stanza 83.

2 Dobson and Taylor, *Rymes*, p. 34. Elements of this chapter have previously appeared in Richard Almond and A. J. Pollard, 'The Yeomanry of Robin Hood and Social Terminology in Fifteenth-century England', *Past and Present*, 170 (2001), pp. 52–77.

3 R. H. Hilton, 'The Origins of Robin Hood', *Past and Present*, 14 (1958), 30–44, reprinted in Hilton, ed., *Peasants, Knights and Heretics: Studies in Medieval English Social History* (Cambridge: Cambridge University Press, 1976); Maurice Keen, 'Robin Hood — Peasant or Gentleman?', *Past and Present*, 19 (1961), 7–15, reprinted in Hilton, *Peasants, Knights and Heretics*, pp. 258–64.

4 J. C. Holt, 'The Origins and Audience of the Ballads of Robin Hood', *Past and Present*, 18 (1960), 89–110, reprinted in R. H. Hilton, ed., *Peasants, Knights and Heretics*, pp. 236–57; J. C. Holt, *Robin Hood* (London, Thames & Hudson 1982),.pp. 118–24, 128–43, and reinforced in his 1989 postscript (p. 197), 'the earliest tales were primarily addressed to yeomen of the household. They reflect the skills, ambitions and social assumptions of these men and the conventions of service and reward of the world in which they moved. The earliest tales fit no other context'.

5 Peter Coss, 'Aspects of Cultural Diffusion in Medieval England: The Early Romances, Local Society and Robin Hood', *Past and Present*, 108 (1985), 66–79, esp, pp. 73–4.

6 Colin Richmond, 'An Outlaw and Some Peasants: The Possible Significance of Robin Hood', *Nottingham Medieval Studies*, 37 (1993), 90–101.

7 Dobson and Taylor, *Rymes*, p. xxxvi.

8 *Statutes of the Realm*, vol. 1, 380. These views are broadly in accord with those of Stephen Knight and Thomas H. Ohlgren, eds, *Robin Hood and Other Outlaw Tales* (Kalamazoo, MI: Western Michigan University Press, 1997), pp. 34, 59, who identify a 'dream of yeomanly community' in *Monk* and an exploration of yeomanly values appropriate to a new social stratum in *Potter*.

9 Holt, *Robin Hood*, pp. 124, 127.

10 *Gest*, stanzas 287–8.

11 Chaucer, *Complete Works*, pp. 658, 660–1; *Gamelyn*, ll. 551–3, 613–58.

12 Ibid., p. 662.

13 M. P. Davies, 'The Tailors of London and their Guild, c.1300–1500', unpublished D Phil thesis, University of Oxford, 1994, pp. 147–56; Davies, 'The Tailors of London: Corporate Charity in the Late-Medieval Town', in R. E. Archer, ed., *Crown, Government and People in the Fifteenth Century* (Stroud: Sutton, 1995), pp. 175–6. The term was also interchangeable with the word bachelor.

14 J. W. Clay, ed., *North Country Wills* (Woodbridge: Surtees Society, 117, 1908), p. 72.

15 North Yorkshire County Record Office, Clervaux Cartulary, fo 55; A. J. Pollard, 'Richard Clervaux of Croft', in Pollard, *The Worlds of Richard III* (Stroud: Tempus, 2001), p. 104.

16 Durham, Dean and Chapter Library, Misc. Ch 625.

17 M. H. Keen, *English Society in the Later Middle Ages*, (Harmondsworth: Penguin, 1990), p. 8.

18 Durham, Dean and Chapter, Misc. Ch. 7012; Pollard, 'Richard Clervaux', p. 105; G. E. Corrie, ed., *Sermons by Hugh Latimer*, 2 vols (Cambridge: Parker Society, 1884–5), p. 101.

19 Sir John Fortescue, *On the Laws and Governance of England*, ed. S. J. Lockwood (Cambridge: Cambridge University Press, 1997), p.43. For jury service of the type Fortescue had in mind, see Anne DeWindt, 'Local Government in a Small Town', *Albion*, 23 (1991), 627–54; R. Goheen, 'Peasant Politics? Village Community and the Crown in Fifteenth-Century England', *American History Review*, 96 (1991), 46–62; Francesca Bumpus, 'The "Middling Sort" in the Lordship of Blakemere, Shropshire, c.1380–c.1420', in T. Thornton, ed., *Social Attitudes and Political Structures in Fifteenth century England* (Stroud: Sutton, 2000), pp. 202–18; Keith Wrightson, *Earthly Necessities: Economic Lives in Early Modern Britain, 1470–1750* (New Haven, CT: Yale University Press, 2000), pp. 99–102, and Pollard, *Fifteenth-Century England*, pp. 188–90.

20 C. L. Kingsford, ed., *The Stonor Letters and Papers* (London: Camden third series, 29, 1919), p. 95. See also the discussion in Dobson and Taylor, *Rymes*, pp. 34–5.

21 Thomas Ohlgren, 'Richard Call, the Pastons, and the Manuscript Context of Robin Hood and the Potter', *Nottingham Medieval Studies*, 45 (2001), pp. 215, 220–25; Colin Richmond, *The Paston Family in the Fifteenth Century: Endings* (Manchester: Manchester University Press, 2000), pp. 94–5.

22 See pp. 22–5.

23 Anne Crawford, ed., *The Household Books of John Howard, Duke of Norfolk, 1462–71, 1481–3* (Stroud: Sutton for Richard III and Yorkist History Trust, 1992), pp. xl-xlii; C. M. Woolgar, *The Great Household in Late Medieval England* (New Haven, CT: Yale University Press, 1999), p. 189.

24 A. R. Myers, ed., *The Household of Edward IV: The Black Book and Ordinances of 1478* (Manchester: Manchester University Press, 1959), pp. 116–17. One can note too that Sir John Paston, en route to Calais in 1473, found himself delayed by the failure of a 'yonge man' to join his retinue. Accordingly he wrote to his brother John asking if he knew of any 'lykly men, and fayr condiycioned, and good archers' (*Paston Letters*, v, no. 834, p. 185)

25 *Potter*, stanza 49.

26 *Gest*, stanzas 163–71, 178.

27 *Gest*, stanzas 80–1.

28 *Gest*, stanza 406.

29 *Adam Bell*, stanza 165.

30 Durham, Dean and Chapter, Misc. Ch. 6253, 6145; Michael Jones and Simon Walker, eds, 'Private Indentures for Life Service in Peace and War, 1278–1476', in *Camden Miscellany*, 32 (London: Royal Historical Society, 1994), pp. 171–2.

31 Coss, 'Aspects of Cultural Diffusion', p. 74, n.145.

32 Holt, *Robin Hood*, p. 122 and 'Origins and Audience', pp. 244–6, 50.

33 Coss, 'Aspects of Cultural Diffusion', p. 74, n.145, pp. 96, 98.

34 *Gest*, stanzas 221–2.

35 *Gest*, stanza 377.

36 The irony of the situation would not have escaped the audience's attention.

37 G. J. Turner, ed., *Select Pleas of the Forest* (London: Selden Society, 13, 1899–1901), introduction; C. R. Young, *The Royal Forests of Medieval England* (Leicester: Leicester University Press, 1979), esp. ch. 8 for the later middle ages.

38 D. J. Stagg, ed., *A Calendar of New Forest Documents: The Fifteenth to the Seventeenth Centuries* (Winchester: Hampshire Record Office, 5, 1983), p. 8; National Archives, DL 39/2/20, m10 (Clarendon); SC 6/1085/20, DL 29/648/10485 (Wensleydale); Westminster Abbey Muniments, 6052 (Durham).

39 Fortescue, *Laws and Governance*, p. 119; Westminster Abbey Muniments, 6052.

40 *Gest*, stanzas 13–14.

41 Nottingham, Special Collections, MiL 3/1&2, Sherwood Forest Book, fo Dxii.

42 Ibid., MS 72/2, p. 108.

43 *Adam Bell*, stanzas 1–2. However, the use of the word 'walk' is more ambiguous in *Gamelyn*. In lines 672–4, describing the hero and his companions when they first enter the forest, the word has the sense of wandering. Later, after he is crowned king of the outlaws, Gamelyn 'walked in whyle under the wode-schawes' (l. 96). This line, so similar to the line in the *Gest*, is, in its context, not easily interpreted as a reference to the forester's occupation (Chaucer, *Complete Works*, pp. 661–2).

44 *Gest*, stanzas 448–9, 356–67. 'Chief governoure' is from a mid-sixteenth century dramatisation of *Robin Hood and the Potter* (Dobson and Taylor, *Rymes*, p. 218).

45 W. A. Baillie-Grohman and F. Baillie-Grohman, eds, *The Master of Game* (London 1909), p. 189; Ralph Whitlock, *Historic Forests of England* (Bradford on Avon, 1979), p. 42; Nottingham, Special Collections, MiL 3/1&2, fo Dxii.v, a late-fifteenth-century copy of the oath of the bowbearer of Sherwood stresses the supervisory role. The bowbearer of the New Forest between 1487 and 1494, Robert Mour, occasionally presented offences against the venison to the forest eyre (Stagg, *New Forest Documents*, pp. 5,14, 18).

46 *Monk*, stanza 33.

47 *Adam Bell*, stanza 162.

48 *Gest*, stanza 211.

49 *Gest*, 421–2.

50 Chaucer, *Complete Works*, vol. 4, p. 4; *Canterbury Tales*, 'Prologue', ll. 103–17.

51 Ibid., pp. 361–2; 'The Friar's Tale', esp. ll. 87–91, 121–5.

52 J. S. Roskell and others, *The History of Parliament: The House of Commons, 1386–1421* (Stroud: Sutton, 1993), p. 518.

53 For fifteenth-century seigneurial forest courts see, e.g., I. M. W. Harvey,

'Bernwood in the Middle Ages', in John Broad and Richard Hoyle, eds, *Bernwood: The Life and Afterlife of a Forest* (Preston: Harris Paper Two, 1997); Christine M. Newman, *Late-Medieval Northallerton* (Stamford, Lincs: Paul Watkins, 1999), pp. 39–40; R. C. Shaw, *The Royal Forest of Lancaster* (Preston: Guardian Press 1956); R. B. Turton, ed., *The Honour and Forest of Pickering* (North Riding Record Society, new series, 1, 1894).

54 John Cummins, *The Hound and the Hawk: The Art of Medieval Hunting* (London: Phoenix, 1988), p. 266; Richard Almond, *Medieval Hunting* (Stroud: Sutton, 2003), pp. 116–20. The master forester was required to warn the sheriff where any hunt was to take place. Somerset and Dorset was a joint shrievalty; Baillie-Gohman and Baillie-Gohman, *Master of Game*, pp. 188–9.

55 Almond and Pollard, 'Yeomanry of Robin Hood', pp. 69–70.

56 *Gest*, stanzas 446–7; *Adam Bell*, stanza 105. A hart of grease was a mature male red deer in his prime, from mid-June to mid-September (Almond, *Medieval Hunting*, pp. 86–7).

57 *Gest*, stanzas 182–8.

58 Pollard and Almond, 'Yeomanry of Robin Hood', pp. 64–6; Almond, *Medieval Hunting*, pp. 82–5.

59 *Gest*, stanzas 387–8. The technical meaning of 'tryst' has eluded editors of the texts. Dobson and Taylor suggest a rendezvous (*Rymes*, p. 99); Knight and Ohlgren, more ingeniously, offer 'trystyll' (trestle or platform) tree, 'presumably suitable for speeches or even hangings' (*Robin Hood and Other Outlaw Tales*, p. 182).

60 *Monk*, stanza 37.

61 Edward Hall, *Chronicle* (1809), p. 582, cited and discussed by Holt, *Robin Hood*, p. 161; Dobson and Taylor, *Rymes*, pp. 42–3; Simon Schama, *Landscape and Memory* (London: HarperCollins, 1995), pp. 152–3. A vivid account is given by Alison Weir, *Henry VIII: King and Court* (London: Jonathan Cape, 2001), pp. 181–2.

62 Corinne J. Saunders, *The Forest of Medieval Romance* (Woodbridge: Boydell & Brewer, 1993), pp. 172–3.

63 Malory, *Works*, p. 375. In this passage, it would seem, Malory used the term 'yeoman' as an intermediate social category.

64 Anne Rooney, *Hunting in Medieval English Literature* (Woodbridge: Boydell & Brewer, 1993), pp. 14–15.

65 C. D'Evelyn, ed., *Peter Idley's Instructions to his Son* (Oxford: Oxford University Press, 1935), p. 160.

66 *Guy*, stanzas 7 and 34.

3 A Greenwood Far Away

1 *Monk*, stanzas 1–2

2 Simon Schama, *Landscape and Memory* (London: HarperCollins, 1995), pp. 142–5.

3   John Broad and Richard Hoyle, eds, *Bernwood: The Life and Afterlife of a Forest* (Preston: Harris Paper Two, 1997) pp. 1–7, 14–18, 23–30.

4   Henry Summerson, *Medieval Carlisle* (Cumberland and Westmorland Antiquarian and Archaeological Society, Extra Series, 25, 2 vols, 1993), pp. 28–9, 325, 393, 413, 508.

5   Nottingham, Special Collections, MiL 3/1&2, fos Bxi–Cxv.v; A. J. Pollard, *North-Eastern England during the Wars of the Roses: War, Politics and Society, 1450–1500* (Oxford: Clarendon Press, 1990), pp. 200–2.

6   Broad and Hoyle, *Bernwood*, p. 14; Pollard, *North-Eastern England*, pp. 36–7; see also Jean Birrell, 'The Forest Economy of the Honour of Tutbury in the Fourteenth and Fifteenth Centuries', *University of Birmingham Historical Journal*, 8 (1962), 114–34, for Needwood and Duffield Firth, adjacent to Sherwood.

7   D. J. Stagg, ed., *A Calendar of New Forest Documents: The Fifteenth to the Seventeenth Centuries* (Winchester: Hampshire Record Office, 5, 1983), pp. 1–29 *passim*.

8   Pollard, *North-East England*, pp. 199–201, 205–6.

9   Ibid., pp. 201–5; J. L. Drury, 'Early Settlement in Stanhope Park, Weardale, c.1406–79', *Archaeologia Aeliana*, 4 (1976), 139–49.

10 J. G. Bellamy, 'The Northern Rebellions in the Later Years of Richard II', *Bulletin of the John Rylands Library*, 47 (1965), 254–61. See also p. 94–5.

11 *Gest*, stanza 447; *Adam Bell*, stanza 105.

12 *Gest*, stanzas 172 and 357.

13 Dobson and Taylor, *Rymes*, p. 161.

14 A Monkbretton charter of 1422 reveals that Robin Hood's Stone had been adopted as a boundary marker (Dobson and Taylor, *Rymes*, pp. 232–4). Northern England might have enjoyed a similar reputation for remoteness, although for them to the south, for the lowland Scots among whom the Robin Hood stories also circulated in the fifteenth century.

15 P. G. Walsh and M. J. Kennedy, eds and trans., *William of Newburgh, The History of English Affairs*, (Warminster: Aris, 1988), p. 75; Richard Muir, *The Lost Villages of Britain* (London: Joseph, 1986), p. 86.

16 http://icg.fas.harvard.edu/-chaucer/canttales/rvt/dialect2.html

17 N. Pronay and J. Cox, eds, *Crowland Chronicle Continuations, 1459–1486* (Gloucester: Sutton, 1986), p. 11.

18 H. Ellis, ed., *The Chronicles of John Hardyng*, (London, 1802), p. 420; Denys Hay, ed., *The Anglica Historia of Polydore Vergil* (London: Camden third series, 74, 1950), p. 11.

19 See A. J. Pollard, 'North, South and Richard III', in Pollard, *The Worlds of Richard III* (Stroud: Tempus, 2001), pp. 45–7, and Pollard, *North-Eastern England*, pp. 26–7 for this paragraph.

20 Pollard, *North-Eastern England*, p. 11; R. B. Dobson, 'Politics and the Church in the Fifteenth-Century North', in A. J. Pollard, ed., *The North of England in the Age of Richard III* (Stroud: Sutton, 1996), p. 10.

21 L. C. Gabel, ed., *The Memoirs of a Renaissance Pope: The Commentaries of Pius II* (London: Allen & Unwin, 1960), p. 35.

22 A. J. L. Winchester, *Harvest of the Hills: Rural Life in Northern England, 1400–1700* (Edinburgh: Edinburgh University Press, 2000), esp. pp. 10–17, 27–9; J. Le Patourel, 'Is Northern History a Subject?', *Northern History*, 12 (1976), 6–8, 12; Pollard, *North-Eastern England*, pp. 397–400; Pollard, *North of England*, pp. x–xiii; Pollard, 'The Characteristics of the Fifteenth-Century North', in J. Appleby and p. Dalton, eds, *Government, Religion and Society in Northern England, 1000–1700* (Stroud: Sutton, 1996), pp. 131–43.

23 A. J. Pollard, 'The North-Eastern Economy and the Agrarian Crisis of 1438–40', *Northern History*, 25 (1989), 88–105; Pollard, *North-Eastern England*, pp. 30–80.

24 R. B. Dobson, *Preserving the Perishable: Contrasting Communities in Medieval England* (Cambridge: Cambridge University Press, 1991); Pollard, 'Characteristics', *passim*; Matthew Davies, *The Merchant Tailors' Company of London: Court Minutes, 1486–1493* (Stamford, Lincs: Paul Watkins, 2000), pp. 32–3. For the hypothesis that the stories originated in the London companies see pp. 159–60.

25 See pp. 91–3.

26 Pollard, *North-Eastern England*, p. 232; Anthony Goodman, *Margery Kempe and her World* (London: Longman, 2002), pp. 135–7, 147–8; Colin Richmond, *The Paston Family in the Fifteenth Century: Fastolf's Will* (Cambridge: Cambridge University Press, 1996), p. 151, and Richmond, *Endings* (Manchester: Manchester University Press, 2000), pp. 134–5.

27 BL, Cotton Julius B.XII, fo 10. An edition of this text is being prepared by Emma Cavell for the Richard III and Yorkist History Trust.

28 Pollard, 'Characteristics', pp. 141–3; Colin Richmond, 'An Outlaw and Some Peasants: The Possible Significance of Robin Hood', *Nottingham Medieval Studies*, 37 (1993), p. 91.

29 *Potter*, stanza 1.

30 *Guy*, stanza 1.

31 *Gest*, stanza 445; see also stanza 329 and *Potter*, stanza 63.

32 *Adam Bell*, stanza 1.

33 M. Y. Offord, ed., *Parlement of the Thre Ages* (London: EETS, original series, 246, 1959), ll. 1–99.

34 F. J. Furnivall, ed., *Early English Meals and Manners* (London, EETS, 32, 1868), pp. 2–3.

35 H. H. Scullard, *Festivals and Ceremonies of the Roman Republic* (London: Thames & Hudson, 1981), pp. 110–11.

36 Chaucer, *Complete Works*, vol. 4, p. 44: 'The Knight's Tale', ll. 639–53. The last three lines were translated by Neville Coghill, *The Canterbury Tales* (Harmondsworth, 1951, p60) as:

> O Month of May, with all thy flowers and green,
> Welcome be thou, o fairest, freshest May,
> Give me thy green in hope of happy day!'

37 Malory, *Works*, pp. 648–50.

38 Dobson and Taylor, *Rymes*, p. 42.

39 Cambridge, Fitzwilliam Museum, MS 74.

40 BL, Add. MS 24098, fo 22b.

41 Martin Cathy, 'May Song', *Because It's There* (Topic Records, 1979, 1995). I owe this reference and the text to Karen Bezella-Bond from an unpublished paper 'Maytime and Revival in Malory's *Morte Darthur*', University of Illinois, 2001.

42 F. J. Furnivall, ed., *Phillip Stubbes' Anatomy of the Abuses in England in Shakespere's Youth* (New Shakespeare Society, 1877–9), p. 147. See also Singman, *Robin Hood*, pp. 94–5.

43 Kathleen Basford, *The Green Man* (Cambridge: D. S. Brewer, 1978), pp. 9–22, esp. 20.

44 See John Matthews, *Robin Hood: Green Lord of the Wildwood* (Glastonbury: Gothic Image, 1993), pp. 2, 35–74; and Maurice Keen, *The Outlaws of Medieval Legend* 2nd edn (London: Routledge, 1977), appendix on 'Supposed Mythological Origin', pp. 219–22.

45 Robert Colls, *Identity of England* (Oxford: Oxford University Press, 2002), pp. 168–271, 300–4; Adam Fox, *Oral and Literate Culture in England, 1500–1700* (Oxford: Clarendon Press, 2000), pp. 213–58.

46 BL, Add. MS 24098, fo 22b.

47 Malory, *Works*, p. 649.

48 Ibid., 673.

49 E. K. Chambers and F. Sidgwick, eds, *Early English Lyrics: Amorous, Divine, Moral and Trivial* (London: Sidgwick & Jackson, 1966), p. 41.

50 William Shakespeare, *As You Like It*, Act V, Scene 4, ll. 200, 202–3.

51 *Gest*, stanza 450. The meaning is ambiguous. It could be in fear of the king; more likely it is for all the authority and power of the king.

52 A. Musson and W. M. Ormrod, *The Evolution of English Justice: Law, Politics and Society in the Fourteenth Century* (London: Macmillan, 1999), p. 170; Schama, *Landscape and Memory*, p. 149; Richmond, 'Outlaw and Some Peasants', pp. 99–101.

4 *Crime, Violence and the Law*

1 *Gest*, stanza 221.

2 For general discussion of the criminal law in late-medieval England see A. Musson and W. M. Ormrod, *The Evolution of English Justice: Law, Politics and Society in the Fourteenth Century* (London: Macmillan, 1999); Edward Powell, 'Law and Justice', in Rosemary Horrox, ed., *Fifteenth-Century Attitudes* (Cambridge: Cambridge University Press, Cambridge, 1994). An earlier version of this chapter was published as A. J. Pollard, 'Idealising Criminality: Robin Hood in the Fifteenth Century', in Rosemary Horrox and Sarah Rees-Jones, eds, *Pragmatic Utopias: Ideals and Communities, 1200–1630* (Cambridge: Cambridge University Press, 2001), pp. 156–73.

3   *Gest*, stanza 377.

4   *Gest*, stanza 366.

5   *Gest*., stanzas 91,121, 172, 357–8, 366; *Monk*, stanza 82.

6   Richard Almond, *Medieval Hunting* (Stroud: Sutton, 2003), pp. 125–42; J.
    Birrell, 'Peasant Deer Poachers in the Medieval Forest', in R. H. Britnell and
    J. Hatcher, eds, *Progress and Problems in Medieval England* (Cambridge:
    Cambridge University Press, 1996), pp. 68–88; Barbara A. Hanawalt, 'Men's
    Games, King's Deer: Poaching in Medieval England', in Hanawalt, '*Of Good
    and Ill Repute': Gender and Social Control in Medieval England* (Oxford: Oxford
    University Press, 1998), 142–55; Nicholas Orme, 'Medieval Hunting: Fact
    and Fancy', in Barbara A. Hanawalt, ed., *Chaucer's England: Literature in Historical
    Context* (Minneapolis, MN: University of Minnesota, 1992), pp. 136–40.

7   David Crook, 'The Records of Forest Eyres in the Public Record Office,
    1179–1670', *Journal of the Society of Archivists*, 17 (1996), pp. 183–93.

8   C. R. Young, *The Royal Forests of Medieval England* (Leicester: Leicester
    University Press, 1979), pp. 149–72.

9   See, for instance, in the second half of the fifteenth century, Bernwood, the
    forest moots of the lordship of Northallerton, the swanimotes of Wyresdale
    and Lonsdale and a surviving forest court roll for Middleham in 1450–1: I.
    M. W. Harvey, 'Bernwood in the Middle Ages', in John Broad and Richard
    Hoyle, eds, *Bernwood: The Life and Afterlife of a Forest* (Preston: Harris Paper Two,
    1997), p. 10; R. C. Shaw, *The Royal Forest of Lancaster* (Preston: Guardian Press,
    1956), pp. 191–6; C. M. Newman, *Late-Medieval Northallerton* (Stamford,
    Lincs.: Paul Watkins, 1999), pp. 39–40; West Riding Archives, DW568.

10 Nottingham, Special Collections, MiL 3/1&2, fo C.xv; note Helen Boulton's
    suggestion that the compiler was William Easingwold, town clerk of
    Nottingham *c.* 1478–1506, who was possibly himself clerk of the forest: H.
    E. Boulton, ed., *The Sherwood Forest Book*, (Nottingham: Thoroton Society,
    record series 23, 1965), p. 12. The book is primarily a set of eighteenth-
    century transcripts of an earlier collection of documents in the National
    Archives.

11 W. Wheater, *Knaresburgh and its Rulers* (Leeds: R. Jackson, 1907), p. 187;
    Broad and Hoyle, *Bernwood*, 7.

12 R. B. Manning, *Hunters and Poachers: A Cultural and Social History of Unlawful
    Hunting in England, 1485–1640* (Oxford: Clarendon Press, 1993), pp. 63–4;
    Crook, 'Forest Eyres', pp. 183–93; H. C. Brentnall, 'Venison trespasses in the
    Reign of Henry VII', *Wiltshire Archaeological and Natural History Society*, 53
    (1949), pp. 191–212, esp. pp. 203–6, 209–11 for presentments in Savernake
    Forest at the same time.

13 J. D. Stagg, ed., *A Calendar of New Forest Documents: The Fifteenth to the Seventeenth
    Centuries* (Winchester: Hampshire Record Society, 5, 1983), pp. 1–29, esp.
    pp. 1–2, 4–5, 7, 11–12, 23–4; National Archives, DL 39/2/20, m15. I am
    grateful to Amanda Richardson for providing me with a transcript of this
    document. The deer taken from both forests were almost all fallow.

14 Stagg, *New Forest Documents*, pp. 3, 22–3; A. J. Pollard, *Richard III and the Princes in the Tower* (Stroud: Sutton, 1991), pp. 145–6; R. E. Horrox and P. W. Hammond, eds., *British Library Harleian Manuscript 433*, 4 vols (Upminster: Richard III Society, 1979–83), i, pp. 185, 243; C. M. Fraser, ed., *Durham Quarter Sessions Rolls, 1471–1625* (Woodbridge: Surtees Society, 194, 1991), p. 25.

15 *Statutes of the Realm*, vol. 1, p. 65.

16 C. Given Wilson, 'Service, Serfdom, and English Labour Legislation, 1350–1500', in Anne Curry and Elizabeth Matthew, eds, *Concepts and Patterns of Service in the Later Middle Ages* (Woodbridge: Boydell & Brewer, 2000), pp. 21–37, esp. 34–5.

17 *Statutes of the Realm*, vol. I, 65; *Rot Parl*, vol. 2, 273.

18 Bertha Putnam, *Proceedings before the Justices of the Peace, Edward III to Richard II* (Cambridge, MA: Ames Foundation, 1938), pp. 404, 411, 413; E. G. Kimball, ed., *The Shropshire Peace Roll, 1400–1414* (Shrewsbury: Shropshire County Council, 1959), pp. 53, 107; Fraser, *Durham Quarter Sessions Rolls*, pp. 41–2, 57, 61; National Archives, JUST 61/8–11. There are few surviving peace or delivery rolls after 1421.

19 Manning, *Hunters and Poachers*, pp. 63–4.

20 Crook, 'Forest Eyres', *passim*; Manning, *Hunters and Poachers*, pp. 63 ff.

21 Charles Ross, *Richard III* (London: Methuen, 1981), p. 149. Edward IV did, however, on behalf of his queen, reprimand the officers of Savernake Forest in 1477 for allowing 'riottous and evil-disposed persones' to hunt therein (Brentnall, 'Venison Trespasses', 198).

22 A. J. Pollard, *North-Eastern England during the Wars of the Roses* (Oxford: Clarendon Press, 1990), pp. 199, 205–6; see also Manning, *Hunters and Poachers*, pp. 15, 64, for similar drives in Savernake Forest and the Weald.

23 Manning, *Hunters and Poachers*, pp. 161–76, 232–5.

24 National Archives KB9 330/27,333/23,334/151,992/95; R. C. E. Hayes, 'Ancient Indictments for the North of England, 1461–1509', in A. J. Pollard, ed., *The North of England in the Age of Richard III* (Stroud: Sutton, 1996), p. 31. See Dobson and Taylor, *Rymes*, pp. 25–7 for further fifteenth-century examples. For the reliability of approvers' appeals see H. Summerson, 'The Criminal Underworld of Medieval England', *Legal History*, 17 (1996), pp. 202–3 and 221, n. 24.

25 V. H. Galbraith, ed., *The Anonimalle Chronicle, 1337 to 1381* (Manchester: Manchester University Press, 1927), p. 152; Rupert Willoughby, 'Sir Adam de Gurdon and the pass of Alton', *The Best of '98* (Winchester: Annual Writers' Conference, 1998), pp. 131–46; M. T. Clanchy, 'Highway Robbery and Trial by Battle in the Hampshire Eyre of 1248', in R. F. Hunnisett and J. B. Post, eds, *Medieval Legal Records Edited in Memory of C. A. F. Meekings* (London: HMSO, 1978), pp. 26–68.

26 *Gest*, stanzas 17–20, 208–17, 375; *Monk*, stanzas 40–41; *Potter*, stanzas 9–17.

27 J. G. Bellamy, 'The Northern Rebellions in the Later Years of Richard II',

Bulletin of the John Rylands Library, 47 (1965), 254–61; Anthony Goodman, *John of Gaunt: The Exercise of Princely Power in Fourteenth Century Europe* (London: Longman, 1992), pp. 331–2.

28   Goodman, *John of Gaunt*, pp. 331–2; Bellamy, 'Northern Rebellions', pp. 254–61; National Archives, SC6/1303/11, E 40/658. Bland, in the Westminster Chronicler's account, is constructed in the same way as the dirty little coward who shot Jesse James in the back.

29   J. C. Holt, *Robin Hood*, 2nd edn (London: Thames & Hudson, 2nd edn, 1989), pp. 58–9.

30   Ibid., p. 150.

31   Pollard, *North-Eastern England*, pp. 171–2; Cynthia J. Neville, *Violence, Custom and Law: The Anglo-Scottish Border Lands in the Later Middle Ages* (Edinburgh: Edinburgh University Press, 1998), pp. 107–11.

32   *Adam Bell*, stanzas 138–40; James Gairdner, ed., *The Historical Collections of a Citizen of London* (London: Camden second series, 5, 1876), p. 214; *Gest*, stanzas 168–7; *Guy*, stanzas 36–41.

33   *Gest*, stanza 257; see also stanza 12.

34   *Guy*, stanza 3. The recurring refrain 'bete and binde' seems to echo the legal formula 'verberaverunt, vulneraverunt et male tractaverunt' used to establish violent assault.

35   *Gest*, stanza 160.

36   *Monk*, stanza 49.

37   *Gest*, stanzas 193–204.

38   *Gest*, stanza 429.

39   *Monk*, stanza 52.

40   *Guy*, stanzas 40–1; Hanawalt, 'Men's Games', p. 153.

41   Peter Coss, 'Aspects of Cultural Diffusion in Medieval England: The Early Romances, Local Society and Robin Hood', *Past and Present*, 108 (1985), pp. 66–79.

42   Richard. W. Kaeuper, *Chivalry and Violence in Medieval Europe* (Oxford: Oxford University Press, 1999), pp. 129–60.

43   P. C. Maddern, *Violence and Social Order: East Anglia, 1422–42* (Oxford: Clarendon Press,1992), pp. 5, 28 (table 2.1), 34 (table 2.3); E. Powell, 'The King's Bench in Shropshire and Staffordshire in 1414', in E. W. Ives and A. H. Manchester eds, *Law, Litigants and the Legal Profession* (Woodbridge: Boydell & Brewer, 1983), p. 97; Powell, *Kingship, Law and Society: Criminal Justice in the Reign of Henry V* (Oxford: Oxford University Press, 1989), pp. 178–80. I have excluded rape from these figures because of the difficulty of definition and because of Robin Hood's own prohibition against harming women.

44   H. Summerson, 'Crime and Society in Medieval Cumberland', *Transactions of the Cumberland and Westmorland Archaeological and Antiquarian Society*, 82 (1982), pp. 111–24; Fraser, *Durham Quarter Sessions*, pp. 47–8; Hayes, 'Ancient Indictments', p. 30.

45   Kimball, *Shropshire Peace Roll*, pp. 53,107; Colin Richmond, 'The Murder of

— *Notes* —

Thomas Dennis', *Common Knowledge*, 2 (1993), 85–98; Fraser, *Durham Quarter Sessions*, 48–9.

46 Hayes, 'Ancient Indictments', pp. 37–42; Fraser, *Durham Quarter Sessions*, pp. 47–8.

47 Nottingham, Special Collections, MiL 3/172, fo Dxii.

48 *Gest*, stanzas 367–9.

49 *Adam Bell*, stanzas 139–40.

50 Manning, *Hunters and Poachers*, pp. 189–95. See also note 6.

51 *Gest*, stanza 222.

52 *Gest*, stanzas 93–124; *Adam Bell*, stanzas 69–79; *Gamelyn*, lines 837–86.

53 Powell, *Kingship, Law and Society*, p. 74; H. M. Jewell, *English Local Administration in the Middle Ages* (Newton Abbot: David and Charles, 1972), pp. 85, 182–97.

54 I. M. W. Harvey, *Jack Cade's Rebellion of 1450* (Oxford: Oxford University Press, 1991), p. 187. A statute of 1445 prohibited the taking of fees for making jury panels. I am grateful to Hannes Kleineke for permission to cite an unpublished paper on under-sheriffs in the fifteenth century.

55 Jewell, *English Local Administration*, p. 199; *Adam Bell*, stanzas 139–40.

56 *Gest*, stanza 326.

57 Powell, *Kingship, Law and Society*, pp. 74–6; I am grateful to Malcolm Mercer for allowing me to consult his unpublished paper, 'Falling Foul of the Law: The Uses and Abuses of the Process of Outlawry in the Fifteenth Century'.

58 *Gest*, stanzas 148, 152, 156, 160, 182, 317–18.

59 S. J. Payling, *Political Society in Lancastrian England: The Greater Gentry of Nottinghamshire* (Oxford: Oxford University Press, 1991), p. 97.

60 *Guy*, stanza 58; *Gest*, stanza 349.

61 Kaeuper, *Chivalry and Violence*, pp. 114–20

62 Maddern, *Violence and the Social Order*, pp. 89, 228–30.

63 Ibid., pp. 154–66.

64 Ibid., pp. 108–9.

65 *Guy*, stanzas 7 and 34

66 Maddern, *Violence and the Social Order*, pp. 108–9.

5 Religion and the Religious

1 *Gest*, stanzas 8–9. But see Colin Richmond, 'An Outlaw and Some Peasants', *Nottingham Medieval Studies*, 37 (1993), p. 97: 'Robin is surely no more a religious enthusiast than he is a lollard . . . He wore his devotion lightly'. Three masses every day before the main meal is, however, somewhat unusual for a layman. I do not think that the passage is a parody of lay piety for the reasons that follow.

2 Dobson and Taylor, *Rymes*, pp. 1–2.

3 *Monk*, stanzas 18–22.

4   Thomas H. Ohlgren, ed., *Medieval Outlaws: Ten Tales in Modern English* (Stroud: Sutton, 1998), pp. 25–6.

5   *Gest*, stanza 10.

6   *Monk*, stanza 180.

7   *Gest*, stanza 441.

8   *Gest*, stanza 193–8.

9   See E. Duffy, *The Stripping of the Altars: Traditional Religion in England, 1400–1580* (New Haven, CT: Yale University Press, 1992), esp. pp. 53–87, 81–5, 131–54.

10 *Gest*, stanza 13.

11 G. R. Owst, *Literature and Pulpit in Late Medieval England*, 2nd edn (Oxford: Basil Blackwell, 1961), pp. 70, 557.

12 *Gest*, stanza 456.

13 *Gest*, stanza 15.

14 See pp. 129–32 for further discussion of this.

15 *Thomas Gascoigne, Loci et libro veritatum* J. E. T. Rogers, ed. , (Oxford: Oxford University Press, 1881), pp. 41–2.

16 *Gest*, stanza 122.

17 Ibid, 216.

18 Ibid, 260.

19 Ibid, 406.

20 *Monk*, esp stanzas 57 and 66.

21 Ibid, 17–23.

22 *Gest*, stanzas 206–51.

23 *Death*, stanza 25.

24 *Gest*, stanzas 86–102. It is possible that this passage, and the belief in the abbey that the knight was 'ferre beyonde the see' (89) indicate that the knight had been on pilgrimage (Peter Coss, 'Aspects of Cultural Diffusion in Medieval England: The Early Romances, Local Society and Robin Hood', *Past and Present*, 108 (1985), pp. 70–1). If so, the story contains another element in which the piety of the laity is contrasted with the avarice of the monks.

25 Chaucer, *Complete Works*, vol 4, *The Canterbury Tales*, pp. 6–7: 'Prologue', ll. 166–207, esp. line 206.

26 Derek Pearsall, 'If heaven be on this earth, it is in cloister or in school' in Rosemary Horrox and Sarah Rees Jones, eds, *Pragmatic Utopias: Ideals and Communities, 1200–1630* (Cambridge: Cambridge University Press, 2001), pp. 11–26; Chaucer, *Complete Works*, vol 4, *The Canterbury Tales*, pp. 167–88.

27 Pearsall, 'If heaven be on this earth', p. 22.

28 I am conscious that this leaves friars unconsidered, especially as Friar Tuck is known to have been the pseudonym of at least one outlaw in the fifteenth century and a character in the surviving play text. He was not central to the cast until the nineteenth century, although the story of 'Robin and the Curtal Friar', recorded after the Reformation, may have originated in the

later middle ages. Exploration of popular attitudes to the friars, the extent to which the stories might have incorporated rivalry between friars and monks, especially Franciscans and Benedictines, and the implications of such lines of inquiry, must wait another day. See Dobson and Taylor, *Rymes*, pp. 40–1, 158–64; Stephen Knight, *Robin Hood: A Mythic Biography* (Ithaca, NY: Cornell University Press, 2003), pp. 11, 32–3, 40–1.

29 *Gest*, stanzas 253–4, 259.

30 *Gest*, stanza 91; *Monk*, stanzas 19, 40, 44, 66.

31 James G. Clark, 'Selling the Holy Places: Monastic Efforts to Win Back the People in Fifteenth-century England', in Tim Thornton, ed., *Social Attitudes and Political Structures in the Fifteenth Century* (Stroud: Sutton, 2000), p. 13.

32 William Page, ed., *The Victoria History of the County of Hertford*, vol. 2 (1908), pp. 478–81; Page, ed., *Victoria History of the County of Suffolk*, vol. 2 (1907), pp. 61–3; E. Miller, 'Medieval York', in P. M. Tillott, ed., *The Victoria History of the County of York* (Oxford: Oxford University Press, 1961), pp. 38–40, 68–9, 81–2; R. S. Gottfried, *Bury St Edmunds and the Urban Crisis, 1290–1539* (Princeton, NJ: Princeton University Press, 1982), pp. 167–72, 215–36; D. M. Knowles, *The Religious Houses in England and Wales*, vol. 1 (Cambridge: Cambridge University Press, 1948), pp. 263–9.

33 Margaret Bonney, *Lordship and the Urban Community: Durham and its Overlords, 1250–1540* (Cambridge: Cambridge University Press, 1990), pp. 229–35; R. B. Dobson, *Durham Priory, 1400–1450* (London: Cambridge University Press, 1973), pp. 49–51; G. Rosser, *Medieval Westminster; 1200–1540* (Oxford: Clarendon Press, 1989), pp. 244–8.

34 I am grateful to Anne DeWindt for providing me with a copy in advance of publication of chapter 3 of her and Edwin DeWindt's important forthcoming study of medieval Ramsey.

35 D. Knowles and R. N. Hadcock, *Medieval Religious Houses* (London: Longman, 1953), p. 359.

36 Christopher Allmand, *Henry V* (London: Methuen, 1992), pp. 277–9.

37 Clark, 'Selling the Holy Places', pp. 13–32; John McKinnell, *The Sequence of the Sacrament at Durham* (Middlesbrough: Papers in North Eastern History, 8, 1998), *passim*.

38 *Gest*, stanzas 219 and 227.

39 S. Raban, *Mortmain Legislation and the English Church, 1279–1500* (Cambridge: Cambridge University Press, 1982), esp. pp. 1–28, 71.

40 Ibid, pp. 75–77, 86–8.

41 Ibid, pp. 92–100, 127, 167–76.

42 Ibid, pp. 44, 54–5; J. R. Maddicott, 'The Birth and Setting of the Ballads of Robin Hood', *EHR*, 93 (1978), 276–99, reprinted in Stephen Knight, ed., *Robin Hood: An Anthology of Scholarship and Criticism* (Woodbridge: Boydell and Brewer, 1999), esp. pp. 239–42.

43 Owst, *Literature and Pulpit*, pp. 232–3, 285.

44 Duffy, *Stripping of the Altars*, Part 1, *passim*; Christopher Haigh, 'Anticlericalism

and the English Reformation', *History*, 68 (1983), 391–407, reprinted in Haigh, *The English Reformation Revised* (Cambridge: Cambridge University Press, 1987); Christopher Harper–Bill, *The Pre-Reformation Church in England, 1400–1530* (London: Longman,1989), *passim*, and Harper-Bill, 'The English Church and English Religion after the Black Death', in Mark Ormrod and Philip Lindley, eds, *The Black Death in England* (Stamford, Lincs.: Paul Watkins, 1996), pp. 79–124.

45 Dobson and Taylor, *Rymes*, p.31, where, it is suggested, the abbot is no more than a personification of the well-worn theme of clerical avarice. Claire Etty has drawn my attention to the role of the abbey as the crown's bank.

46 Anthony Fletcher and Diarmaid MacCulloch, *Tudor Rebellions*, 4th edn (London: Longman, 1997), pp. 36–9; C. S. L. Davies, 'Popular Religion and the Pilgrimage of Grace', in A. Fletcher and J. Stevenson, eds, *Order and Disorder in Early Modern England* (Cambridge: Cambridge University Press, 1985); R. W. Hoyle, *The Pilgrimage of Grace and the Politics of the 1530s* (Oxford: Oxford University Press, 2001), pp. 282–342, for Norfolk and Henry; M. Bateson, 'Aske's Examination', *EHR*, 5 (1890), pp. 561–2; A. G. Dickens, 'Robert Parkyn's Narrative of the Reformation', *EHR*, 62 (1947), p. 65.

47 D. M. Loades, *Revolution in Religion: The English Reformation, 1530–1570* (Cardiff: University of Wales Press, 1992); Hoyle, *Pilgrimage*, pp. 41–52 for the most recent and sceptical assessment of the religious conservatism of the north; D. M. Knowles, *The Religious Orders in England*, vol. 3 (Cambridge: Cambridge University Press, 1959), pp. 268–90, and Duffy, *Stripping of the Altars*, pp. 383–6, on the commissions of 1535.

48 A. G. Dickens, 'The Shape of Anti-Clericalism and the English Reformation', in E. I. Kouri and T. Scott, eds, *Politics and Society in Western Europe* (London: Macmillan, 1987), reprinted in Dickens, *Late-Medieval Monasticism and the Reformation* (London: Hambledon, 1994); Ethan Shagan, *Popular Politics and the English Reformation* (Cambridge: Cambridge University Press, 2003), pp. 162–96, for the spoliation of Hailes Abbey and pp. 193–4 for Marshall.

49 Shagan, *Popular Politics*, pp. 135–40; R. N. Swanson, 'Problems of the Priesthood in Pre-Reformation England', *EHR*, 105 (1990), 845–69; Katherine L. French, *The People of the Parish: Community Life in a Late-medieval English Diocese* (Philadelphia, PA: University of Pennsylvania Press, 2001), ch. 3 and pp. 335, 37–8, 42–3 and 158–60 for the assertive laity of Taunton and Dunster; B. Kumin, *The Shaping of a Community: The Rise and Reformation of the English Parish c. 1400–1560* (Aldershot: Scolar Press, 1996), esp. pp. 128–40.

50 James D. Stokes, 'Robin Hood and the Churchwardens in Yeovil', *Medieval and Renaissance Drama in England*, 3 (1986), p. 5; J. H. Betty, *The Suppression of the Monasteries in the West Country* (Stroud: Sutton, 1989), pp. 142, 183.

51 Sean Field, 'Devotion, Discontent, and the Henrician Reformation: The Evidence of the Robin Hood Stories', *Journal of British Studies*, 41 (2002),

6–22, goes over some of the same ground as this chapter. However, his objective is to demonstrate that 'the points of contact between Henry [VIII]'s [religious] positions and those reflected in the Robin Hood stories are evident' (p. 21). Although the conceit is pleasing, I'm not entirely convinced that 'Henry VIII might well have envisioned himself as the Robin Hood of the Reformation' (p. 22). The significance of the stories lies not in explaining Henry VIII's own religious outlook, surely shaped by other influences, but in throwing light on popular attitudes towards the monasteries in the early sixteenth century.

6 *Fellowship and Fraternity*

1 *Gest*, stanza 14.
2 *Gest*, stanza 7.
3 E.g. Colin Richmond, 'An Outlaw and Some Peasants: The Possible Significance of Robin Hood', *Nottingham Medieval Studies*, 37 (1993), p. 94: the knight proves to be a 'good chap'.
4 I am grateful to Felicity Riddy for pointing this out to me.
5 I am grateful to Maurice Keen for his comment on this.
6 *PL*, iv, p. 155.
7 Chaucer, *Complete Works*, vol. 4, p. 311, 'Pardoner's Tale', lines 672–3; p. 372, 'Summoner's Tale', l. 1740.
8 Ibid., p. 12, 'Prologue', ll. 395–7.
9 Ibid., pp. 337–8, 'Wife of Bath's Prologue', ll. 615–18.
10 G. R. Owst, *Literature and Pulpit in Late Medieval England*, 2nd edn (Oxford: Basil Blackwell, 1961), pp. 46–7, from a fifteenth-century homily preserved in Gloucester Cathedral Library.
11 *PL*, ii, no. 169, p. 206; Jeffrey L. Singman, *Robin Hood: The Shaping of the Legend* (Westport, CT: Greenwood, 1998), p. 37.
12 *PL*, iv, p. 155; v, no. 740, p. 65.
13 *PL*, iv, p. 137; *Monk*, stanza 46.
14 A. B. Cobban, 'Colleges and Halls', in J. Catto and T. A. R. Evans, eds, *The History of the University of Oxford, vol. II, Later Medieval England* (Oxford: Oxford University Press, 1992), pp. 581–633; Cobban, *The Medieval English Universities: Oxford and Cambridge to c.1500* (Aldershot: Scolar Press, 1988), pp. 112–28.
15 Margaret S. Blayney, ed., *A Familiar Dialogue of the Friend and the Fellow* (Oxford: EETS, 295, 1989), p. 1. I am grateful to Craig Taylor for bringing this work to my attention.
16 E. W. Ives, 'The Common Lawyers', in C. H. Clough, ed., *Profession, Vocation and Culture in Later Medieval England* (Liverpool: Liverpool University Press, 1982); D. S. Bland, *Early Records of Furnival's Inn, Edited from a Middle Temple Manuscript* (Newcastle upon Tyne: Department of Extra Mural Studies, King's College, Newcastle, 1957), pp. 26, 40. I have Linda Clark to thank for this second reference.

17 *Gest*, stanza 229.

18 *Potter*, stanza 24.

19 *PL*, iv, no. 610, pp. 191–5; no. 613, pp. 197–200.

20 *PL*, ii, nos 217–19, pp. 271–3.

21 *PL*, v, no. 724, p. 45; no. 730, p. 55; no. 736, p. 61.

22 *PL*, v, no. 839, pp. 194–5. Is there possibly a joke intended by Hastings signing himself as a 'felaw' in a letter written at Nottingham?

23 *PL*, iv, no. 533, p. 61.

24 J. G. Nichols, ed., *Chronicle of the Rebellion in Lincolnshire, 1470* (Camden, 1839), p. 12.

25 J. Bruce, ed., *The Historie of the Arrivall of Edward IV* (Camden, 1830), pp. 18–20.

26 *PL*, v, no. 781, p. 111.

27 Malory, *Works*, pp. 78, 650.

28 A. Ayton, 'Military Service and the Development of the Robin Hood Legend in the Fourteenth Century', *Nottingham Medieval Studies*, 36 (1992), 126–47, esp. p. 146; K. DeVries, 'Longbow Archery and the Earliest Robin Hood Legends', in T. Hahn, ed., *Robin Hood in Popular Culture: Violence, Transgression, and Justice* (Cambridge: D. S. Brewer, 2000), pp. 53–4.

29 *Gest*, stanzas 130–4, 309–21.

30 One should note, too, that throughout the stories Robin is never 'captain', as one would expect of a military retinue, as clearly John Paston III was of the thirty men he commanded at Caister in 1469. Robin Hood, on the contrary, is always master. He is master, just as the head of the company of the Staple, another fellowship, was addressed as 'my maister the Maire' (Alison Hanham, ed., *The Cely Letters, 1472–1488* (Oxford: EETS, 273, 1975), no. 224, p. 224.

31 *Gest*, stanzas 95 and 97: it may be noted that the knight leaves the forest accompanied only by Little John, but arrives the following day with a full meyny.

32 *Gest*, stanza 262.

33 *Gest*, stanza 23.

34 J. C. Holt, *Robin Hood*, 2nd edn (London: Thames & Hudson, 1989), p. 150; *PL*, ii, no. 126, p. 155; Payn also referred to Fastolf's meyny of soldiers who during the rising withdrew to the Tower. On 2 April 1473 Sir John informed his brother John that 'off beyond the see, it is seyd that the Frense Kyngs host hath kyllyd the Erle of Armenak and all hys myrry mene'. Is this a joking reference to Robin Hood's merry men/meyny? Sir John seems to have had Robin Hood on his mind that month, for two weeks later, writing to say that one of his servants had deserted him, he again joked about Robin Hood (*PL*, v, no. 830, pp. 179–80; no. 833, p. 185).

35 *PL*, ii, no. 241, p. 308.

36 *Gest*, stanza 170. Little John had earlier been retained by the sheriff for the same fee. This is another example of how the story of 'Little John and the Sheriff' parodies gentility.

37 *Potter*, stanzas 1–21.

38 *Potter*, stanzas 24–5.

39 *Potter*, stanzas 15, 17, 24, 27, 28.

40 *Monk*, stanzas 1–14.

41 *Monk*, stanza 15.

42 *Monk.*, stanza 77.

43 *Monk*, stanzas 79–81

44 *Potter*, stanza 22; *Monk*, stanza 87.

45 Nottingham, Special Collections, MiL 3/1&2. The full text of the relevant part of the forester's oath runs: 'all wayfes and strayes founden in thyn office yu shal saise and then present to the officers assigned therefore (by) the kynges counsel, the lieu tenaunt, the maistre forester, thy fellows and thy nawne trewly kepe'. It would seem that in the transcription a word or two was lost between 'thy nawne' (thine own) and 'trewly kepe'.

46 The complex story, interrupted by the interlude of 'Little John and the Sheriff', runs from stanzas 1 to 143, and 206 to 280.

47 *Gest*, stanzas 22–3.

48 *Gest*, stanza 269.

49 *Gest*, stanza 81.

50 *Gest*, stanzas 310–18.

51 *Gest*, stanza 314.

52 *Gest*, stanza 316.

53 There is now a substantial literature on fraternities and guilds. Of these see in particular, V. R. Bainbridge, *Gilds in the Medieval Countryside: Social and Religious Change in Cambridgeshire, c.1350–1558* (Woodbridge: Boydell & Brewer, 1996); David J. F. Crouch, *Piety, Fraternity and Power: Religious Gilds in Late-medieval Yorkshire, 1389–1547* (Woodbridge: Boydell & Brewer, 2000); Ken Farnhill, *Guilds and the Parish Community in Late Medieval East Anglia, 1470–1550* (Woodbridge: Boydell & Brewer, 2001); Barbara A. Hanawalt and Ben R. McCree, 'The Guilds of *Homo Prudens* in Late-medieval England', *Continuity and Change*, 7 (1992), 163–79; J. Mattingly, 'The Medieval Parish Guilds of Cornwall', *Journal of the Royal Institute of Cornwall*, new series 10 (1989), 290–329; A. G. Rosser, 'Communities of Parish and Guild in the Late Middle Ages', in S. J. Wright, ed., *Parish, Church and People: Local Studies in Lay Religion, 1350–1750* (London; Hutchinson, 1988); A. G. Rosser, 'Going to the Fraternity Feast: Commensuality and Social Relations in Late-medieval England', *Journal of British Studies*, 33 (1994), 430–46; M. Rubin, *Charity and Community in Medieval Cambridge* (Cambridge: Cambridge University Press, 1991).

54 Thomas H. Ohlgren, The "Marchaunt" of Sherwood: Mercantile Ideology in *A Gest of Robyn Hode*', in Hahn, ed., *Robin Hood in Popular Culture* (Cambridge: D. S. Brewer, 2000) pp. 175–90.

55 M. Grant, ed., *Records of the Gild of St George in Norwich, 1389–1547* (Norwich: Norfolk Records Society, 9, 1937), pp. 29–30, 37. One might note that there were no sisters in the forest fraternity.

56 G. Templeman, ed., *Records of Holy Trinity Guild, Coventry* (Stratford-upon-Avon: Dugdale Society, 1944), pp. 25, 38–45.

57 A. H. Thomas and I. D. Thornley, eds, *Great Chronicle of London* (London, 1938), pp. 246, 323.

58 M. Davies, ed., *The Merchant Tailors' Company of London: Court Minutes, 1486–1493* (Stamford, Lincs.: Paul Watkins for Richard III and Yorkist History Trust, 2000) p. 158.

59 L. Lyell and F. D. Watney, eds, *Acts of Court of the Mercers Company, 1453–1527* (Cambridge: Cambridge University Press, 1936), p. 305.

60 Hanham, *Cely Letters*, p. 224.

61 M. D. Harris, ed. *The Coventry Leet Book. AD 1450–1555*, (EETS, 4 vols, 1907) p. 743; J. McKinnell, *The Sequence of the Sacrament at Durham* (Middlesbrough: Papers in North Eastern History, 8, 1998), p. 5.

62 Malory, *Works*, p. 699; H. E. L. Collins, *The Order of the Garter, 1348–1461: Chivalry and Politics in Late Medieval England* (Oxford: Clarendon Press, 2000), pp. 15–33, esp. pp. 23, 25–6; M. H. Keen, *Chivalry* (New Haven, CT: Yale University Press, 1984), pp. 179–99, esp. pp. 181–5.

63 *Gest*, stanza 27.

64 Ohlgren, '"Marchaunt" of Sherwood', pp. 187–8.

7 *Authority and the Social Order*

1 Julian Barnes, *England, England* (London: Picador, 1999), pp. 149–50, 223, 248.

2 E. J. Hobsbawm, *Bandits* (Harmondsworth: Penguin, 1970), pp. 13–15, 34–5, 44–48.

3 Ibid., pp. 46–8, 111–14.

4 R. H. Hilton, 'The Origins of Robin Hood', *Past and Present*, 14 (1958), 30–44, reprinted in Hilton, ed., *Peasants, Knights and Heretics: Studies in Medieval English Social History* (Cambridge: Cambridge University Press, 1976).

5 Maurice Keen, *The Outlaws of Medieval Legend* (London: Routledge, 1961, ch.11, 'The Outlaw Ballad as an Expression of Peasant Discontent', esp. pp. 148–59, and also Keen, 'Robin Hood – Peasant or Gentleman?', *Past and Present*, 19 (1961), 7–15, reprinted in Hilton, *Peasants, Knights and Heretics*.

6 J. C. Holt, 'The Origins and Audience of the Ballads of Robin Hood', *Past and Present*, 18 (1960), 89–110, reprinted in Hilton, *Peasant, Knights and Heretics*, and in Holt, *Robin Hood* (London: Thames & Hudson, 1982 and 1989), esp. pp. 109–58.

7 Maurice Keen, *Outlaws of Medieval Legend*, 2nd edn (London: Routledge, 1977), Introduction, pp. xiii–xv.

8 See pp. 22–4.

9 R. Tardiff, 'The "Mistery" of Robin Hood: A New Social Context for the Texts', in S. Knight and S. N. Mukherjee, eds, *Words and Worlds: Studies in the Social Role of Verbal Culture*. (Sydney: Association for Studies in Society and Culture, 1983) pp. 130–45.

10 Thomas H. Ohlgren, 'The "Marchaunt" of Sherwood: Mercantile Ideology in *A Gest of Robyn Hode*', in Thomas Hahn, ed., *Robin Hood in Popular Culture* (Cambridge: Cambridge University Press, 2000), pp. 175–90, and Ohlgren, 'Edwardus redivivus in *A Gest of Robyn Hode*', *Journal of English and Germanic Philology*, 99 (2000), pp. 19–25.

11 See pp. 149–51.

12 C. C. Dyer, 'Were There any Capitalists in Fifteenth-Century England?', in Jennifer Kermode, ed., *Enterprise and Individuals in Fifteenth-Century England* (Stroud: Sutton, 1991), p. 16; M. R. McCarthy and C. M. Brooks, *Medieval Pottery in Britain, AD 900–1600* (Leicester: Leicester University Press, 1988), pp. 75–7; I. M. W. Harvey, 'Bernwood in the Middle Ages', in John Broad and Richard Hoyle, eds, *Bernwood: The Life and Afterlife of a Forest* (Preston: Harris Paper Two, 1997), p. 4.

13 Colin Richmond, 'An Outlaw and Some Peasants: The Possible Significance of Robin Hood', *Nottingham Medieval Studies*, 37 (1993), 90–101; one might note, too, that being courteous in the texts often has a specific meaning of showing respect, and not necessarily possessing the attributes of gentility.

14 Stephen Knight, *Robin Hood: A Mythic Biography* (Ithaca, NY: Cornell University Press, 2003), pp. 208–10.

15 P. R. Coss, 'Aspects of Cultural Diffusion in Medieval England: The Early Romances, Local Society and Robin Hood', *Past and Present*, 108 (1985), pp. 74–6; Keen, *Outlaws of Medieval Legend*, pp. 145–73, modified by his comments in the preface to the 2nd edition in 1977, which still leave an emphasis on the context of the late-fourteenth century.

16 L. A. Coote, *Prophecy and Public Affairs in Later Medieval England* (York: York Medieval Press, 2000), p. 166; P. Strohm, *England's Empty Throne: Usurpation and the Language of Legitimation, 1399–1422* (New Haven, CT: Yale University Press, 1998), pp. 1–31.

17 Dobson and Taylor, *Rymes*, pp. 71–2.

18 Thomas Ohlgren, 'Richard Call, the Pastons, and the Manuscript Context of Robin Hood and the Potter (Cambridge: Cambridge University Press, University Library Ee.4.35.1)', *Nottingham Medieval Studies*, 45 (2001), 210–33. For a suggested alternative provenance for a later date see Dobson and Taylor, *Rymes*, pp. 123–4. The text was not printed until 1795.

19 *PL*, v, no. 833, pp. 185. He was not one of the men John asked his brother to take into his service, or recommend to others, on 5 October 1469. But the text surely reveals he was one of those in the fellowship which garrisoned Caister in 1468–9, and was thereafter taken on as a stable groom as well as an entertainer (*PL*, v, no. 735, p. 60); Colin Richmond, *The Paston Family in the Fifteenth Century: Fastolf's Will* (Cambridge: Cambridge University Press, 1996), pp. 192–209.

20 John Marshall, '"goon in-to Bernysdale": The Trail of the Paston Robin Hood Play', *Leeds Studies in English*, 29 (1998), 185–217.

21 George Unwin, *The Gilds and Companies of London*, 4th edn (London: Cass, 1963), p. 125. There were other factors, including the extension of taxation and bringing them under the scope of mortmain legislation.

22 See p. 128.

23 Unwin, *Gilds*, pp. 224–31; Matthew Davies, 'The Tailors of London: Corporate Charity in the Late-Medieval Town', in R. E. Archer, ed., *Crown, Government and People in the Fifteenth Century* (Stroud: Sutton, 1995), pp. 175–6, and Davies, ed., *The Merchant Tailors' Company of London: Court Minutes, 1486–1493* (Stamford, Lincs.: Paul Watkins for Richard III and Yorkist History Trust, 2000), pp. 232–4.

24 See pp. 150–1.

25 F. J. Furnivall, ed., *The Gild of St Mary, Lichfield* (London: EETS, 114, 1920 for 1914), pp. 11–15; Barbara A. Hanawalt and Ben R. McRee, 'The Guilds of *Homo Prudens* in Late Medieval England', *Continuity and Change*, 7 (1992), pp. 163–79.

26 Chris Given Wilson, 'Service, Serfdom and English Labour Legislation, 1350–1500', in Anne Curry and Elizabeth Matthew, eds, *Concepts and Patterns of Service in the Later Middle Ages* (Woodbridge: Boydell & Brewer, 2000), p. 36; M. K. McIntosh, *Controlling Misbehavior in England, 1370–1600* (Cambridge: Cambridge University Press, 1998), pp. 54–197, and McIntosh, 'Local Change and Community Control in England, 1465–1500', *Huntingdon Library Quarterly*, 49 (1986), 219–242.

27 Nottingham, Special Collections, MS 72/2, p. 98.

28 *Monk*, stanza 88.

29 D. G. Shaw, *The Creation of a Community: The City of Wells in the Middle Ages* (Oxford: Oxford University Press, 1993), pp. 94–6.

30 R. Hutton, *The Rise and Fall of Merry England: The Ritual Year 1400–1700* (Oxford: Oxford University Press, 1994), pp. 31–3; Jeffrey L. Singman, *Robin Hood: The Shaping of the Legend* (Westport, CT: Greenwood, 1998), pp. 61–104; John Wasson, 'The St George and Robin Hood Plays in Devon', *Medieval English Theatre*, 2 (1980), 67–8; Eamon Duffy, *The Voices of Morebath: Reformation and Rebellion in an English Village* (New Haven, CT: Yale University Press, 2001), pp. 26–7: a Young Men's Store, but no record of Robin Hood revels; James D. Stokes, 'Robin Hood and the Churchwardens in Yeovil', *Medieval and Renaissance Drama in England*, 3 (1986), p. 7.

31 A. H. Thompson, *The History of the Hospital and the New College of the Annunciation of St Mary in the Newarke, Leicester* (Leicester: Leicestershire Archaeological Society, 1937), p. 156. I am grateful to Carole Rawcliffe for drawing this evidence to my attention.

32 See note 29.

33 T. Serel, *Historical Notes on the Church of Saint Cuthbert in Wells* (Wells, 1875), p. 48. Katherine L. French, *The People of the Parish: Community Life in a Late-medieval English Diocese* (Philadelphia, PA: University of Pennsylvania Press, 2001), p. 131, suggests that Robin Hood was linked with the dancing girls in

performance, but the text quoted by Serel, and now missing, leaves open the possibility that dancing girls were a separate fund-raising custom. For the association between Robin Hood and dancing girls, linked with the apocryphal St Penket, see Colin Richmond, ' A William Sponne Deed at Towcester: Further Light on the Cult of St Penket', in Richmond, *The Penket Papers* (Gloucester: Sutton, 1986), pp. 35–9.

34 J. Marshall, '"Comyth in Robyn Hode": Paying and Playing the Outlaw at Croscombe', *Leeds Studies in English*, 32 (2001), 345–68.

35 Singman, *Robin Hood*, p. 93.

36 Ibid., pp. 144–57; Hanawalt and McRee, 'Guilds of *Homo Prudens*', p. 163; French, *People of the Parish*, pp. 130–2.

37 *Gest*, stanza 154.

38 Ibid., stanzas 153–179.

39 Ibid., stanza 190.

40 F. J. Furnivall, ed., *Early English Meals and Manners*, (London: EETS, original series, 32, 1868). The work opens with an encounter between the narrator and the masterless young man who is poaching in the forest in the merry month of May. He coaches the young man so that he can find a master and enter service. In the *Gest*, the story is reversed: the cook is persuaded to abandon his master and go to the greenwood.

41 *Gest*, stanza 144.

42 See , pp. 9–11, 163.

43 Singman, *Robin Hood*, pp. 68, 92–3, 119–20, 160–1, 187–92, 193–6. On 17 April 1518, Francis Bothwell excused himself from the part of Little John 'for to mak sportis and jocosities' in Edinburgh because of other pressing business (p. 188). The 'Records of Early Scottish Drama' project, currently being undertaken at the University of Southampton, will add to our knowledge of Robin Hood in Scotland.

44 Singman, *Robin Hood*, p. 81.

45 The text, given in full by Holt, *Robin Hood*, pp. 148–9, is printed in *Collections for a History of Staffordshire* (Stafford: William Salt Archaeological Society, new series, x, Part 1, 1907), pp. 80–1. The 'abbot of Marram' is perhaps the equivalent of the Scottish abbot of unreason. One may note that twenty-first-century football fans have their own camaraderie and codes that enable them, with tongue similarly in cheek perhaps, to describe their fights with rivals as 'good cheer'.

46 Barbara A. Hanawalt, '"The Childe of Bristowe" and the Making of Middle Classs Adolescence', in Hanawalt, *'Of Good and Ill Repute': Gender and Social Conftrol in Medieval England* (Oxford: Oxford University Press, 1998), pp. 178–201, esp. pp. 180, 190, 193.

47 A. H. Thomas and I. D. Thornley, eds, *Great Chronicle of London* (London, 1938), p. 319. It is worth noting, pace Ohlgren, '"Marchaunt" of Sherwood', the disparaging comment of the author, an eminent Draper of the City of London, that Robin Hood was of 'the common fame of the people'.

48 G. R. Owst, *Literature and Pulpit in Late Medieval England,* 2nd edn (Oxford: Basil Blackwell, 1961), pp. 45–6. See pp. 135–6.

49 R. H. Hilton, *Bond Men Made Free: Medieval Peasant Movements and the English Rising of 1381* (London: Temple Smith, 1973), pp. 214–16. Also see above, pp. 138–40.

50 M. Mate, 'The Economic and Social Roots of Medieval Popular Rebellions: Sussex in 1450–51', *Economic History Review,* 45 (1992), p. 664; R. F. Hunnisett, 'Treason by Words', *Sussex Notes and Queries,* 14 (1954–7), p. 119.

51 L. R. Poos, *A Rural Society after the Black Death: Essex, 1350–1525* (Cambridge: Cambridge University Press, 1991), pp. 277–8. Poos argues that this is a case of personal anticlericalism, but the text suggests that the fellows with which the parishioner associated were lollards.

52 P. C. Maddern, *Violence and Social Order: East Anglia, 1422–42* (Oxford: Clarendon Press, 1992), pp. 108–9. Also see above, pp. 174–5.

53 S. Justice, *Writing and Rebellion: England in 1381* (Berkeley, CA: University of California Press, 1994), pp. 12–66, offers the fullest discussion of these texts.

54 See for example Hilton, *Bond Men Made Free,* pp. 176–85; C. C. Dyer, 'The Social and Economic Background to the Rural Revolt of 1381', in R. H. Hilton and T. H. Ashton, eds, *The English Rising of 1381* (Cambridge: Cambridge University Press, 1984), pp. 15–22; I. M. W. Harvey, *Cade's Rebellion of 1450* (Oxford: University Press, 1991), pp. 102–11; R. A. Griffiths, *The Reign of Henry VI: The Exercise of Royal Power, 1422–1461* (London: Benn, 1981), pp. 619–22 on 1450; Poos, *Rural Society,* pp. 239–40, 258–9, 261; I. Arthurson, 'The Rising of 1497 – A Revolt of the Peasantry?', in J. T. Rosenthal and C. F. Richmond, eds, *People, Politics and Community in the Later Middle Ages* (Gloucester: Sutton, 1987), pp. 1–18, on 1497; R. W. Hoyle, *The Pilgrimage of Grace and the Politics of the 1530s* (Oxford: Oxford University Press, 2001), esp. pp. 423–47 on 1536.

55 E. H. Shagan, *Popular Politics and the English Reformation* (Cambridge: Cambridge University Press, 2003), p. 19. For discussion of popular politics in the century before the Reformation see ibid., pp. 1–25; I. M. W. Harvey, 'Was there Popular Politics in Fifteenth-century England?', in R. H. Britnell and A. J. Pollard, eds, *The McFarlane Legacy* (Stroud: Sutton, 1995); A. J. Pollard, *Late-Medieval England, 1399–1509* (London: Longman, 2000), pp. 253–5, and further references therein.

56 D. Starkey, 'Which Age of Reform?', in C. Coleman and D. Starkey, eds, *Revolution Reassessed: Revisions in the History of Tudor Government and Administration* (Oxford: Clarendon Press, 1986), pp. 13–28. See also Keith Wrightson's discussion of Edmund Dudley's The Tree of the Commonwealth emphasising the communitarian ideal in which everyone, accepting their degree or place in the hierarchy, contributed to and shared in the benefits of society (*Earthly Necessities: Economic Lives in Early Modern Britain, 1470–1750* (Harmondsworth: Penguin, 2000), pp. 27–9).

57 M. A. Hicks, *English Political Culture in the Fifteenth Century* (London:Routledge, 2002), pp. 194–202.

58 J. L. Watts, 'Ideas, Principles and Politics', in A. J. Pollard, ed.,*The Wars of the Roses* (London: Macmillan, 1995); Watts, '"A New Ffundatation of is Crowne": Monarchy in the Age of Henry VII', in B. Thompson, ed.,*The Reign of Henry VII* (Stamford, Lincs.: Paul Watkins, 1996); 'Bishop Russell's Parliamentary Sermons of 1483–84', in G. W. Bernard and S. J. Gunn, eds, *Authority and Consent in Tudor England: Essays Presented to C. S. L. Davies* (Aldershot: Ashgate, 2002), esp. p. 51 for the democratic implications. See also Watts, 'Politics, War and Public Life', in Richard Marks and Paul Williamson, eds, *Gothic: Art for England, 1400–1547* (London: V&A, 2003), pp. 35–6, in which he refers to a 'mass public with an interest in its own political, moral and spiritual health'.

59 Harvey, *Cade's Rebellion*, p. 189.

60 M. L. Kekewich and others, eds, *The Politics of Fifteenth-century England: John Vale's Book*, (Stroud: Sutton for the Richard III and Yorkist History Trust, 1995), pp. 208–15, 218–21.

61 This paragraph draws upon John Marshall, 'Comyth in Robyn Hode', *passim*, and a private communication from Ian Arthurson, who generously provided me with details of villagers of Croscombe fined in the aftermath of the rebellions of 1497.

62 Ian Arthurson, *The Perkin Warbeck Conspiracy, 1491–1499* (Stroud: Sutton, 1994), pp. 181–8; Arthurson, *Cornwall Marches On! Keskerdh Kernow 500*, ed. S. Parker (Truro, 1998), pp. 22–9; Shaw, *Wells*, p. 205.

63 A. F. Pollard, ed., *The Reign of Henry VII from Contemporary Sources*, 3 vols (London, 1913), vol. 1, p. 153.

64 See M. L. Bush, 'The Risings of the Commons in England, 1381–1549', in J. Denton, ed., *Orders and Hierarchies in Late Medieval and Renaissance Europe* (London: Macmillan, 1999). Montgomery Bohna, 'Armed Force and Civic Legitimacy in Jack Cade's Revolt, 1450', *EHR*, 118 (2003), 563–82, appeared too late for me to incorporate. His argument that the revolt was an expression of political violence grounded in a customary right to bear arms as a way of registering political opinion is clearly germane to my discussion.

8 *History and Memory*

1 *Gest*, stanza 2.

2 J. C. Bellamy, *Robin Hood: An Historical Inquiry* (London: Croom Helm, 1985).

3 J. R. Maddicott, 'The Birth and Setting of the Ballads of Robin Hood', *EHR*, 93 (1978), 276–99.

4 Thomas H. Ohlgren, 'Edwardus redivivus in *A Gest of Robyn Hode*', *Journal of English and German Philology*, 99 (2000), pp. 5–9. The hypothesis depends on interpreting 'he is' in stanza 89 of the *Gest*, 'The knight is ferre beyonde the

see/In Englonde he is ryght', as meaning England 'his' right, or England's, i.e. Edward III's, right. Dobson and Taylor (*Rymes*, p. 85, n. 6.), however, gloss the words as an error for 'is his'. The knight's right, in this reading, would be his estates, which the abbot of St Mary's hopes to acquire because the knight is aboad and cannot redeem his mortgage.

5 Andrew Ayton, 'Military Service and the Development of the Robin Hood Legend in the Fourteenth Century', *Nottingham Medieval Studies*, 36 (1992), 126–47.

6 See pp. 126–8.

7 R. B. Dobson, 'Robin Hood: The Genesis of a Popular Hero', in Thomas Hahn, ed., *Robin Hood in Popular Culture* (Cambridge: D. S. Brewer, 2000), p. 69.

8 Dobson and Taylor, *Rymes*, p. xxxiii.

9 J. C. Holt inclined, in his second edition, to an earlier formation and evolution of the legend from 1261–2: *Robin Hood* (London: Thames & Hudson, 1989), pp. 191–2.

10 For which see Dobson and Taylor, *Rymes*, pp. 36–65; Holt, *Robin Hood*, pp. 159–86; Stephen Knight, *Robin Hood: A Complete Study of the English Outlaw* (Oxford: Basil Blackwell, 1994), pp. 115–201.

11 Adam Fox, *Oral and Literate Culture in England, 1500–1700* (Oxford: Clarendon Press, 2000), pp. 1–49.

12 Adam Fox, 'Remembering the Past in Early Modern England: Oral and Written Traditions', *TRHS*, sixth series, 9 (1999), pp. 255–6.

13 Dobson and Taylor, *Rymes*, p. 5;, eds Stephen Knight and Thomas H. Ohlgren, *Robin Hood and Other Outlaw Tales* (Kalamazoo, MI: Western Michigan University Press, 1997), p. 27.

14 I owe this suggestion to David Ditchburn. One might note how the invention of Robin as the dispossessed Anglo–Saxon earl of Huntingdon mirrors the manner in which Alfred the Great invented an Anglo–Saxon past for the kingdom of Wessex (Sarah Foot, 'Remembering, Forgetting and Inventing: Attitudes to the Past in England at the End of the First Viking Age', *TRHS*, sixth series, 9 (1999), pp. 197–200.

15 See Thorlac Turville–Petre, *England and Nation: Language, Literature and National Identity, 1290–1340* (Oxford: Clarendon Press, 1996), p. 28.

16 Dobson and Taylor, *Rymes*, p. 254.

17 Ibid., pp. 251–4, esp.stanza 24, p. 254; *Gest*, stanza 456. For a discussion of the likely authorship and circulation of the Outlaw Song see J. R. Maddicott, 'Poems of Social Protest in Early-Fourteenth Century England', in W. M. Ormrod, ed., *England in the Fourteenth Century* (Woodbridge: Boydell and Brewer, 1986), pp. 130–44.

18 E. L. G. Stones, 'The Folvilles of Ashby-Folville, Leicestershire, and their Associates in Crime, 1326–41', *TRHS*, fifth series, 7 (1957), p. 131.

19 Barbara A. Hanawalt, 'Ballads and Bandits: Fourteenth-Century Outlaws and the Robin Hood Poems', in Hanawalt, ed., *Chaucer's England: Literature in*

Historical Context (Minneapolis, MN: University of Minnesota Press, 1992), pp. 154–75.

20 V. H. Galbraith, ed., *The Anonimalle Chronicle, 1337–1381,* (Manchester: Manchester University Press, 1927), p. 152; Antonia Gransden, *Historical Writing in England, II, c.1307 to the Early Sixteenth Century* (London: Routledge, 1982), pp. 111–12. Also see above, p. 92–3.

21 A. Musson and W. M. Ormrod, *The Evolution of English Justice: Law, Politics and Society in the Fourteenth Century* (London: Macmillan, 1994), pp. 36–40.

22 See , pp. 102–3.

23 Maurice Keen, *The Outlaws of Medieval Legend,* 2nd edn (London: Routledge, 1977), p. 78; Knight and Ohlgren, *Robin Hood and Other Outlaw Tales,* p. 185.

24 Dobson and Taylor, *Rymes,* pp. 258–9.

25 Keen, *Outlaws of Medieval Legend,* pp. 130–1; Peter Coss, 'Aspects of Cultural Diffusion in Medieval England: The Early Romances, Local Society and Robin Hood', *Past and Present,* 108 (1985), passim. Also see above pp. 171–3.

26 Rupert Willoughby, 'Sir Adam de Gurdon and the Pass of Alton', *The Best of '98* (Winchester: Annual Writers' Conference, 1998), pp. 134–6. Also see above pp. 92–3.

27 Knight and Ohlgren, *Robin Hood and Other Outlaw Tales,* pp. 25–6; Keen, *Outlaws of Medieval Legend,* p. 177.

28 *Thomas Wright's Political Songs of England,* reissued with an introduction by Peter Coss (Cambridge: Cambridge University Press for the Royal Historical Society, 1996), ll. 126–37, p. 329.

29 See p. 128. In the *Simony* the porter turns them away; in the *Gest* he welcomes them.

30 P. R. Coss, 'Sir Geoffrey de Langley and the Crisis of the Knightly Class in Thirteenth-Century England', *Past and Present,* 68 (1975), pp. 5–17, 24–5, 33–4; D. A. Carpenter, 'Was There a Crisis of the Knightly Class in the Thirteenth Century?', *EHR,* 95 (1980), 721–52, esp. p. 724.

31 Local memory, as the histories of these disputes show, was long. How widely knowledge of them spread elsewhere is hard to tell. See pp. 123–4.

32 See p. 95.

33 *Thomas Wright's Political Songs,* p. 198; but one might doubt whether anyone alive then could remember the victories.

34 Katherine L. French, *The People of the Parish: Community Life in a Late-medieval English Diocese* (Philadelphia, PA: University of Pennsylvania Press, 2001), p. 54. See pp. 45–67 passim for a discussion of written and oral memory at parochial level.

35 J. Smyth, *The Lives of the Berkeleys,* ed. Sir John Maclean, 3 vols (Gloucester, 1883–5), vol 2, pp. 114–15.

36 See for example Oscar de Ville, 'The Deyvilles and the Genesis of the Robin Hood Legend', *Nottingham Medieval Studies,* 43 (1999), pp. 90–109.

37 *Thomas Wright's Political Songs,* pp. 149–52; J. Stephenson, ed., *The Townley*

Mysteries (Woodbridge: Surtees Society, 3, 1836), pp. 98–9. It has recently been proposed that the composition should be dated c.1500 (P. J. P. Goldberg, 'Performing the Word of God', in D. Wood, ed., *Life and Thought in the Northern Church* (Studies in Church History, Subsidia 12, Woodbridge: Boydell & Brewster, 1999).

38 Knight and Ohlgren, *Robin Hood and Other Outlaw Tales*, p. 27.

39 Turville-Petre, *England the Nation*, p. 96 (my modernisation).

40 Ibid, pp. 91–100.

41 This paragraph draws on Ohlgren, 'Edwardus redivivus', pp. 4–5, 10–12, in which detailed references are given. My argument here and later is not based on the ambiguity of the second line of stanza 89 of the *Gest*, for which see note 4, and its possible specific reference to military service under Edward III, but on Edward III's known reputation. Elements of *Edward and the Hermit* are recycled in the story of 'Little John and the Sheriff'.

42 One can reconstruct from the narrative that the king was on the throne for at least twenty-four years. This is based on the statements that the king dwelt at Nottingham for six months and more when trying to track Robin down (*Gest*, stanza 365), that Robin was at court for fifteen months (stanza 433) and that Robin lived for a further twenty two years after he fled the court (stanza 450). All numbers fit the rhyming scheme, and should not, perhaps, be taken literally, but the impression is given that the king reigned for an exceptionally long time. Edward III reigned for fifty years. Neither Edward II nor Edward IV for more than twenty-two. Edward I, who reigned for thirty-five years, is, for reasons I suggest later, too early.

43 D. A. L. Morgan, 'The Political After-Life of Edward III: The Apotheosis of a Warmonger', *EHR*, (1997), p. 861. The following paragraphs draw heavily on this important assessment of Edward's late-medieval reputation.

44 F. W. D. Brie, ed., *The Brut or the Chronicles of England* (Oxford, EETS, old series, 196, 1908), vol. 2, p. 334.

45 *Gest*, stanzas 410–11.

46 Morgan, 'Political After-Life', p. 873.

47 The words are those of Musson and Ormrod, *Evolution of English Justice*, p. 163, in their characterisation of the 'didactic discourse' on fourteenth-century justice.

48 *Great Chronicle*, p. 338. The context is an obituary notice on Henry VII, who, in comparison with Edward III, in the authors' opinion, did not quite make the grade. See Morgan, 'Political After-Life', p. 858.

49 *Gest*, stanzas 436 and 438.

50 *Gest*, stanza 250.

51 *The Brut*, vol. 2, p. 334. Here lies another reason for supposing that the central thread of the *Gest* began to take shape in the last quarter of the fourteenth century.

52 *Adam Bell*, stanzas 165–73.

53 Musson and Ormrod, *Evolution of English Justice*, pp. 169–70.

54 Fox, 'Remembering the Past', pp. 239–40.
55 See pp. 180–2.
56 *Monk*, stanza 84.
57 *Monk*, stanza, 88.
58 *Gest*, stanzas 384–5. Mark Ormrod has pointed out in an unpublished paper that the *Gest* contains much that is reverential of the king, his office and his authority. This, it seems to me, makes the ultimate challenge to and rejection of royal authority all the more significant.
59 *Gest*, stanza 391.
60 *Gest*, stanza 417.
61 *Gest*, stanza 449.
62 *Gest*, stanza 324.
63 Thomas More, *Utopia*, ed. Edward Surz (New Haven, CT: University of Yale Press, 1964), p.148.

9 *Farewell to Merry England*

1 *Henry VI, Part 2*, Act IV, Scene 2. Holland's words, almost verbatim, were reportedly spoken in a Sussex pub in 1450 (see pp. 176–7).
2 *Gest*, stanzas 145 and 445; *Monk*, stanza 1.
3 *Gest*, stanza 437.
4 *Monk*, stanza 86.
5 *Gest*, stanza 306.
6 *Gest*, stanza 198.
7 *Gest*, stanza 361. The text deploys part of the standard formula of a title deed.
8 E. Shagan, *Popular Politics and the English Reformation* (Cambridge: Cambridge University Press, 2003), pp. 239–66.
9 For an evocative and empathetic account of how one parish, Morebath, which did resist as much as it could, resigned itself to revolutionary times see Eamon Duffy, *The Voices of Morebath: Reformation and Rebellion in an English Village* (New Haven, CT: University of Yale Press, 2001).
10 Jeffrey L. Singman, *Robin Hood: The Shaping of the Legend* (Westport, CT: Greenwood, 1998), p. 70; James D. Stokes, 'Robin Hood and the Churchwardens in Yeovil', *Medieval and Renaissance Drama in England*, 3 (1986), p. 6.
11 Singman, *Robin Hood*, p. 70; see also R. Hutton, *The Rise and Fall of Merry England: The Ritual Year, 1400–1700* (Oxford: Oxford University Press, 1994), pp. 111–152, esp. pp. 143 ff, but note also his suggestion, p. 67, that by the mid-1520s the popularity of the Robin Hood theme in May Games was waning all over the West Midlands and the Thames basin.
12 Dobson and Taylor, *Rymes*, pp. 46–53.
13 Julian Barnes, *England, England* (London: Picador, 1999), p. 146.

BIBLIOGRAPHY

Allmand, C. T., *Henry V* (London: Methuen, 1992).

Almond, R. L, *Medieval Hunting* (Stroud: Sutton, 2003).

Almond, R. L. and A. J. Pollard, 'The Yeomanry of Robin Hood and Social Terminology in Fifteenth-century England', *Past and Present*, 170 (2001), 52–77.

Arber, E., ed., *Hugh Latimer, Seven Sermons before Edward VI* (London: Murray, 1869).

Arthurson, I., 'The Rising of 1497 – A Revolt of the Peasantry?', in J. T. Rosenthal and C. F. Richmond, eds, *People, Politics and Community in the Later Middle Ages* (Gloucester: Sutton, 1987), 1–18.

——, *The Perkin Warbeck Conspiracy, 1491–1499* (Stroud: Sutton, 1994).

——, '"as able we be to depose him" . . . Rebellion in the South West, 1497' in *Cornwall Marches On! Keskerdh Kernow 500*, ed. S. Parker (Truro: 1998), 22–8.

Ayton, A., 'Military Service and the Development of the Robin Hood Legend in the Fourteenth Century', *Nottingham Medieval Studies*, 36 (1992), 126–47.

Baillie-Grohman, W. A. and F. Baillie-Grohman, eds, *The Master of Game* (London, 1909).

Bainbridge, V. R., *Gilds in the Medieval Countryside: Social and Religious Change in Cambridgeshire, c.1350–1558* (Woodbridge, Boydell & Brewer, 1996).

Barker, B. A., 'The Claxtons: A North-Eastern Gentry Family in the Fourteenth and Fifteenth Centuries', unpublished PhD thesis, University of Teesside, 2003.

Barnes, J., *England, England* (London: Picador, 1999).

Basford, K., *The Green Man* (Cambridge: D. S. Brewer, 1978).

Bateson, M., 'Aske's Examination', *EHR*, 5 (1890), 550–73.

Bellamy, J. G., 'The Northern Rebellions in the Later Years of Richard II', *Bulletin of the John Rylands Library*, 47 (1965), 254–61.

——, *Robin Hood: An Historical Inquiry* (London: Croom Helm, 1985).

Betty, J. H., *The Suppression of the Monasteries in the West Country* (Stroud: Sutton, 1989).

Birrell, J., 'The Forest Economy of the Honour of Tutbury in the Fourteenth and Fifteenth Centuries', *University of Birmingham Historical Journal*, 8 (1962), 114–34.

——, 'Peasant Deer Poachers in the Medieval Forest', in R. H. Britnell and J. Hatcher (eds), *Progress and Problems in Medieval England* (Cambridge: Cambridge University Press, 1996).

Bland, D. S., *Early Records of Furnival's Inn, Edited from a Middle Temple Manuscript*, (Newcastle upon Tyne: Department of Extra Mural Studies, King's College, Newcastle, 1957).

Blayney, M. S., ed., *A Familiar Dialogue of the Friend and the Fellow* (Oxford: EETS, 295, 1989).

Bohna, M., 'Armed Force and Civic Legitimacy in Jack Cade's Revolt, 1450', *EHR*, 118 (2003), 563–82.

Bonney, M., *Lordship and the Urban Community: Durham and its Overlords, 1250–1540* (Cambridge: Cambridge University Press, 1990).

Boulton, H. E., ed., *The Sherwood Forest Book* (Nottingham: Thoroton Society, record series 23, 1965).

Brentnall, H. C., 'Venison Trespasses in the Reign of Henry VII', *Wiltshire Archaeological and Natural History Society*, 53 (1949), 191–212.

Brie, F. W. D, ed., *The Brut or the Chronicles of England* (Oxford: EETS, old series, 196, 1908).

Britnell, R. H., *The Closing of the Middle Ages? England, 1471–1529* (Oxford: Blackwell, 1995).

——, *The Commercialisation of English Society, 1000–1500*, 2nd edn (Manchester University Press, 1996).

Broad, J. and R. Hoyle, eds, *Bernwood: The Life and Afterlife of a Forest* (Preston: Harris Paper Two, 1997).

Bruce, J., ed., *Historie of the Arrivall of Edward IV* (Camden, 1830).

Bumpus, F., 'The "Middling Sort" in the Lordship of Blakemere, Shropshire, c.1380–c. 1420', in T. Thornton, ed., *Social Attitudes and Political Structures in the Fifteenth Century* (Stroud: Sutton, 2000).

Bush, M. L. 'The Risings of the Commons in England, 1381–1549', in J. Denton, ed., *Orders and Hierarchies in Late Medieval and Renaissance Europe* (London: Macmillan, 1999).

Carpenter, D. A., 'Was There a Crisis of the Knightly Class in the Thirteenth Century?', *EHR*, 95 (1980), 721–52.

Chambers, E. K. and F. Sidgwick, eds, *Early English Lyrics: Amorous, Divine, Moral and Trivial* (London: Sidgwick & Jackson, 1966).

Clanchy, M. T., 'Highway Robbery and Trial by Battle in the Hampshire Eyre of 1248', in R. F. Hunnisett and J. B. Post, eds, *Medieval Legal Records Edited in Memory of C. A. F. Meekings* (London: HMSO, 1978).

Clark, J. G., 'Selling the Holy Places: Monastic Efforts to Win Back the People in Fifteenth-century England', in Tim Thornton, ed., *Social Attitudes and Political Structures in the Fifteenth Century* (Stroud: Sutton, 2000).

Clay, J. W., ed., *North Country Wills*, (Durham: Surtees Society, 117, 1908).

Cobban, A. B., *The Medieval English Universities: Oxford and Cambridge to c.1500* (Aldershot: Scolar Press, 1988).

——, 'Colleges and Halls', in J. Catto and T .A. R. Evans, eds, *The History of the University of Oxford, vol. II, Later Medieval England* (Oxford: Oxford, University Press, 1992).

Collins, H. E. L., *The Order of the Garter, 1348–1461: Chivalry and Politics in Late Medieval England* (Oxford: Clarendon Press, 2000).

Colls, R., *Identity of England* (Oxford: Oxford University Press, 2002).

— Bibliography —

Coote, L. A., *Prophecy and Public Affairs in Later Medieval England* (York: York Medieval Press, 2000).

Corrie, G. E., ed., *Sermons by Hugh Latimer*, 2 vols (Cambridge: Parker Society, 1844–5).

Coss, P. R., 'Sir Geoffrey de Langley and the Crisis of the Knightly Class in Thirteenth-Century England', *Past and Present*, 68 (1975), 3–37.

——, 'Aspects of Cultural Diffusion in Medieval England: The Early Romances, Local Society and Robin Hood', *Past and Present*, 108 (1985), 66–79.

Crawford, A., ed., *The Household Books of John Howard, Duke of Norfolk, 1462–71, 1481–3* (Stroud: Sutton for Richard III and Yorkist History Trust, 1992).

Crook, D., 'Some Further Evidence Concerning the Dating of the Origins of the Legend of Robin Hood', *EHR*, 99 (1984), 530–4.

——, 'The Sheriff of Nottingham and the Robin Hood Stories: The Genesis of the Legend?', in P. R. Coss and S. D. Lloyd, eds, *Thirteenth Century England*, vol. 2 (Woodbridge: Boydell & Brewer, 1988).

——, 'The Records of Forest Eyres in the Public Record Office, 1179–1670', *Journal of the Society of Archivists*, 17 (1996), 183–93.

Crouch, D. J. F., *Piety, Fraternity and Power: Religious Gilds in Late-medieval Yorkshire, 1389–1547*, (Woodbridge, Boydell & Brewer, 2000).

Cummins, J., *The Hound and the Hawk: The Art of Medieval Hunting* (London: Phoenix, 1988).

Davies, C. S. L., 'Popular Religion and the Pilgrimage of Grace', in A. Fletcher and J. Stevenson, eds, *Order and Disorder in Early Modern England* (Cambridge: Cambridge University Press, 1985).

Davies, M. P., 'The Tailors of London and their Guild, c.1300–1500', unpublished D. Phil. thesis, University of Oxford, 1994.

——, 'The Tailors of London: Corporate Charity in the Late-Medieval Town', in R. E. Archer, ed., *Crown, Government and People in the Fifteenth Century* (Stroud: Sutton, 1995).

——, ed., *The Merchant Tailors' Company of London: Court Minutes, 1486–1493* (Stamford, Lincs.: Paul Watkins for Richard III and Yorkist History Trust, 2000).

Davies, N., *The Isles: A History of Britain* (London: Macmillan, 1999).

D'Evelyn, C., ed., *Peter Idley's Instructions to his Son* (Oxford: Oxford, University Press, 1935).

DeVille, O. 'The Deyvilles and the Genesis of the Robin Hood Legend', *Nottingham Medieval Studies*, 43 (1999), 90–109.

DeVries, K., 'Longbow Archery and the Earliest Robin Hood Legends', in T. Hahn, ed., *Robin Hood in Popular Culture: Violence, Transgression, and Justice* (Cambridge: D. S. Brewer, 2000).

DeWindt, A., 'Local Government in a Small Town', *Albion*, 23 (1991), 627–54.

Dickens, A. G., 'Robert Parkyn's Narrative of the Reformation', *EHR*, 62 (1947), 58–83.

——, 'The Shape of Anti-Clericalism and the English Reformation', in E. I. Kouri and T. Scott, eds, *Politics and Society in Western Europe* (London: Macmillan,

1987), reprinted in Dickens, *Late-Medieval Monasticism and the Reformation* (London: Hambledon, 1994).

Dobson, R. B., *Durham Priory, 1400–1450* (London: Cambridge University Press, 1973).

——, *Preserving the Perishable: Contrasting Communities in Medieval England* (Cambridge: Cambridge University Press, 1991).

——, 'Politics and the Church in the Fifteenth-Century North', in A. J. Pollard, ed., *The North of England in the Age of Richard III* (Stroud: Sutton, 1996).

——, 'Robin Hood: The Genesis of a Popular Hero', in T. Hahn, ed., *Robin Hood in Popular Culture* (Cambridge: D. S. Brewer, 2000).

Dobson, R. B. and J. Taylor, 'Robin Hood of Barnsdale: A Fellow Thou has Long Sought', *Northern History*, 19 (1983), 210–20.

——, *Rymes of Robyn Hood: An Introduction to the English Outlaw*, 3rd edn (Stroud: Sutton, 1997).

Drury, J. L., 'Early Settlement in Stanhope Park, Weardale, *c.*1406–79', *Archaeologia Aeliana*, 4 (1976), 139–49.

Duffield, G. E., ed., *The Works of William Tyndale* (Appleford, Berks: Marcham Manor Press, 1964).

Duffy, E., *The Stripping of the Altars: Traditional Religion in England, 1400–1580* (New Haven, CT: Yale University Press, 1992).

——, *The Voices of Morebath: Reformation and Rebellion in an English Village* (New Haven, CT: Yale University Press, 2001).

Dyer, C. C., 'The Social and Economic Background to the Rural Revolt of 1381', in R. H. Hilton and T. H. Ashton, eds, *The English Rising of 1381* (Cambridge: Cambridge University Press, 1984).

——, 'Were There any Capitalists in Fifteenth-Century England?', in Jennifer Kermode, ed., *Enterprise and Individuals in Fifteenth-Century England* (Stroud: Sutton, 1991).

——, *Making a Living in the Middle Ages: The People of Britain, 850–1520* (New Haven, CT: Yale University Press, 2002).

Ellis, H., ed., *The Chronicles of John Hardyng* (London: 1802).

Farnhill, K., *Guilds and the Parish Community in Late Medieval East Anglia, 1470–1550* (Woodbridge: Boydell & Brewer, 2001).

Field, S., 'Devotion, Discontent, and the Henrician Reformation: The Evidence of the Robin Hood Stories', *Journal of British Studies*, 41 (2002), 6–22.

Fletcher, A. J. and D. MacCulloch, *Tudor Rebellions*, 4th edn (London: Longman, 1997).

Foot, S., 'Remembering, Forgetting and Inventing: Attitudes to the Past in England at the End of the First Viking Age', *TRHS*, sixth series, 9 (1999), 185–200.

Fortescue, J., *On the Laws and Governance of England*, ed. S. J. Lockwood (Cambridge: Cambridge University Press, 1997).

Fox, A., 'Remembering the Past in Early Modern England: Oral and Written Traditions', *TRHS*, sixth series, 9, (1999), 233–56.

—— *Oral and Literate Culture in England, 1500–1700* (Oxford, University Press, 2000).

Fraser, C. M., ed., *Durham Quarter Sessions Rolls, 1471–1625* (Newcastle upon Tyne: Surtees Society, 194, 1991).

French, K. L., *The People of the Parish: Community Life in a Late-medieval English Diocese* (Philadelphia, PA: University of Pennsylvania Press, 2001).

Furnivall, F. J., ed., *Early English Meals and Manners* (London: EETS, original series, 32, 1868).

——, ed., *Phillip Stubbes' Anatomy of the Abuses in England in Shakespere's Youth* (New Shakespeare Society, 1877–9.

——, ed., *The Gild of St Mary, Lichfield*, (London: EETS, 114 1920 for 1914).

Gabel, L. C., ed., *The Memoirs of a Renaissance Pope: The Commentaries of Pius II* (London: Allen & Unwin, 1960).

Gairdner, J., ed., *The Historical Collections of a Citizen of London* (London: Camden second series, 5, 1876).

——, ed., *The Paston Letters*, 6 vols (London, 1904).

Galbraith, V. H., ed. *The Anonimalle Chronicle, 1337 to 1381* (Manchester: Manchester University Press, 1927).

Given Wilson, C., 'Service, Serfdom and English Labour Legislation, 1350–1500', in A. E. Curry and E. Matthew, eds, *Concepts and Patterns of Service in the Later Middle Ages* (Woodbridge: Boydell & Brewer, 2000).

Goheen, R., 'Peasant Politics? Village Community and the Crown in Fifteenth-Century England', *American History Review*, 96 (1991), 46–62.

Goldberg, P. J. P., 'Performing the Word of God', in D. Wood, ed., *Life and Thought in the Northern Church* (Studies in Church History, Subsidia 12, Woodbridge: Boydell & Brewer, 1999).

Goodman, A. E., *John of Gaunt: The Exercise of Princely Power in Fourteenth Century Europe* (London: Longman, 1992).

——, *Margery Kempe and her World* (London: Longman, 2002).

Gottfried, R. S., *Bury St Edmunds and the Urban Crisis, 1290–1539* (Princeton: NJ: Princeton University Press, 1982).

Gransden, A., *Historical Writing in England, II, c.1307 to the Early Sixteenth Century* (London: Routledge, 1982).

Grant, M., ed., *Records of the Gild of St George in Norwich, 1389–1547* (Norwich: Norfolk Records Society, 9, 1937).

Gray, D., 'The Robin Hood Poems', *Poetica*, 18 (1984), 1–18.

Greatorex, V., 'Robin Hood: Birth of a Legend', *Medieval History Magazine*, 4 (2003).

Griffiths, R. A., *The Reign of Henry VI: The Exercise of Royal Power, 1422–1461* (London: Benn, 1981).

Haigh, C., 'Anticlericalism and the English Reformation', *History*, 68 (1983), 391–407.

Hall, E., *Chronicle* (1809).

Hanawalt, B. A., 'Ballads and Bandits: Fourteenth-Century Outlaws and the

Robin Hood Poems', in Hanawalt, ed., *Chaucer's England: Literature in Historical Context* (Minneapolis, MN: University of Minnesota Press, 1992).

——, 'Men's Games, King's Deer: Poaching in Medieval England', in Hanawalt, *'Of Good and Ill Repute': Gender and Social Control in Medieval England* (Oxford: Oxford University Press, 1998).

——, '"The Childe of Bristowe" and the Making of Middle Class Adolescence', in Hanawalt, *'Of Good and Ill Repute'*.

Hanawalt, B. A. and B. R. McRee, 'The Guilds of *Homo Prudens* in Late-medieval England', *Continuity and Change*, 7 (1992), 163–79.

Hanham, A., ed., *The Cely Letters, 1472–1488* (Oxford: EETS, 273, 1975).

Harper-Bill, C., *The Pre-Reformation Church in England, 1400–1530* (London: Longman, 1989).

——, 'The English Church and English Religion after the Black Death', in Mark Ormrod and Philip Lindley, eds, *The Black Death in England* (Stamford, Lincs.: Paul Watkins, 1996).

Harvey, I. M. W., *Cade's Rebellion of 1450* (Oxford: Oxford University Press, 1991).

——, 'Was there Popular Politics in Fifteenth-century England?', in R. H. Britnell and A. J. Pollard, eds, *The McFarlane Legacy* (Stroud: Sutton, 1995).

——, 'Bernwood in the Middle Ages', in J. Broad and R. Hoyle, eds., *Bernwood: The Life and Afterlife of a Forest* (Preston: Harris Paper Two, 1997).

Hatcher, J., 'The Great Slump of the Mid-Fifteenth Century', in R. H. Britnell and J. Hatcher, eds, *Progress and Problems in Medieval England* (Cambridge: Cambridge University Press, 1996).

Hay, D., ed., *The Anglica Historia of Polydore Vergil* (London: Camden third series, 74, 1950).

Hayes, R. C. E., 'Ancient Indictments for the North of England, 1461–1509', in A. J. Pollard, ed., *The North of England in the Age of Richard III* (Stroud: Sutton, 1996).

Hicks, M. A., *English Political Culture in the Fifteenth Century* (London: Routledge, 2002).

Hilton, R. H., 'The Origins of Robin Hood', *Past and Present*, 14 (1958), 30–44.

——, *Bond Men Made Free: Medieval Peasant Movements and the English Rising of 1381* (London: Temple Smith, 1973).

——, ed., *Peasants, Knights and Heretics: Studies in Medieval English Social History* (Cambridge: Cambridge University Press, 1976).

Hobsbawm, E. J., *Bandits* (Harmondsworth: Penguin, 1970).

Holt, J. C., 'The Origins and Audience of the Ballads of Robin Hood', *Past and Present*, 18 (1960), 89–110.

——, *Robin Hood*, 2nd edn (London: Thames & Hudson, 1982).

——, 'The Origins of the Legend', in K. Carpenter, ed., *Robin Hood: The Many Faces of that Celebrated English Outlaw* (Oldenberg: BIS, 1995).

Horrox, R. E. and P. W. Hammond, eds, *British Library Harleian Manuscript 433*, 4 vols (Upminster: Richard III Society, 1979–83).

Hoyle, R. W., *The Pilgrimage of Grace and the Politics of the 1530s* (Oxford: Oxford University Press, 2001).

Hunnisett, R. F., 'Treason by Words', *Sussex Notes and Queries*, 14 (1954–7), 116–20.

Hutton, R., *The Rise and Fall of Merry England: The Ritual Year 1400–1700* (Oxford: Oxford University Press, 1994).

Ives, I. W., 'The Common Lawyers', in C. H. Clough, ed., *Profession, Vocation and Culture in Later Medieval England* (Liverpool: Liverpool University Press, 1982).

Jamieson, T. H., ed., *The Shyp of Folys of the Worlde* (London, 1874).

Jewell, H. M., *English Local Administration in the Middle Ages* (Newton Abbot: David and Charles, 1972).

Jones, M. and S. Walker, eds, 'Private Indentures for Life Service in Peace and War, 1278–1476', in *Camden Miscellany*, 32 (London: Royal Historical Society, 1994).

Justice, S., *Writing and Rebellion: England in 1381* (Berkeley, University of California Press, 1994).

Kaeuper, R. W., 'An Historian's Reading of the Tale of Gamelyn', *Medium Aevium*, 52 (1983), 51–62.

——, *Chivalry and Violence in Medieval Europe* (Oxford: Oxford, University Press, 1999).

Keen, M. H., 'Robin Hood – Peasant or Gentleman?', *Past and Present*, 19 (1961), 7–15.

——, *The Outlaws of Medieval Legend*, 2nd edn (London: Routledge, 1977).

——, *Chivalry* (New Haven, CT: Yale University Press, 1984).

Kekewich, M. L. and others, eds, *The Politics of Fifteenth-century England: John Vale's Book* (Stroud: Sutton for the Richard III and Yorkist History Trust, 1995).

Kimball, E. G., ed., *The Shropshire Peace Roll, 1400–1414* (Shrewsbury: Shropshire County Council, 1959).

Kingsford, C.L., ed., *The Stonor Letters and Papers* (London: Camden third series, 29, 1919).

Knight, S., *Robin Hood: A Complete Study of the English Outlaw* (Oxford: Basil Blackwell, 1994).

——, *Robin Hood: A Mythic Biography* (Ithaca, NY: Cornell University Press, 2003).

Knight, S. and T. Ohlgren, eds, *Robin Hood and Other Outlaw Tales* (Kalamazoo, MI: Western Michigan University Press, 1997).

Knowles, D. M., *The Religious Orders in England*, 3 vols (Cambridge: Cambridge University Press, 1948–59).

Knowles, D. M. and R. N. Hadcock, *Medieval Religious Houses* (London: Longman, 1953).

Kumin, B., *The Shaping of a Community: The Rise and Reformation of the English Parish, c. 1400–1560* (Aldershot: Scolar Press, 1996).

Le Patourel, L., 'Is Northern History a Subject?', *Northern History*, 12 (1976) pp. 1–16.

Loades, D. M., *Revolution in Religion: The English Reformation, 1530–1570* (Cardiff: University of Wales Press, 1992).

Lyell, L. and F. D. Watney, eds, *Acts of Court of the Mercers Company, 1453–1527* (Cambridge: Cambridge University Press, 1936).

McCarthy, M. R. and C. M. Brooks, *Medieval Pottery in Britain, AD 900–1600* (Leicester: Leicester University Press, 1988).

McFarlane, A., *The Origins of English Individualism* (Oxford: Blackwell, 1976).

McIntosh, M. K., 'Local Change and Community Control in England, 1465–1500', *Huntingdon Library Quarterly*, 49 (1986), 219–242.

——, *Controlling Misbehavior in England, 1370–1600* (Cambridge: Cambridge University Press, 1998).

McKinnell, J., *The Sequence of the Sacrament at Durham* (Middlesbrough: Papers in North Eastern History, 8, 1998).

Maddern, P. C., *Violence and Social Order: East Anglia, 1422–42* (Oxford: Clarendon Press, 1992).

Maddicott, J. R., 'The Birth and Setting of the Ballads of Robin Hood', *EHR*, 93 (1978), 276–99.

——, 'Poems of Social Protest in Early-Fourteenth Century England', in W. M. Ormrod, ed., *England in the Fourteenth Century* (Woodbridge: Boydell & Brewer, 1986).

Malory, T., *Works*, ed. E. Vinaver, 2nd edn (Oxford: Clarendon Press, 1971).

Manning, R. B., *Hunters and Poachers: A Cultural and Social History of Unlawful Hunting in England, 1485–1640* (Oxford: Clarendon Press, 1993).

Marshall, J. '"goon in-to Bernysdale": The Trail of the Paston Robin Hood Play', *Leeds Studies in English*, 29 (1998), 185–217.

——, 'Playing the Game: Reconstructing *Robin Hood and the Sheriff of Nottingham*', in T. Hahn, ed., *Robin Hood in Popular Culture* (Cambridge: D. S. Brewer, 2000, 161–74).

——, '"Comyth in Robyn Hode": Paying and Playing the Outlaw at Croscombe', *Leeds Studies in English*, 32 (2001), 345–68.

Mate, M. E., 'The Economic and Social Roots of Medieval Popular Rebellions: Sussex in 1450–51', *Economic History Review*, 45 (1992), 661–76.

Matthews, J., *Robin Hood: Green Lord of the Wildwood* (Glastonbury: Gothic Image, 1993).

Mattingly, J., 'The Medieval Parish Guilds of Cornwall', *Journal of the Royal Institute of Cornwall*, new series 10 (1989), 290–329.

Miller, E., 'Medieval York', in P. M. Tillott, ed., *The Victoria History of the County of York* (Oxford: Oxford, University Press, 1961).

More, T., *Utopia*, ed. Edward Surz (New Haven, CT: University of Yale Press, 1964).

Morgan, D. A. L., 'The Political After-Life of Edward III: The Apotheosis of a Warmonger', *EHR*, 112 (1997), 856–81.

Muir, R., *The Lost Villages of Britain*, (London: Joseph, 1986).

Musson, A. and W. M. Ormrod, *The Evolution of English Justice: Law, Politics and Society in the Fourteenth Century* (London: Macmillan, 1999).

Myers, A. R., ed., *The Household of Edward IV: The Black Book and Ordinances of 1478* (Manchester: Manchester, University Press, 1959).

Neville, C. J., *Violence, Custom and Law: The Anglo-Scottish Border Lands in the Later Middle Ages* (Edinburgh: Edinburgh University Press, 1998).

Newman, C. M., *Late-Medieval Northallerton* (Stamford, Lincs.: Paul Watkins, 1999).

Nichols, J. D., ed., *Chronicle of the Rebellion in Lincolnshire, 1470* (Camden, 1839).

Offord, M. Y., ed., *Parlement of the Thre Ages*, (London: EETS, 246, 1959).

Ohlgren, T. H., ed., *Medieval Outlaws: Ten Tales In Modern English* (Stroud: Sutton, 1998).

——, 'Edwardus redivivus in *A Gest of Robyn Hode*', *Journal of English and Germanic Philology*, 99 (2000), 1–29.

——, 'The "Marchaunt" of Sherwood: Mercantile Ideology in *A Gest of Robyn Hode*', in T. Hahn, ed., *Robin Hood in Popular Culture* (Cambridge: D. S. Brewer, 2000).

——, 'Richard Call, the Pastons and the Manuscript Context of Robin Hood and the Potter (Cambridge, University Library Ee.4.35.1)', *Nottingham Medieval Studies*, 45 (2001), 210–33.

Orme, N., 'Medieval Hunting: Fact and Fancy', in B. A. Hanawalt, ed., *Chaucer's England: Literature in Historical Context* (Minneapolis, MN: University of Minnesota Press, 1992).

Ormrod, W. M. and P. Lindley, eds, *The Black Death in England* (Stamford, Lincs., Paul Watkins, 1996).

Owst, G. R., *Literature and Pulpit in Late Medieval England*, 2nd edn (Oxford: Basil Blackwell, 1961).

Page, W., ed., *The Victoria History of the County of Suffolk*, vol. 2 (1907).

—— ed., *The Victoria History of the County of Hertford*, vol. 2 (1908).

Payling, S. J., *Political Society in Lancastrian England: The Greater Gentry of Nottinghamshire* (Oxford: Oxford, University Press, 1991).

Pearsall, D., 'If heaven be on this earth, it is in cloister or in school', in R. E. Horrox and S. Rees Jones, eds, *Pragmatic Utopias: Ideals and Communities, 1200–1630* (Cambridge: Cambridge University Press, 2001).

Pollard, A. F., ed., *The Reign of Henry VII from Contemporary Sources*, 3 vols (London, 1913).

Pollard, A. J., 'The North-eastern Economy and the Agrarian Crisis of 1438–40', *Northern History*, 25, (1989), 88–105.

——, *North-Eastern England during the Wars of the Roses: War, Politics and Society, 1450–1500* (Oxford: Clarendon Press, 1990).

——, *Richard III and the Princes in the Tower* (Stroud: Sutton, 1991).

——, 'The Characteristics of the Fifteenth-Century North', in J. Appleby and P. Dalton, eds, *Government, Religion and Society in Northern England, 1000–1700* (Stroud: Sutton, 1996), 131–43.

——, *Late-Medieval England, 1399–1509* (London: Longman, 2000).

——, *The Wars of the Roses*, 2nd edn (Basingstoke: Palgrave, 2000).

——, 'Idealising Criminality: Robin Hood in the Fifteenth Century', in R. E. Horrox and S. Rees-Jones, eds, *Pragmatic Utopias: Ideals and Communities, 1200–1630* (Cambridge: Cambridge University Press, 2001).

——, 'North, South and Richard III', in Pollard, *The Worlds of Richard III* (Stroud: Tempus, 2001).

——, 'Richard Clervaux of Croft', in *The Worlds of Richard III* (Stroud: Tempus, 2001).

Poos, L. R., *A Rural Society after the Black Death: Essex, 1350–1525* (Cambridge: Cambridge University Press, 1991).

Powell, E., 'The King's Bench in Shropshire and Staffordshire in 1414', in E. W. Ives and A. H. Manchester, eds, *Law, Litigants and the Legal Profession* (Woodbridge: Boydell & Brewer, 1983).

——, *Kingship, Law and Society: Criminal Justice in the Reign of Henry V* (Oxford: Oxford University Press, 1989).

——, 'Law and Justice', in R. E. Horrox, ed., *Fifteenth-Century Attitudes* (Cambridge: Cambridge University Press, 1994).

Pronay, N. and J. Cox, eds, *Crowland Chronicle Continuations, 1459–1486* (Gloucester: Sutton, 1986).

Putnam, B., *Proceedings before the Justices of the Peace, Edward III to Richard II* (Cambridge: MA: Ames Foundation, 1938).

Raban, S., *Mortmain Legislation and the English Church, 1279–1500* (Cambridge: Cambridge University Press, 1982).

Richmond, C. F., ' A William Sponne Deed at Towcester: Further Light on the Cult of St Penket', in Richmond, *The Penket Papers* (Gloucester, Sutton, 1986).

——, 'The Murder of Thomas Dennis', *Common Knowledge*, 2 (1993), 85–98.

——, 'An Outlaw and Some Peasants: The Possible Significance of Robin Hood', *Nottingham Medieval Studies*, 37 (1993), 90–101.

——, *The Paston Family in the Fifteenth Century: Fastolf's Will* (Cambridge: Cambridge University Press, 1996).

——, *The Paston Family in the Fifteenth Century: Endings* (Manchester: Manchester, University Press, 2000).

Rogers, J. E. T., ed., *Thomas Gascoigne, Loci et libro veritatum* (Oxford: Oxford, University Press, 1881).

Rooney, A., *Hunting in Medieval English Literature* (Woodbridge: Boydell & Brewer, 1993).

Roskell, J. S. and others, *The History of Parliament: The House of Commons, 1386–1421* (Stroud: Sutton, 1993).

Ross, C. D., *Richard III* (London: Methuen, 1981).

Rosser, A. G., 'Communities of Parish and Guild in the Late Middle Ages', in S. J. Wright, ed., *Parish, Church and People: Local Studies in Lay Religion, 1350–1750* (London: Hutchinson, 1988).

——, *Medieval Westminster, 1200–1540* (Oxford: Clarendon Press, 1989).

——, 'Going to the Fraternity Feast: Commensuality and Social Relations in late-medieval England', *Journal of British Studies*, 33 (1994), 430–46.

Rubin, M., *Charity and Community in Medieval Cambridge* (Cambridge: Cambridge University Press, 1991).

Saunders, C. J., *The Forest of Medieval Romance* (Woodbridge: Boydell & Brewer, 1993).

Schama, S., *Landscape and Memory* (London: HarperCollins, 1995).

Schofield, P. R., *Peasant and Community in Medieval England* (Basingstoke: Palgrave, 2003).

Scullard, H. H., *Festivals and Ceremonies of the Roman Republic* (London: Thames & Hudson, 1981).

Serel, T., *Historical Notes on the Church of Saint Cuthbert in Wells* (Wells, 1875).

Shagan, E., *Popular Politics and the English Reformation* (Cambridge: Cambridge University Press, 2003).

Shaw, D. G., *The Creation of a Community: The City of Wells in the Middle Ages*, (Oxford, University Press, 1993).

Shaw, R. C., *The Royal Forest of Lancaster* (Preston: Guardian Press, 1956).

Singman, J. L., *Robin Hood: The Shaping of a Legend* (Westport, CT: Greenwood, 1998).

Skeat, W.W., ed., *The Complete Works of Geoffrey Chaucer*, 6 vols, 2nd edn (Oxford, 1900).

Smyth, J., *The Lives of the Berkeleys, 1066–1618*, ed. J. Maclean, 3 vols (Gloucester, 1883–5).

Stagg, D. J., ed., *A Calendar of New Forest Documents: The Fifteenth to the Seventeenth Centuries* (Winchester: Hampshire Record Office, 5, 1983).

Starkey, D., 'Which Age of Reform?', in C. Coleman and D. Starkey, eds, *Revolution Reassessed: Revisions in the History of Tudor Government and Administration* (Oxford: Clarendon Press, 1986).

Stephenson, J., ed., *The Townley Mysteries* (Durham: Surtees Society, 3, 1836).

Stokes, J. D., 'Robin Hood and the Churchwardens in Yeovil', *Medieval and Renaissance Drama in England*, 3 (1986), 1–25.

Stones, E. L. G., 'The Folvilles of Ashby-Folville, Leicestershire, and their Associates in Crime, 1326–41', *TRHS*, fifth series, 7 (1957), 117–36.

Strohm, P., *England's Empty Throne: Usurpation and the Language of Legitimation, 1399–1422* (New Haven, CT: Yale University Press, 1998).

Summerson, H., 'Crime and Society in Medieval Cumberland', *Transactions of the Cumberland and Westmorland Archaeological and Antiquarian Society*, 82 (1982), 111–24.

——, *Medieval Carlisle* (Cumberland and Westmorland Antiquarian and Archaeological Society, Extra Series, 25, 2 vols, 1993).

——, 'The Criminal Underworld of Medieval England', *Legal History*, 17 (1996), 197–224.

Swanson, R. N., 'Problems of the Priesthood in Pre-Reformation England', *EHR*, 105 (1990), 845–69.

Tardiff, R., 'The "Mistery" of Robin Hood: A New Social Context for the Texts', in S. Knight and S. N. Mukherjee, eds, *Words and Worlds: Studies in the Social Role of Verbal Culture* (Sydney: Association for Studies in Society and Culture, 1983).

Templeman, G., ed., *Records of Holy Trinity Guild, Coventry*, vol. 2 (Stratford-upon-Avon: Dugdale Society, 19, 1944).

Thomas, A. H. and I. D. Thornley, eds, *Great Chronicle of London* (London, 1938).

Thomas Wright's Political Songs of England, reissued with an introduction by Peter Coss (Cambridge: Cambridge University Press for the Royal Historical Society, 1996).

Thompson, A. H., *The History of the Hospital and the New College of the Annunciation of St Mary in the Newarke, Leicester* (Leicester: Leicestershire Archaeological Society, 1937).

Turner, G. J., ed., *Select Pleas of the Forest* (London: Selden Society, 13, 1899–1901).

Turton, R. B, ed., *The Honour and Forest of Pickering* (North Riding Record Society, new series, 1, 1894).

Turville-Petre, T., *England and Nation: Language, Literature and National Identity, 1290–1340* (Oxford: Clarendon Press, 1996).

Unwin, G., *The Gilds and Companies of London*, 4th edn (London: Cass, 1963).

Walsh, P. G. and M. J. Kennedy, eds and trans., *William of Newburgh, The History of English Affairs* (Warminster: Aris, 1988).

Wasson, J., 'The St George and Robin Hood Plays in Devon', *Medieval English Theatre*, 2 (1980), 67–8.

Watts, J. L., 'Ideas, Principles and Politics', in A. J. Pollard, ed.,*The Wars of the Roses* (London: Macmillan, 1995).

——, '"A New Ffundatation of is Crowne": Monarchy in the Age of Henry VII', in B. Thompson, ed.,*The Reign of Henry VII* (Stamford, Lincs: Paul Watkins, 1996).

——, 'Bishop Russell's Parliamentary Sermons of 1483–84', in G. W. Bernard and S. J. Gunn, eds, *Authority and Consent in Tudor England: Essays Presented to C. S. L. Davies* (Aldershot: Ashgate, 2002).

——, 'Politics, War and Public Life', in Richard Marks and Paul Williamson, eds, *Gothic: Art for England, 1400–1547* (London: V&A, 2003).

Weir, A. *Henry VIII: King and Court* (London: Jonathan Cape, 2001).

Wheater, W., *Knaresburgh and its Rulers* (Leeds: R. Jackson, 1907).

Whitlock, R., *Historic Forests of England* (Bradford on Avon, 1979).

Whittle, J., *The Development of Agrarian Capitalism: Land and Labour in Norfolk, 1440–1580* (Oxford: Clarendon Press, 2000).

Wiles, D., *The Early Plays of Robin Hood* (Cambridge: D. S. Brewer, 1981.

Willoughby, R., 'Sir Adam de Gurdon and the Pass of Alton', *The Best of '98* (Winchester: Annual Writers' Conference, 1998).

Winchester, A. J. L., *Harvest of the Hills: Rural Life in Northern England, 1400–1700* (Edinburgh: Edinburgh University Press, 2000).

Woolgar, C. M., *The Great Household in Late Medieval England* (New Haven, CT: Yale University Press, 1999).

Wrightson, K., *Earthly Necessities: Economic Lives in Early Modern Britain, 1470–1750* (Harmondsworth: Penguin, 2000; New Haven, CT: Yale University Press, 2000).

Young, C. R., *The Royal Forests of Medieval England* (Leicester: Leicester University Press, 1979).

INDEX